DEVELOPMENTAL PSYCHOLOGY

DEVELOPMENTAL PSYCHOLOGY

Dr. Punam Singh

CENTRUM PRESS
NEW DELHI-110002 (INDIA)

CENTRUM PRESS
H.O.: 4360/4, Ansari Road, Daryaganj,
New Delhi-110002 (India)
Tel: 23278000, 23261597, 23255577, 23286875
B.O.: No. 1015, Ist Main Road, BSK IIIrd Stage,
IIIrd Phase, IIIrd Block, Bangalore-560085 (INDIA)
Tel: 080-41723429
Email: centrumpress@gmail.com
Visit us at: www.centrumpress.com

Developmental Psychology

First Edition, 2011

ISBN 978-93-80921-61-7

PRINTED IN INDIA

Printed at Tarun Offset Printers, Delhi-110053

Contents

Preface

Developmental psychology is a subfield within psychology which focuses on the study of age-based behavioural changes. Historically, the term has been used specifically to refer to the behavioural development of children, but developmental psychologists actually study people of all ages, looking at behaviour from the womb until death. Researchers in this field can apply their skills to the treatment of children with psychological disorders, the analysis of psychological issues which pertain to criminal cases, education, elder care, and a number of other situations. Researchers in this field primarily gather evidence through observation, with each study adding to the overall body of material in developmental psychology. Experimentation under controlled circumstances may be used by some researchers, but most focus on watching humans in natural environments and learning about the ways in which development can be influenced or altered. Since many experiments involving the manipulation of environment could involve unethical methods such as subjecting children to sensory deprivation or malnourishing infants to determine the role of diet in infant development, observation is often the only way to gather data.

Developmental psychologists are interested in the emotional, intellectual, and moral development of people throughout their lifespan, looking at everything from the age infants first respond to specific stimuli to the behavioural changes which occur in the elderly. Developmental psychology is also concerned with physical and social development, such as the age at which boys and girls start differentiating between each other, or the dynamics of middle aged adults. They also study humans in the womb, especially in the later phases of pregnancy when the fetus appears to be engaging in conscious actions.

The study of developmental psychology is critical to understanding how humans mature, and to identifying issues with human maturation. Developmental psychologists, for example, can set basic milestones which can be used to determine whether or not a child is developing normally. Lagging behind normal development or failing to meet development targets by a specific age can be an early sign that a child is experiencing problems which need to be addressed.

Research in developmental psychology can also be used to explore the developmental differences between different populations, and the reasons why some groups seem to develop more quickly than others. This research can be valuable when people are deciding how to allocate funding and which social and educational issues need the most attention, as developmental psychology has illustrated that people need sound developmental building blocks to grow into healthy, well-adjusted adults.

This book contains the fundamental and basic information of subject and the selection of contents makes it an appropriate textbook for the students.

1

Introduction

Developmental psychology, also known as human development, is the scientific study of systematic psychological changes that occur in human beings over the course of their life span. Originally concerned with infants and children, the field has expanded to include adolescence, adult development, aging, and the entire life span. This field examines change across a broad range of topics including motor skills and other psycho-physiological processes; cognitive development involving areas such as problem solving, moral understanding, and conceptual understanding; language acquisition; social, personality, and emotional development; and self-concept and identity formation.

Developmental psychology includes issues such as the extent to which development occurs through the gradual accumulation of knowledge versus stage-like development, or the extent to which children are born with innate mental structures versus learning through experience. Many researchers are interested in the interaction between personal characteristics, the individual's behaviour, and environmental factors including social context, and their impact on development; others take a more narrowly focused approach.

Developmental psychology informs several applied fields, including: educational psychology, child psychopathology, and forensic developmental psychology. Developmental psychology complements several other basic research fields in psychology including social psychology, cognitive psychology, ecological psychology, and comparative psychology.

Approaches

Many theoretical perspectives attempt to explain development; among the most prominent are; Jean Piaget's Stage Theory, Lev Vygotsky's Social Contextualism (and its heirs, the Cultural Theory of Development of Michael Cole, and the Ecological Systems Theory of Urie Bronfenbrenner), Albert Bandura's Social learning theory, and the information processing framework employed by cognitive psychology.

To a lesser extent, historical theories continue to provide a basis for additional research. Among them are Erik Erikson's eight stages of psychosocial development and John B. Watson's and B. F. Skinner's behaviourism.

Many other theories are prominent for their contributions to particular aspects of development. For example, attachment theory describes kinds of interpersonal relationships and Lawrence Kohlberg describes stages in moral reasoning.

Piagetian Stages of Cognitive Development

Piaget was a French speaking Swiss theorist who posited that children learn through actively constructing knowledge through hands-on experience. He suggested that the adult's role in helping the child learn was to provide appropriate materials for the child to interact and construct. He would use Socratic questioning to get the children to reflect on what they were doing. He would try to get them to see contradictions in their explanations. He also developed stages of development. His approach can be seen in how the curriculum is sequenced in schools, and in the pedagogy of preschool centres across the United States.

Vygotsky's Cultural-historical Theory

Vygotsky was a theorist from the Soviet era, who posited that children learn through hands-on experience, as Piaget suggested. However, unlike Piaget, he claimed that timely and sensitive intervention by adults when a child is on the edge of learning a new task (called the "zone of proximal development") could help children learn new tasks. This technique is called "scaffolding," because it builds upon knowledge children already have with new knowledge that adults can help the child learn.

Vygotsky was strongly focused on the role of culture in determining the child's pattern of development, arguing that development moves from the social level to the individual level.

Ecological Systems Theory

Also called "Development in Context" or "Human Ecology" theory, Ecological Systems Theory, originally formulated by Urie Bronfenbrenner specifies four types of nested environmental systems, with bi-directional influences within and between the systems. The four systems are Microsystem, Mesosystem, Exosystem, and Macrosystem. Each system contains roles, norms and rules that can powerfully shape development. Since its publication in 1979, Bronfenbrenner's major statement of this theory, *The Ecology of Human Development* has had widespread influence on the way psychologists and others approach the study of human beings and their environments. As a result of this conceptualization of development, these environments — from the family to economic and political structures — have come to be viewed as part of the life course from childhood through adulthood.

Attachment Theory

Attachment theory, originally developed by John Bowlby, focuses on open, intimate, emotionally meaningful relationships. Attachment is described as a biological system or powerful survival impulse that evolved to ensure the survival of the infant. A child who is threatened or stressed will move toward caregivers who create a sense of physical, emotional and psychological safety for the individual. Attachment feeds on body contact and familiarity. Later Mary Ainsworth developed the Strange Situation Protocol and the concept of the secure base. Unfortunately, there are situations that inhibit a child from forming attachments. Some babies are raised without the stimulation and attention of a regular caregiver, or locked away under conditions of abuse or extreme neglect. The possible short-term effects of this deprivation are anger, despair, detachment, and temporary delay in intellectual development. Long-term effects include increased aggression, clinging behaviour, detachment, psychosomatic disorders, and an increased risk of depression as an adult.

Nature/Nurture

A significant issue in developmental psychology is the relationship between innateness and environmental influence in regard to any particular aspect of development. This is often referred to as "nature versus nurture" or nativism versus empiricism. A nativist account of development would argue that the processes in question are innate, that is, they are specified by the organism's genes.

An empiricist perspective would argue that those processes are acquired in interaction with the environment. Today developmental psychologists rarely take such extreme positions with regard to most aspects of development; rather they investigate, among many other things, the relationship between innate and environmental influences. One of the ways in which this relationship has been explored in recent years is through the emerging field of evolutionary developmental psychology.

One area where this innateness debate has been prominently portrayed is in research on language acquisition. A major question in this area is whether or not certain properties of human language are specified genetically or can be acquired through learning.

The empiricist position on the issue of language acquisition suggests that the language input provides the necessary information required for learning the structure of language and that infants acquire language through a process of statistical learning. From this perspective, language can be acquired via general learning methods that also apply to other aspects of development, such as perceptual learning.

The nativist position argues that the input from language is too impoverished for infants and children to acquire the structure of language. Linguist Noam Chomsky asserts that, evidenced by the lack of sufficient information in the language input, there is a universal grammar that applies to all human languages and is pre-specified. This has led to the idea that there is a special cognitive module suited for learning language, often called the language acquisition device. Chomsky's critique of the behaviorist model of language acquisition is regarded by many as a key turning point in the decline in the prominence of the theory of behaviourism generally. But Skinner's conception of "Verbal Behaviour" has not died, perhaps in part because it has generated successful practical applications.

Mechanisms of Development

Developmental psychology is concerned not only with describing the characteristics of psychological change over time, but also seeks to explain the principles and internal workings underlying these changes. Psychologists have attempted to better understand these factors by using models. Developmental models are sometimes computational, but they do not need to be. A model must simply account for the means by which a process takes place. This is sometimes done in reference to changes in the brain that may correspond to changes in behaviour over the course of the development. Computational accounts of development often use either symbolic, connectionist (neural network), or dynamical systems models to explain the mechanisms of development.

Research Areas

Cognitive Development

Cognitive development is primarily concerned with the ways in which infants and children acquire, develop, and use internal mental capabilities such as problem solving, memory, and language. Major topics in cognitive development are the study of language acquisition and the development of perceptual and motor skills. Piaget was one of the influential early psychologists to study the development of cognitive abilities. His theory suggests that development proceeds through a set of stages from infancy to adulthood and that there is an end point or goal. Other accounts, such as that of Lev Vygotsky, have suggested that development does not progress through stages, but rather that the developmental process that begins at birth and continues until death is too complex for such structure and finality. Rather, from this viewpoint, developmental processes proceed more continuously, thus development should be analysed, instead of treated as a product to be obtained.

Modern cognitive development has integrated the considerations of cognitive psychology and the psychology of individual differences into the interpretation and modeling of development. Specifically, the neo-Piagetian theories of cognitive development showed that the successive levels or stages of cognitive development are associated with increasing processing efficiency and working memory capacity. These increases explain progression to higher stages, and individual differences in such increases by same-age persons explain differences in cognitive performance. Other theories have moved away from Piagetian stage theories, and are influenced by accounts of domain-specific information processing, which posit that development is guided by innate evolutionarily specified and content-specific information processing mechanisms.

Social and Emotional Development

Developmental psychologists who are interested in social development examine how individuals develop social and emotional competencies. For example, they study how children form friendships, how they understand and deal with emotions, and how identity develops. Research in this area may involve study of the relationship between cognition or cognitive development and social behaviour.

Research Methods

Developmental psychology employs many of the research methods used in other areas of psychology. However, infants and children cannot always be tested in the same ways as adults, so different methods are often used to study their development.

Methods and Techniques

Techniques for Studying Infants

Psychologists often use the habituation methodology to assess infant ability. Typically, infants prefer stimuli that are novel relative to those they have encountered previously. Demonstrating a preference for one stimulus over another demonstrates that the infant can discriminate between them. Several methods are used to measure infants' preference. In the high-amplitude sucking procedure infants suck on a pacifier more or less depending on their level of interest. In other methods, infants kick their legs to indicate preference, or their level of interest is measured by the amount of time spent looking in a particular direction.

Habituation has been used to discover the resolution of perceptual systems by habituating an infant to a particular stimulus. If an infant is able to discriminate between an initial "habituated" stimulus and a novel stimulus, they will show a preference for the novel stimulus after habituation. More and more similar stimuli are presented to determine the smallest degree of difference detectable by the infant.

Children

Adolescents: When studying older children, especially adolescents, adult measurements of behaviour can often be used, but they may need to be simplified to allow children to perform certain tasks.

Research Design

Developmental psychologists have a number of methods to study changes in individuals over time.

In a longitudinal study, a researcher observes many individuals born at or around the same time (a cohort) and carries out new observations as members of the cohort age. This method can be used to draw conclusions about which types of development are universal (or normative) and occur in most members of a cohort. As an example a longitudinal study of early literacy development examined in detail the early literacy experiences of one child in each of 30 families. Researchers may also observe ways in which development varies between individuals and hypothesize about the causes of variation observed in their data. Longitudinal studies often require large amounts of time and funding, making them unfeasible in some situations. Also, because members of a cohort all experience historical events unique to their generation, apparently normative developmental trends may in fact be universal only to their cohort.

In a cross-sectional study, a researcher observes differences between individuals of different ages at the same time. This generally requires less resources than the longitudinal method, and because the individuals come from different cohorts, shared historical events are not so much of a confounding factor. By the same token, however, cross-sectional research may not be the most effective way to study differences between participants, as these differences may result not from their different ages but from their exposure to *different* historical events.

An accelerated longitudinal design or cross-sequential study or cohort-sequential design combines both methodologies. Here, a researcher observes members of different birth cohorts at the same time, and then tracks all participants over time, charting changes in the groups. By comparing differences and similarities in development, one can more easily determine what changes can be attributed to individual or historical environment, and which are truly universal. Clearly such a study can be even more resource-consuming than a longitudinal study.

Additionally, these are all correlational, not experimental, designs, and so one cannot readily infer causation from the data they yield. Nonetheless, correlational research methods are common in the study of development, in part due to ethical concerns. In a study of the effects of poverty on development, for instance, one cannot easily randomly assign certain families to a poverty condition and others to an affluent one, and so observation alone has to suffice.

Stages of Development

Child development stages describe theoretical milestones of child development. Many stage models of development have been proposed, used as working concepts and in some cases asserted as nativist theories.

Specifications Sorted by Reached Age

1–4 Months

Physical

- Head and chest circumference are nearly equal to the part of the abdomen.
- Head circumference increases approximately 2 cm per month until two months, then increases 1.5 cm per month until four months. Increases are an important indication of continued brain growth.

- Continues to breathe using abdominal muscles.
- Posterior fontanel closes by the second month.
- Anterior fontanel closes to approximately 1.3 cm.
- Skin remains sensitive and easily irritated.
- Legs may appear slightly bowed.
- Cries with tears.
- Eyes begin moving together in unison (binocular vision).

Motor Development

- Rooting and sucking reflexes are well developed.
- Swallowing reflex and tongue movements are still immature; continued drooling and inability to move food to the back of the mouth.
- Grasp reflex gradually disappears.
- *Landau reflex* appears near the middle of this period; when baby is held in a prone (face down) position, the head is held upright and legs are fully extended.
- Grasps with entire hand; strength insufficient to hold items. Holds hands in an open or semi-open position.
- Muscle strength and control improving; early movements are large and jerky; gradually become smoother and more purposeful.
- Raises head and upper body on arms when in a prone position.
- Turns head side to side when in a supine (face up) position; near the end of this period can hold head up and in line with the body.
- Upper body parts are more active: clasps hands above face, waves arms about, reaches for objects.

4–8 Months

Physical

- Head and chest circumferences are basically equal.
- Head circumference increases approximately 1 cm per month until six to seven months, then 0.5 cm per month;

head circumference should continue to increase steadily, indicating healthy, ongoing brain growth.

- Breathing is abdominal; respiration rate depending on activity; rate and patterns vary from infant to infant.
- Teeth may begin to appear, with upper and lower incisors coming in first. Gums may become red and swollen, accompanied by increased drooling, chewing, biting, and mouthing of objects.
- Legs may appear bowed; bowing gradually disappears as infant grows older.
- Fat rolls ("Baby Fat") appear on thighs, upper arms and neck.
- True eye color is established.

Motor development

- Reflexive behaviours are changing:
- Blinking reflex is well established
- Sucking reflex becomes voluntary
- Moro reflex disappears
- When lowered suddenly, infant throws out arms as a protective measure.
- Swallowing reflex appears and allows infant to move solid foods from front of mouth to the back for swallowing.
- Picks up objects using finger and thumb (pincer grip).
- Reaches for objects with both arms simultaneously; later reaches with one hand or the other.
- Transfers objects from one hand to the other; grasps object using entire hand (palmar grasp).
- Handles, shakes, and pounds objects; puts everything in mouth.
- Able to hold bottle.
- Sits alone without support, holding head erect, back straightened, and arms propped forward for support
- Pulls self into a crawling position by raising up on arms and drawing knees up beneath the body; rocks back and forth, but generally does not move forward.

- Lifts head when placed on back.
- Can roll over from back or stomach position.
- May accidentally begin scooting backwards when placed on stomach; soon will begin to crawl forward.
- Looks for fallen objects by 7 months
- Plays 'peek-a-boo' games
- Cannot understand "no" or "danger"

8–12 Months

Physical

- Respiration rates vary with activity
- Environmental conditions, weather, activity, and clothing still affect variations in body temperature.
- Head and chest circumference remain equal.
- Continues to use abdominal muscles for breathing.
- Anterior fontanel begins to close.
- More teeth appear, often in the order of two lower incisors then two upper incisors followed by four more incisors and two lower molars but some babies may still be waiting for their first.
- Arm and hands are more developed than feet and legs (cephalocaudal development); hands appear large in proportion to other body parts.
- Legs may continue to appear bowed.
- "Baby Fat" continues to appear on thighs, upper arms and neck.
- Feet appear flat as arch has not yet fully developed.
- Both eyes work in unison (true binocular coordination).
- Can see distant objects (4 to 6 m or 13 to 20 ft away) and points at them.

Motor Development

- Reaches with one hand leading to grasp an offered object or toy.
- Manipulates objects, transferring them from one hand to the other.

- Explores new objects by poking with one finger.
- Uses deliberate pincer grasp to pick up small objects, toys, and finger foods.
- Stacks objects; also places objects inside one another
- Releases objects or toys by dropping or throwing; cannot intentionally put an object down.
- Beginning to pull self to a standing position.
- Beginning to stand alone, leaning on furniture for support; moves around obstacles by side-stepping.
- Has good balance when sitting; can shift positions without falling.
- Creeps on hands and knees; crawls up and down stairs.
- Walks with adult support, holding onto adult's hand; may begin to walk alone.
- Watches people, objects, and activities in the immediate environment.
- Shows awareness of distant objects (4 to 6 m or 13 to 20 ft away) by pointing at them.
- Responds to hearing tests (voice localization); however, loses interest quickly and, therefore, may be difficult to test informally.
- Follows simple instructions
- Reaches for toys that are out of reach but visible
- Recognizes objects in reverse
- Drops thing intentionally and repeats and watches object
- Imitates activities like playing drum

Toddlers (12–24 Months)

Physical

- Weight is now approximately 3 times the child's birth weight.
- Respiration rate varies with emotional state and activity.
- Rate of growth slows

- Head size increases slowly; grows approximately 1.3 cm every six months; anterior fontanelle is nearly closed at eighteen months as bones of the skull thicken.
- Chest circumference is larger than head circumference.
- Rapid eruption of teeth; six to ten new teeth will appear.
- Legs may still appear bowed.
- Toddler will begin to lose the "Baby Fat" once he/she begins walking.
- Body shape changes; takes on more adult-like appearance; still appears top-heavy; abdomen protrudes, back is swayed.

Motor Development

- Crawls skilfully and quickly.
- Stands alone with feet spread apart, legs stiffened, and arms extended for support.
- Gets to feet unaided.
- Most children walk unassisted near the end of this period; falls often; not always able to manoeuvre around obstacles, such as furniture or toys.
- Uses furniture to lower self to floor; collapses backwards into a sitting position or falls forward on hands and then sits.
- Enjoys pushing or pulling toys while walking.
- Repeatedly picks up objects and throws them; direction becomes more deliberate.
- Attempts to run; has difficulty stopping and usually just drops to the floor.
- Crawls up stairs on all fours; goes down stairs in same position.
- Sits in a small chair.
- Carries toys from place to place.
- Enjoys crayons and markers for scribbling; uses whole-arm movement.
- Helps feed self; enjoys holding spoon (often upside down) and drinking from a glass or cup; not always accurate

in getting utensils into mouth; frequent spills should be expected.

- Helps turn pages in book.
- Stacks two to six objects per day.

Cognitive Development

- Enjoys object-hiding activities
- Early in this period, the child always searches in the same location for a hidden object (if the child has watched the hiding of an object). Later, the child will search in several locations.
- Passes toy to other hand when offered a second object (referred to as "crossing the midline"-an important neurological development).
- Manages three to four objects by setting an object aside (on lap or floor) when presented with a new toy.
- Puts toys in mouth less often.
- Enjoys looking at picture books.
- Demonstrates understanding of functional relationships (objects that belong together): Puts spoon in bowl and then uses spoon as if eating; places teacup on saucer and sips from cup; tries to make doll stand up.
- Shows or offers toy to another person to look at.
- Names many everyday objects.
- Shows increasing understanding of spatial and form discrimination: puts all pegs in a pegboard; places three geometric shapes in large formboard or puzzle.
- Places several small items (blocks, clothespins, cereal pieces) in a container or bottle and then dumps them out.
- Tries to make mechanical objects work after watching someone else do so.
- Responds with some facial movement, but cannot truly imitate facial expression.
- Most children with autism are diagnosed at this age.

Language

- Produces considerable "jargon": puts words and sounds together into speech-like (inflected) patterns.
- Holophrastic speech: uses one word to convey an entire thought; meaning depends on the inflection ("me" may be used to request more cookies or a desire to feed self). Later; produces two-word phrases to express a complete thought (telegraphic speech): "More cookie," "Daddy bye-bye."
- Follows simple directions, "Give Daddy the cup."
- When asked, will point to familiar persons, animals, and toys.
- Identifies three body parts if someone names them: "Show me your nose (toe, ear)."
- Indicates a few desired objects and activities by name: "Bye-bye," "cookie"; verbal request is often accompanied by an insistent gesture.
- Responds to simple questions with "yes" or "no" and appropriate head movement.
- Speech is 25 to 50 percent intelligible during this period.
- Locates familiar objects on request (if child knows location of objects).
- Acquires and uses five to fifty words; typically these are words that refer to animals, food, and toys.
- Uses gestures, such as pointing or pulling, to direct adult attention.
- Enjoys rhymes and songs; tries to join in.
- Seems aware of reciprocal (back and forth) aspects of conversational exchanges; some turn-taking in other kinds of vocal exchanges, such as making and imitating sounds.

Social

- less wary of strangers.
- Helps pick up and put away toys.
- Plays by themselves

- Enjoys being held and read to.
- Often imitates adult actions in play.
- Enjoys adult attention; likes to know that an adult is near; gives hugs and kisses.
- Recognizes self in mirror.
- Enjoys the companionship of other children, but does not play cooperatively.
- Beginning to assert independence; often refuses to cooperate with daily routines that once were enjoyable; resists getting dressed, putting on shoes, eating, taking a bath; wants to try doing things without help.
- May have a tantrum when things go wrong or if overly tired or frustrated.
- Exceedingly curious about people and surroundings; toddlers need to be watched carefully to prevent them from getting into unsafe situations.

Psychological

Autonomy vs. Shame and Doubt (will) (J. Chasse, 2008) Psychosocial stimulation is vital during the toddler years. Play begins to become interactive. Toddlers begin to learn and exhibit independence, but ironically they enjoy sharing this discovery with others. Another important advancement is active social play with adults including mirroring and repeating. Songs, rhymes, and finger plays (e.g. incy wincy spider, little teapot, etc.) are a great way to encourage and stimulate this area of development.

Two Year Old

Physical

- Posture is more erect; abdomen still large and protruding, back swayed, because abdominal muscles are not yet fully developed.
- Respirations are slow and regular
- Body temperature continues to fluctuate with activity, emotional state, and environment.
- Brain reaches about 80 percent of its adult size.

- 15 baby teeth almost finished growing out

Motor Development

- Can walk around obstacles and walk more erect
- Squats for long periods while playing.
- Climbs stairs unassisted (but not with alternating feet).
- Balances on one foot (for a few moments), jumps up and down, but may fall.
- Often achieves toilet training during this year (depending on child's physical and neurological development) although accidents should still be expected; the child will indicate readiness for toilet training.
- Throws large ball underhand without losing balance. Holds cup or glass (be sure it is unbreakable) in one hand. Unbuttons large buttons; unzips large zippers.
- Opens doors by turning doorknobs.
- Grasps large crayon with fist; scribbles enthusiastically on large paper.
- Climbs up on chair, turns around and sits down.
- Enjoys pouring and filling activities-sand, water, styrofoam peanuts.
- Stacks four to six objects on top of one another.
- Uses feet to propel wheeled riding toys.

Cognitive

- Eye–hand movements better coordinated; can put objects together, take them apart; fit large pegs into pegboard.
- Begins to use objects for purposes other than intended (may push a block around as a boat).
- Does simple classification tasks based on one dimension (separates toy dinosaurs from toy cars).
- Stares for long moments; seems fascinated by, or engrossed in, figuring out a situation: where the tennis ball has rolled where the dog has gone, what has caused a particular noise.

- Attends to self-selected activities for longer periods of time. Discovering cause and effect: squeezing the cat makes her scratch.
- Knows where familiar persons should be; notes their absence; finds a hidden object by looking in last hiding place first. (This is what Piaget termed object permanence, which usually occurs during the sensorimotor stage of Piaget's childhood theory of cognitive development)
- Names objects in picture books; may pretend to pick something off the page and taste or smell it.
- Recognizes and expresses pain and its location.
- Is expected to use magical thinking, such as believing that a toy bear is a real bear.
- Tells about objects and events not immediately present (this is both a cognitive and linguistic advance).

Language

- Enjoys being read to if allowed to participate by pointing, making relevant noises, turning pages.
- Realizes that language is effective for getting others to respond to needs and preferences.
- Uses fifty to three hundred different words; vocabulary continuously increasing.
- Has broken the linguistic code; in other words, much of a two-year-old's talk has meaning to him or her.
- Receptive language is more developed than expressive language; most two-year olds understand significantly more than they can talk about.
- Utters three-and four-word statements; uses conventional word order to form more complete sentences.
- Refers to self as "me" or sometimes "I" rather than by name: "Me go bye-bye"; has no trouble verbalizing "mine."
- Expresses negative statements by tacking on a negative word such as "no" or "not": "Not more milk."

- Repeatedly asks, "What's that?"
- Uses some plurals.
- Some stammering and other dysfluencies are common.
- Speech is as much as 65 to 70 percent intelligible.
- Is able to verbalize needs.

Social and Emotional

- Shows signs of empathy and caring: comforts another child if hurt or frightened; appears to sometimes be overly affectionate in offering hugs and kisses to children
- Continues to use physical aggression if frustrated or angry (for some children, this is more exaggerated than for others); Physical aggression usually lessens as verbal skills improve.
- Temper tantrums likely to peak during this year; cannot be reasoned with while tantrum is in progress.
- Impatient; finds it difficult to wait or take turns.
- Enjoys "helping" with household chores; imitates everyday activities: may try to toilet a stuffed animal, feed a doll.
- "Bossy" with parents and caregivers; orders them around, makes demands, expects immediate compliance from adults.
- Watches and imitates the play of other children, but seldom interacts directly; plays near others, often choosing similar toys and activities (parallel play); solitary play is often simple and repetitive.
- Offers toys to other children, but is usually possessive of playthings; still tends to hoard toys.
- Making choices is difficult; wants it both ways.
- Often defiant; shouting "no" becomes automatic.
- Ritualistic; wants everything "just so"; routines carried out exactly as before; belongings placed "where they belong."

Three Year Old

Physical

- Growth is steady though slower than in first two years.
- Adult height can be predicted from measurements of height at three years of age; males are approximately 53% of their adult height and females, 57%.
- Legs grow faster than arms,
- Circumference of head and chest is equal; head size is in better proportion to the body.
- "Baby fat" disappears as neck appears.
- Posture is more erect; abdomen no longer protrudes.
- Slightly knock-kneed.
- can jump from low step
- can stand up and walk around on tiptoes
- "baby" teeth stage over.
- Needs to consume approximately 6,300 J (1,500 calories) daily.

Motor Development

- Walks up and down stairs unassisted, using alternating feet; may jump from bottom step, landing on both feet.
- Can walk on one foot, balance momentarily.
- Can kick big ball-shaped objects.
- Needs minimal assistance eating.
- Jumps on the spot.
- Pedals a small tricycle.
- Throws a ball overhand; aim and distance are limited.
- Catches a large bounced ball with both arms extended.
- Enjoys swinging on a swing (not too high or too fast).
- Shows improved control of crayons or markers; uses vertical, horizontal and circular strokes.
- Holds crayon or marker between first two fingers and thumb (tripod grasp), not in a fist as earlier.
- Can turn pages of a book one at a time

- Enjoys building with blocks.
- Builds a tower of eight or more blocks.
- Enjoys playing with clay; pounds, rolls, and squeezes it.
- May begin to show hand dominance.
- Carries a container of liquid, such as a cup of milk or bowl of water, without much spilling; pours liquid from pitcher into another container.
- Manipulates large buttons and zippers on clothing.
- Washes and dries hands; brushes own teeth, but not thoroughly.
- Usually achieves complete bladder control during this time.

Cognitive Development

- Listens attentively to age-appropriate stories.
- Makes relevant comments during stories, especially those that relate to home and family events.
- Likes to look at books and may pretend to "read" to others or explain pictures.
- Enjoys stories with riddles, guessing, and "suspense."
- Speech is understandable most of the time.
- Produces expanded noun phrases: "big, brown dog."
- Produces verbs with "ing" endings; uses "-s" to indicate more than one; often puts "-s" on already pluralized forms: geeses, mices.
- Indicates negatives by inserting "no" or "not" before a simple noun or verb phrase: "Not baby."
- Answers "What are you doing?", "What is this?", and "Where?" questions dealing with familiar objects and events.

Four Year Old

Physical Development

- Head circumference is usually not measured after age three.

- Requires approximately 1,700 calories daily.
- Hearing acuity can be assessed by child's correct usage of sounds and *Language also, by the child's appropriate responses to questions and instructions.

Motor Development

- Walks a straight line (tape or chalk line on the floor).
- Hops on one foot.
- Pedals and steers a wheeled toy with confidence; turns corners, avoids obstacles and oncoming "traffic."
- Climbs ladders, trees, playground equipment.
- Jumps over objects 12 to 15 cm (5 to 6 in) high; lands with both feet together.
- Runs, starts, stops, and moves around obstacles with ease.
- Throws a ball overhand; distance and aim improving.
- Builds a tower with ten or more blocks.
- Forms shapes and objects out of clay: cookies, snakes, simple animals.
- Reproduces some shapes and letters.
- Holds a crayon or marker using a tripod grasp.
- Paints and draws with purpose; may have an idea in mind, but often has problems implementing it so calls the creation something else.
- Becomes more accurate at hitting nails and pegs with hammer.
- Threads small wooden beads on a string.
- Can run in a circle

Cognitive

- Can recognize that certain words sound similar
- Names eighteen to twenty uppercase letters. Writes several letters and sometimes their name.
- A few children are beginning to read simple books, such as alphabet books with only a few words per page and many pictures.

- Likes stories about how things grow and how things operate.
- Delights in wordplay, creating silly Language.
- Understands the concepts of "tallest," "biggest," "same," and "more"; selects the picture that has the "most houses" or the "biggest dogs."
- Rote counts to 20 or more.
- Understands the sequence of daily events: "When we get up in the morning, we get dressed, have breakfast, brush our teeth, and go to school."
- When looking at pictures, can recognize and identify missing puzzle parts (of person, car, animal).
- Very good storytellers.
- Counts 1 to 7 objects out loud, but not always in order
- follows two to three step directions given individually or in a group
- may put the "ed" on the end of words such as "I goed outside and I played."

Language

- Uses the prepositions "on," "in," and "under."
- Uses possessives consistently: "hers," "theirs," "baby's."
- Answers "Whose?", "Who?", "Why?", and "How many?"
- Produces elaborate sentence structures: "The cat ran under the house before I could see what color it was."
- Speech is almost entirely intelligible.
- Begins to correctly use the past tense of verbs: "Mommy closed the door," "Daddy went to work."
- Refers to activities, events, objects, and people that are not present.
- Changes tone of voice and sentence structure to adapt to listener's level of under-standing: To baby brother, "Milk gone?" To Mother, "Did the baby drink all of his milk?"
- States first and last name, gender, siblings' names, and sometimes own telephone number.

- Answers appropriately when asked what to do if tired, cold, or hungry. Recites and sings simple songs and rhymes.

Social Development

- Outgoing; friendly; overly enthusiastic at times.
- Moods change rapidly and unpredictably; laughing one minute, crying the next; may throw tantrum over minor frustrations (a block structure that will not balance); sulk over being left out.
- Imaginary playmates or companions are common; holds conversations and shares strong emotions with this invisible friend.
- Boasts, exaggerates, and "bends" the truth with made-up stories or claims of boldness; tests the limits with "bathroom" talk.
- Cooperates with others; participates in group activities.
- Shows pride in accomplishments; seeks frequent adult approval.
- Often appears selfish; not always able to take turns or to understand taking turns under some conditions; tattles on other children.
- Insists on trying to do things independently, but may get so frustrated as to verge on tantrums when problems arise: paint that drips, paper airplane that will not fold right.
- Enjoys role-playing and make-believe activities.
- Relies (most of the time) on verbal rather than Physical aggression; may yell angrily rather than hit to make a point; threatens: "You can't come to my birthday party"
- Name-calling and taunting are often used as ways of excluding other children.
- Establishes close relationships with playmates; beginning to have "best" friends.

Five Year Old

Physical

- Head size is approximately that of an adult's.
- May begin to lose "baby" (deciduous) teeth.
- Body is adult-like in proportion.
- Requires approximately 7,500 J (1,800 calories) daily
- Visual tracking and binocular vision are well developed.

Motor Development

- Walks backwards, toe to heel.
- Walks unassisted up and down stairs, alternating feet.
- May learn to turn somersaults (should be taught the right way in order to avoid injury).
- Can touch toes without flexing knees.
- Walks a balance beam.
- Learns to skip using alternative feet.
- Catches a ball thrown from 1 m (3.3 ft) away.
- Rides a tricycle or wheeled toy with speed and skilful steering; some children learning to ride bicycles, usually with training wheels.
- Jumps or hops forward ten times in a row without falling.
- Balances on either foot with good control for ten seconds.
- Builds three-dimensional structures with small cubes by copying from a picture or model.
- Reproduces many shapes and letters: square, triangle, A, I, O, U, C, H, L, T.
- Demonstrates fair control of pencil or marker; may begin to color within the lines.
- Cuts on the line with scissors (not perfectly).
- Hand dominance is fairly well established.

Cognitive

- Forms rectangle from two triangular cuts.

- Builds steps with set of small blocks.
- Understands concept of same shape, same size.
- Sorts objects on the basis of two dimensions, such as color and form.
- Sorts a variety of objects so that all things in the group have a single common feature (classification skill: all are food items or boats or animals).
- Understands the concepts of smallest and shortest; places objects in order from shortest to tallest, smallest to largest.
- Identifies objects with specified serial position: first, second, last.
- Rote counts to 20 and above; many children count to 100.
- Recognizes numerals from 1 to 10.
- Understands the concepts of less than: "Which bowl has less water?"
- Understands the terms dark, light, and early: "I got up early, before anyone else. It was still dark."
- Relates clock time to daily schedule: "Time to turn on TV when the little hand points to 5."
- Some children can tell time on the hour: five o'clock, two o'clock.
- Knows what a calendar is for.
- Recognizes and identifies coins; beginning to count and save money.
- Many children know the alphabet and names of upper- and lowercase letters.
- Understands the concept of half; can say how many pieces an object has when it's been cut in half.
- Asks innumerable questions: Why? What? Where? When?
- Eager to learn new things.

Language Development

- Vocabulary of 1,500 words plus.

- Tells a familiar story while looking at pictures in a book.
- Defines simple words by function: a ball is to bounce; a bed is to sleep in.
- Identifies and names four to eight colours.
- Recognizes the humour in simple jokes; makes up jokes and riddles.
- Produces sentences with five to seven words; much longer sentences are not unusual.
- States the name of own city or town, birthday, and parents' names.
- Answers telephone appropriately; calls person to phone or takes a brief message
- Speech is almost entirely intelligible.
- Uses "would" and "could" appropriately.
- Uses past tense of irregular verbs consistently: "went," "caught," "swam."
- Uses past-tense inflection (-ed) appropriately to mark regular verbs: "jumped," "rained," "washed."

Social Development

- Enjoys and often has one or two focus friendships.
- Plays cooperatively (can lapse), is generous, takes turns, shares toys.
- Participates in group play and shared activities with other children; suggests imaginative and elaborate play ideas.
- Shows affection and caring towards others especially those "below" them or in pain
- Generally subservient to parent or caregiver requests.
- Needs comfort and reassurance from adults but is less open to comfort.
- Has better self-control over swings of emotions.
- Likes entertaining people and making them laugh.
- Boasts about accomplishments.

Six Year Old

Physical

- Weight gains reflect significant increases in muscle mass.
- Heart rate and respiratory rates are close to adults.
- Body may appear lanky as through period of rapid growth.
- Baby teeth beginning to be replaced by permanent ones, starting with the two lower front teeth
- 20/20 eyesight; if below 20/40 should see a professional.
- The most common vision problem during middle childhood is myopia, or nearsightedness. (Berk, 2007).
- Uses 6,700 J to 7,100 J (1,600 to 1,700 calories) a day.

Motor Development

- Gains greater control over large and fine motor skills; movements are more precise and deliberate, though some clumsiness persists.
- Enjoys vigorous running, jumping, climbing, and throwing est.
- Has trouble staying still.
- Span of attention increases; works at tasks for longer periods of time, though
- Can concentrate effort but not always consistently.
- Understands time (toda; tomorrow, yesterday) and simple motion (things go faster than others).
- Recognizes seasons and major activities done in the times.
- Has fun with problem solving and sorting activities like stacking, puzzles and mazes
- Enjoys the challenge of puzzles, counting and sorting activities, paper-and-pencil mazes, and games that involve matching letters and words with pictures.
- Recognizes some words by sight; attempts to sound out words

- In some cases the child may be reading well.
- functioning which facilitates learning to ride a bicycle, swim, swing a bat, or kick a ball.
- Making things is enjoyed.
- Reverses or confuse certain letters: b/d, p/g, g/q, t/f.
- Able to trace objects.
- Folds and cuts paper into simple shapes.
- Can Tie Laces, string (like shoes).

Language

- Can identify right and left hands fairly consistently.
- Holds onto positive beliefs involving the unexplainable (magic or fantasy)
- Arrives at some understanding about death and dying; expresses fear that parents may die.
- Talks a lot.
- Loves telling jokes and riddles; often, the humour is far from subtle.
- Experiments with slang and profanity and finds it funny.
- Enthusiastic and inquisitive about surroundings and everyday events.
- Able to carry on adult-like conversations; asks many questions.
- Learns 5 to 10 words a day; vocabulary of 10,000–14,000.
- Uses appropriate verb tenses, word order, and sentence structure.

Social and Emotional

- Uses language rather than tantrums or physical aggression to express displeasure: "That's mine! Give it back, you dummy."
- Talks self through steps required in simple problem-solving situations (though the "logic" may be unclear to adults).

- Has mood swings towards primary caregiver depending on the day
- Friendship with parent is less depended on but still needs closeness and nurturing.
- Anxious to please; needs and seeks adult approval, reassurance, and praise; may complain excessively about minor hurts to gain more attention.
- Often can't view the world from another's point of view
- Self-perceived failure can make the child easily disappointed and frustrated.
- Can't handle things not going their own way
- Does not understand ethical behaviour or moral standards especially when doing things that have not been given rules
- Understands when he or she has been thought to be "bad"; values are based on others enforced values.
- May be increasingly fearful of the unknown like things in the dark, noises, and animals.

Pre-natal Development

Pre-natal development is of interest to psychologists investigating the context of early psychological development. For example, some primitive reflexes arise before birth and are still present in newborns. One hypothesis is that these reflexes are vestigial and have limited use in early human life. Piaget's Theory of cognitive development suggested that some early reflexes are building blocks for infant sensorimotor development. For example the tonic neck reflex may help development by bringing objects into the infant's field of view. Other reflexes, such as the walking reflex disappear to be replaced by more sophisticated voluntary control later in infancy. This may be because the infant gains too much weight after birth to be strong enough to use the reflex, or because the reflex and subsequent development are functionally different. It has also been suggested that some reflexes (for example the moro and walking reflexes) are predominantly adaptations to life in the womb with little connection to early infant development. Primitive reflexes reappear in adults under certain conditions, such as neurological conditions like dementia or traumatic lesions.

Ultrasound has shown that infants are capable of a range of movements in the womb, many of which appear to be more than simple reflexes. By the time they are born, infants can recognise and have a preference for their mother's voice suggesting some pre-natal development of auditory perception. Pre-natal development and birth complications may also be connected to neurodevelopmental disorders, for example in schizophrenia. With the advent of cognitive neuroscience, embryology and the neuroscience of pre-natal development is of increasing interest to developmental psychology research.

Infancy

From birth until the onset of speech, the child is referred to as an infant. Developmental psychologists vary widely in their assessment of infant psychology, and the influence the outside world has upon it, but certain aspects are relatively clear.

The majority of a newborn infant's time is spent in sleep. At first this sleep is evenly spread throughout the day and night, but after a couple of months, infants generally become diurnal.

Infants can be seen to have 6 states, grouped into pairs:

- quiet sleep and active sleep (dreaming, when REM occurs)
- quiet waking, and active waking
- fussing and crying

Infants respond to stimuli differently in these different states.

Habituation has been used to discover the resolution of perceptual systems, suggesting that infants' basic perceptual abilities develop before acquisition of object permanence.

- Vision is significantly worse in infants than in older children. Infant sight, blurry in early stages, improves over time. Colour perception similar to that seen in adults has been demonstrated in infants as young as four months, using habituation methods.

- Hearing is well-developed prior to birth, however, and a preference for the mother's heartbeat is well established. Infants are fairly good at detecting the direction from which a sound comes, and by 18 months their hearing ability is approximately equal to that of adults.
- Smell and taste are present, with infants showing different expressions of disgust or pleasure when presented with pleasant odors (honey, milk, etc.) or unpleasant odors (rotten egg) and tastes (e.g. sour taste). There is good evidence for infants preferring the smell of their mother to that of others.
- Language : infants of around six months can differentiate between phonemes in their own language, but not between similar phonemes in another language. At this stage infants also start to babble, producing phonemes.
- Touch is one of the better developed senses at birth, being one of the first to develop inside the womb. This is evidenced by the primitive reflexes described above, and the relatively advanced development of the somatosensory cortex.
- Pain : Infants feel pain similarly, if not more strongly than older children but pain-relief in infants has not received so much attention as an area of research.

An early theory of infant development was the Sensorimotor stage of Piaget's Theory of cognitive development. Piaget suggested that an infant's perception and understanding of the world depended on their motor development, which was required for the infant to link visual, tactile and motor representations of objects. According to this view, it is through touching and handling objects that infants develop object permanence, the understanding that objects are solid, permanent, and continue to exist when out of sight.

Piaget's Sensorimotor Stage comprised six sub-stages. In the early stages, development arises out of movements caused by primitive reflexes. Discovery of new behaviours results from classical and operant conditioning, and the formation of habits.

From eight months the infant is able to uncover a hidden object but will persevere when the object is moved. Piaget's evidence for an incomplete understanding of object permanence before 18 months was the infant's failure to look for an object where it was last seen. Instead infants continue to look for an object where it was first seen, committing the "A-not-B error".

Later researchers have developed a number of other tests which suggest that younger infants understand more about objects than first thought. These experiments usually involve a toy, and a crude barrier which is placed in front of the toy, and then removed, repeatedly. Before the age of eight to nine months, infants inability to understand object permanence extends to people, which explains why infants at this age do not cry when their mothers are gone ("Out of sight, out of mind.").

There are critical periods in infancy and childhood during which development of certain perceptual, sensorimotor, social and language systems depends crucially on environmental stimulation. Feral children such as Genie, deprived of adequate stimulation, fail to acquire important skills which they are then unable to learn in later childhood. The concept of critical periods is also well established in neurophysiology, from the work of Hubel and Wiesel among others. Some feel that classical music, particularly Mozart is good for an infant's mind. While some tentative research has shown it to be helpful to older children, no conclusive evidence is available involving infants.

Babyhood

Intelligence is demonstrated through the use of symbols, language use matures, and memory and imagination are developed. Thinking is done in a nonlogical, nonreversible manner. Egocentric thinking predominates.

Socially, toddlers are little people attempting to become independent at this stage, which they are commonly called the " terrible twos". They walk, talk, use the toilet, and get food for themselves. Self-control begins to develop. If taking the initiative to explore, experiment, risk mistakes in trying new things, and test their limits is encouraged by the caretaker(s) the child will become autonomous, self-reliant, and confident.

If the caretaker is overprotective or disapproving of independent actions, the toddler may begin to doubt their abilities and feel ashamed for the desire for independence. The child's autonomic development will be inhibited, and be less prepared to successfully deal with the world in the future.

Early Childhood

When children attend preschool, they broaden their social horizons and become more engaged with those around them. Impulses are channeled into fantasies, which leaves the task of the caretaker to balance eagerness for pursuing adventure, creativity and self expression with the development of responsibility. If caretakers are properly encouraging and consistently disciplinary, children are more likely to develop positive self-esteem while becoming more responsible, and will follow through on assigned activities. If not allowed to decide which activities to perform, children may begin to feel guilt upon contemplating taking initiative. This negative association with independence will lead them to let others make decisions in place of them.

Late Childhood

In middle childhood, intelligence is demonstrated through logical and systematic manipulation of symbols related to concrete objects. Operational thinking develops, which means actions are reversible, and egocentric thought diminishes.

Children go through the transition from the world at home to that of school and peers. Children learn to make things, use tools, and acquire the skills to be a worker and a potential provider. Children can now receive feedback from outsiders about their accomplishments. If children can discover pleasure in intellectual stimulation, being productive, seeking success, they will develop a sense of competence. If they are not successful or cannot discover pleasure in the process, they may develop a sense of inferiority and feelings of inadequacy that may haunt them throughout life. This is when children think of them selves as industrious or as inferior.

Adolescence

Adolescence is the period of life between the onset of puberty and the full commitment to an adult social role, such as worker, parent, and/or citizen. It is the period known for the formation of personal and social identity and the discovery of moral purpose. Intelligence is demonstrated through the logical use of symbols related to abstract concepts and formal reasoning. A return to egocentric thought often occurs early in the period. Only 35% develop the capacity to reason formally during adolescence or adulthood.

It is divided into two parts namely:

1. Early Adolescence: 13 to 17 years and
2. Late Adolescence: 17 to 18 years

The adolescent unconsciously explores questions such as "Who am I? Who do I want to be?" Like toddlers, adolescents must explore, test limits, become autonomous, and commit to an identity, or sense of self. Different roles, behaviours and ideologies must be tried out to select an identity. Role confusion and inability to choose vocation can result from a failure to achieve a sense of identity.

Early Adulthood

The person must learn how to form intimate relationships, both in friendship and love. The development of this skill relies on the resolution of other stages. It may be hard to establish intimacy if one has not developed trust or a sense of identity. If this skill is not learned the alternative is alienation, isolation, a fear of commitment, and the inability to depend on others.

A related framework for studying this part of the life span is that of Emerging adulthood, introduced in 2000 by Jeffrey Arnett. Scholars of emerging adulthood are interested not only in relationship development (focusing on the role of dating in helping individuals settle on a long-term spouse/partner), but also the development of sociopolitical views and occupational choice.

Middle Age

Middle adulthood generally refers to the period between ages 40 to 60. During this period, the middle-aged experience a conflict between generativity and stagnation. They may either feel a sense of contributing to the next generation and their community or a sense of purposelessness. Physically, the middle-aged experience a decline in muscular strength, reaction time, sensory keenness, and cardiac output. Also, women experience menopause and a sharp drop in the hormone estrogen. Men do have an equivalent to menopause, it is called "Andropause," which is a hormone fluctuation with physical and psychological effects similar to menopause. Lowered testosterone levels result in mood swings and a decline in sperm count and speed of ejaculation and erection. Most men and women remain capable of sexual satisfaction after middle age.

Old Age

This stage generally refers to those over 60–80 years. During old age, people experience a conflict between integrity vs. despair. When reflecting on their life, they either feel a sense of accomplishment or failure.

Physically, older people experience a decline in muscular strength, reaction time, stamina, hearing, distance perception, and the sense of smell. They also are more susceptible to severe diseases such as cancer and pneumonia due to a weakened immune system. Mental disintegration may also occur, leading to Dementia or Alzheimer's Disease. However, partially due to a lifetime's accumulation of antibodies, the elderly are less likely to suffer from common diseases such as the cold.

Whether or not intellectual powers increase or decrease with age remains controversial. Longitudinal studies have suggested that intellect declines, while cross-sectional studies suggest that intellect is stable. It is generally believed that crystallized intelligence increases up to old age, while fluid intelligence decreases with age.

Other Findings

Parenting

In Western developed societies, mothers (and women generally) were emphasized to the exclusion of other caregivers, particularly as the traditional role of the father was more the breadwinner, and less the direct caregiver of an infant, he has been traditionally viewed as impacting an infant indirectly through interactions with the mother of the child.

The emphasis of study has shifted to the primary caregiver (regardless of gender or biological relation), as well as all persons directly or indirectly influencing the child (the family system). The roles of the mother and father are more significant than first thought as we moved into the concept of primary caregiver.

Affirming a role for fathers, studies have shown that children as young as 15 months benefit significantly from substantial engagement with their father. In particular, a study in the U.S.A. and New Zealand found the presence of the natural father was the most significant factor in reducing rates of early sexual activity and rates of teenage pregnancy in girls. Covariate factors used included early conduct problems, maternal age at first childbirth, race, maternal education, father's occupational status, family living standards, family life stress, early mother-child interaction, measures of psychosocial adjustment and educational achievement, school qualifications, mood disorder, anxiety disorder, suicide attempts, violent offending, and conduct disorder. Further research has found fathers have an impact on child academic performance, including involved nonresident fathers. However, father absence is associated with a range of negative outcomes for children, including child and later criminal behaviour.

Historical Antecedents

The modern form of developmental psychology has its roots in the rich psychological tradition represented by Aristotle, Tabari, Rhazes, and Descartes. William Shakespeare had his melancholy character *Jacques* (in As You Like It) articulate the seven ages of man: these included three stages of childhood and four of adulthood. In the mid-eighteenth century Jean Jacques Rousseau described three stages of childhood: *infans* (infancy), *puer* (childhood) and *adolescence* in *Emile: Or, On Education*. Rousseau's ideas were taken up strongly by educators at the time.

In the late nineteenth century, psychologists familiar with the evolutionary theory of Darwin began seeking an evolutionary description of psychological development; prominent here was G. Stanley Hall, who attempted to correlate ages of childhood with previous ages of mankind.

A more scientific approach was initiated by James Mark Baldwin, who wrote essays on topics that included *Imitation: A Chapter in the Natural History of Consciousness* and *Mental Development in the Child and the Race: Methods and Processes*. In 1905, Sigmund Freud articulated five psychosexual stages. Later, Rudolf Steiner articulated stages of psychological development throughout human life. By the early to mid-twentieth century, the work of Vygotsky and Piaget, mentioned above, had established a strong empirical tradition in the field.

2

Childhood Development

Childhood is the age span ranging from birth to adolescence. In developmental psychology, childhood is divided up into the developmental stages of toddlerhood (learning to walk), early childhood (play age), middle childhood (school age), and adolescence (post-puberty).

Age Ranges of Childhood

The term *childhood* is non-specific and can imply a varying range of years in human development. Developmentally, it refers to the period between infancy and adulthood. In common terms, childhood is considered to start from birth. Some consider that childhood, as a concept of play and innocence, ends at adolescence. In many countries, there is an age of majority when childhood officially ends and a person legally becomes an adult. The age ranges anywhere from 13 to 21, with 18 being the most common.

Developmental Stages of Childhood

Early Childhood

Early childhood follows the infancy stage, and begins with toddlerhood when the child begins speaking or taking steps independently. While toddlerhood ends around age three when the child becomes less dependent on parental assistance for basic needs, early childhood continues approximately through years seven or eight. According to the National Association for the Education of Young Children, early childhood spans the human life from birth to age eight.

Early childhood is a stage in human development. It generally includes toddlerhood and some time afterwards. Play age is an unspecific designation approximately within the scope of early childhood.

Education

Early childhood education is the organized practice of educating those who are in early childhood, one of the most vulnerable stages in life. According to the NAEYC (National Association for the Education of Young Children), it spans the human life from birth to age eight.

Early childhood education often focuses on children learning through play.

According to UNESCO ECCE (Early Childhood Care and Education) Unit, Early childhood is defined as the period from birth to 8 years old. A time of remarkable brain development, these years lay the foundation for subsequent learning.

The terms preschool education and kindergarten emphasize education around the ages of 3–6 years. The terms "early childhood learning," "early care," and "early education" are comparable with *early childhood education*. The terms Day care and Childcare do not embrace the educational aspects. Many childcare centres are now using more educational approaches. They are creating curricula and incorporating it into their daily routines to foster greater educational learning.

Researchers in the field and early childhood educators both view the parents as an integral part of the early childhood education process. Early childhood education takes many forms depending on the beliefs of the educator or parent.

Much of the first two years of life are spent in the creation of a child's first "sense of self" or the building of a first identity. This is a crucial part of children's makeup—how they first see themselves, how they think they should function, how they expect others to function in relation to them.

For this reason, early care must ensure that in addition to employing carefully selected and trained caretakers, program policy must emphasize links with family, home culture, and home language, meaning caregivers must uniquely care for

each child using Developmentally Appropriate Practice, Individually Appropriate Practice and Culturally Appropriate Practice. Care should support families rather than be a substitute for them.

If a young child doesn't receive sufficient nurturing, nutrition, parental/caregiver interaction, and stimulus during this crucial period, the child may be left with a developmental deficit that hampers his or her success in preschool, kindergarten, and beyond.

Worst-case scenarios such as those found in Russian and Romanian orphanages demonstrate how the lack of proper social interaction and development of attachment affect the developing child. Children must receive attention and affection to develop in a healthy manner.

Developmental Domains

There are five different developmental domains of children which all relate to each other. They are easily referred to as the SPICE of life:

- Social-Refers mostly to the ability to form attachments, play with others, co-operation and sharing, and being able to create lasting relationships with others.
- Physical-Development of Fine (small) and Gross (large) Motor Skills.
- Intellectual-The process of making sense of the world around them.
- Creative-The development of special abilities creating talents. Music, Art, Writing, Reading, and Singing are all ways for creative development to take place.
- Emotional-Development of self-awareness, self-confidence, and coping with feelings as well as understanding them.

Psychosocial According to Jean Piaget, there are four major stages of cognitive development:

1. Sensorimotor Stage. This stage occurs between the ages of birth and two years of age. Sensorimotor (infancy): During this stage, which includes six distinct substages,

intelligence is demonstrated through motor activity with limited use of symbols, including language; the infant's knowledge of the world is primarily based on physical interactions and experiences.

2. Preoperational Stage. The second stage occurs between the ages of 2 – 7 years. During this stage, intelligence is increasingly demonstrated through the use of symbols; memory and imagination are developed as language use matures; thinking is nonlogical, nonreversible, and egocentric.
3. Concrete Operations Stage. Occurring between ages 7 and about 12 years. During this stage—characterized by conservation of number, length, liquid, mass, weight, area, volume—intelligence is increasingly demonstrated through logical and systematic manipulation of symbols relating to concrete objects; thinking is operational, reversible, and less egocentric.
4. Formal Operations Stage. The final stage of cognitive development (from age 12 and beyond). During this final stage, intelligence is demonstrated through the logical use of symbols related to abstract concepts; thinking is abstract, hypothetical, and early on, quite egocentric; it is commonly held that the majority of people never complete this stage.
   - Emotional Development-Concerning children's increasing awareness and control of their feelings and how they react to these feelings in a given situation.
   - Social Development-Concerning the children's identity, their relationships with others, and understanding their place within a social environment

There are many other reformers of education that have contributed to what early childhood education means today. Although Piaget had a great impact on early childhood education, people like John Locke, Horace Mann and Jane Addams contributed a lifetime of work to reform education and learning in this country.

Benefits of Early Childhood Education

Chicago's publicly-funded Child-Parent Centres have served almost 100,000 3-and 4-year-olds since 1967. Researchers tracked 989 of those children and 550 similar children not in the program for 14 years. The children who did not participate were 70 percent more likely to be arrested for a violent crime by age 18. This program also cut child abuse and neglect. In Ypsilanti, Michigan, 3-and 4-year-olds from low-income families who were randomly assigned to a group that did not receive preschool who were five times more likely to have become chronic lawbreakers by age 27 than those who were assigned to the High/Scope Educational Research Foundation's Perry Preschool program. The overarching goals of the World Conference on Early Childhood Care and Education (WCECCE) are to:

- Reaffirm ECCE as a right of all children and as the basis for development;
- Take stock of the progress of Member States towards achieving the EFA Goal 1;
- Identify binding constraints toward making the intended equitable expansion of access to quality ECCE services;
- Establish, more concretely, benchmarks and targets for the EFA Goal 1 toward 2015 and beyond
- Identify key enablers that should facilitate Member States to reach the established targets; and
- Promote global exchange of good practices.

Infants and toddlers experience life more holistically than any other age group. Social, emotional, cognitive, language, and physical lessons are not learned separately by very young children. Adults who are most helpful to young children interact in ways that understand that the child is learning from the whole experience, not just that part of the experience to which the adult gives attention..

Middle Childhood

Middle childhood begins at around age seven or eight, approximating primary school age and ends around puberty, the beginning of adolescence.

Adolescence

Adolescence, or late childhood, begins around the time of puberty. The end of adolescence and the beginning of adulthood varies by country and by function, and even within a single nation-state or culture there may be different ages at which an individual is considered to be (chronologically and legally) mature enough to be entrusted by society with certain tasks.

History of Childhood

It has been argued that childhood is not a natural phenomenon but a creation of society. Philippe Ariès, an important French medievalist and historian, pointed this out in his book *Centuries of Childhood*. This theme was then taken up by Cunningham in his book the *Invention of Childhood* (2006) which looks at the historical aspects of childhood from the Middle Ages to what he refers to as the Post War Period of the 1950s, 1960s and 1970s.

Ariès published a study in 1961 of paintings, gravestones, furniture, and school records. He found that before the 17th-century, children were represented as mini-adults. Since then historians have increasingly researched childhood in past times. Before Ariès, George Boas had published *The Cult of Childhood*.

During the Renaissance, artistic depictions of children increased dramatically in Europe. This did not impact the social attitude to children much, however—see the article on child labour.

The man usually credited with-or accused of-creating the modern notion of childhood is Jean Jacques Rousseau. Building on the ideas of John Locke and other 17th-century liberal thinkers, Rousseau formulated childhood as a brief period of sanctuary before people encounter the perils and hardships of adulthood. "Why rob these innocents of the joys which pass so quickly," Rousseau pleaded. "Why fill with bitterness the fleeting early days of childhood, days which will no more return for them than for you?"

The Victorian Era has been described as a source of the modern institution of childhood. Ironically, the Industrial Revolution during this era led to an increase in child labour, but due to the campaigning of the Evangelicals, and efforts of author Charles Dickens and others, child labour was gradually reduced and halted in England via the Factory Acts of 1802-1878. The Victorians concomitantly emphasized the role of the family and the sanctity of the child, and broadly speaking, this attitude has remained dominant in Western societies since then.

In the contemporary era Joe L. Kincheloe and Shirley R. Steinberg have constructed a critical theory of childhood and childhood education that they have labeled kinderculture. Kincheloe and Steinberg make use of multiple research and theoretical discourses (the bricolage) to study childhood from diverse perspectives—historiography, ethnography, cognitive research, media studies, cultural studies, political economic analysis, hermeneutics, semiotics, content analysis, etc. Based on this multiperspectival inquiry, Kincheloe and Steinberg contend that new times have ushered in a new era of childhood. Evidence of this dramatic cultural change is omnipresent, but many individuals in the late 20th century and early 21st century have not yet noticed it. When Steinberg and Kincheloe wrote the first edition of Kinderculture: The Corporate Construction of Childhood in 1997 (second edition, 2004) many people who made their living studying, teaching, or caring for children were not yet aware of the nature of the changes in childhood that they encountered daily.

In the domains of psychology, education, and to a lesser degree sociology and cultural studies few observers before kinderculture had studied the ways that the information explosion so characteristic of our contemporary era (hyperreality) had operated to undermine traditional notions of childhood and change the terrain of childhood education. Those who have shaped, directed and employed contemporary information technology have played an exaggerated role in the reformulation of childhood. Of course, information technology alone, Kincheloe and Steinberg maintain, has not produced a new era of childhood. Obviously, numerous social, cultural, and political economic factors have operated to produce such changes. The central purpose of kinderculture is to socially, culturally, politically, and economically situate the changing historical status of childhood and to specifically interroge the ways diverse media have helped construct what Kincheloe and Steinberg call "the new childhood." Kinderculture understands that childhood is an ever-changing social and historical artifact—not simply a biological entity. Because many psychologists have argued that childhood is a natural phase of growing up, of becoming an adult, Kincheloe and Steinberg coming from an educational context saw kinderculture as a corrective to such a "psychologization" of childhood.

Geographies of Childhood

The geographies of childhood involves how (adult) society perceives the very idea of childhood and the many ways the attitudes and behaviours of adults affects children's lives. This includes ideas about the surrounding environment of children and its related implications. This is similar in some respects to children's geographies which examines the places and spaces in which children live.

Modern Concepts of Childhood

The concept of childhood appears to evolve and change shape as lifestyles change and adult expectations alter. Some believe that children should not have any worries and should not have to work; life should be happy and trouble-free. Childhood is usually a mixture of happiness, wonder, angst and resilience. It is generally a time of playing, learning, socializing, exploring, and worrying in a world without much adult interference, aside from parents. It is a time of learning about responsibilities without having to deal with adult responsibilities.

Childhood is often retrospectively viewed as a time of innocence, which is generally viewed as a positive term, connoting an optimistic view of the world, in particular one where the lack of knowledge stems from a lack of wrongdoing, whereas greater knowledge comes from doing wrong.

A "loss of innocence" is a common concept, and is often seen as an integral part of coming of age. It is usually thought of as an experience or period in a child's life that widens their awareness of evil, pain or the world around them. This theme is demonstrated in the novels *To Kill a Mockingbird* and *Lord of the Flies*. The fictional character Peter Pan was the embodiment of a childhood that never ends.

Nature Deficit Disorder

Nature Deficit Disorder, a term coined by Richard Louv in his 2005 book *Last Child in the Woods,* refers to the alleged trend in the United States that children are spending less time outdoors, resulting in a wide range of behavioral problems. With the advent of the computer, video games and television, children have more reasons to stay inside rather than outdoors exploring. "The average American child spends 44 hours a week with electronic media". Parents are also keeping children indoors in order to protect them from their growing fear of "stranger danger". Recent research has drawn a further contrast between the declining number of National Park visits in the United States and increasing consumption of electronic media by children.

Healthy Childhoods

Role of Parents

Parenting is the process of promoting and supporting the physical, emotional, social, and intellectual development of a child from infancy to adulthood. Parenting refers to the activity of raising a child rather than the biological relationship.

In the case of humans, it is usually done by the biological parents of the child in question, although governments and society take a role as well. In many cases, orphaned or abandoned children receive parental care from non-parent blood relations. Others may be adopted, raised by foster care, or be placed in an orphanage.

The goals of human parenting are debated. Usually, parental figures provide for a child's physical needs, protect them from harm, and impart in them skills and cultural values until they reach legal adulthood, usually after adolescence. Among non-human species, parenting is usually less lengthy and complicated, though mammals tend to nurture their young extensively. The degree of attention parents invest in their offspring is largely inversely proportional to the number of offspring the average adult in the species produces.

Parenting Models, Tools, Philosophies and Practices

Although race may be a significant contributing factor, social class, wealth, and income have the strongest impact on what methods of child rearing are used by parents. Lack of money is found to be the defining factor in the style of child rearing that is chosen, and minorities are more likely to have less wealth or assets available for use in their children's upbringing. Societal values and norms of a generation also have an effect, as in the United States where authoritarian parenting was the most popular until the 1960s when a backlash made permissive parenting the most popular in the 1970s.

Models of Parenting

Developmental psychologist Diana Baumrind identified three main parenting styles in early child development: authoritative, authoritarian, and permissive. Maccoby and Martin expanded the styles to four: authoritative, authoritarian, indulgent and neglectful. These four styles of parenting involve combinations of acceptance and responsiveness on the one hand and demand and control on the other.

There is no single or definitive model of parenting. What may be right for one family or one child may not be suitable for another. With authoritative and permissive (indulgent) parenting on opposite sides of the spectrum, most conventional and modern models of parenting fall somewhere in between.

- Attachment parenting – Seeks to create strong emotional bonds, avoiding physical punishment and accomplishing discipline through interactions recognizing a child's emotional needs all while focusing on holistic understanding of the child.
- Historic Developmental (Child as Apprentice) Skill Based Model – As a child's independent capacities emerge, ever more complex opportunities for parental instruction in or modeling of the widest possible number of essential skills and knowledge are presented. The child gains self-worth simultaneous to the emergence of various physical and mental competencies in an ever-growing number of essential venues, as adulthood is approached. From the initial highly dependent

relationship with parents and direct community support, high levels of independence are attained seamlessly while special skills and abilities of the child have emerged in a manner relevant to successful adult vocational choices, leisure pursuits, expanded life interests, and contributions to the community.

- Nurturant parent model – A family model where children are expected to explore their surroundings with protection from their parents.
- Single Parent Model – The percentage of children being raised by single parents has been flat for the last 20 years but it remains nearly double the rate of 1970. Obstacles which create difficulty for single parents relate primarily to a halving of the numerous resources fundamental to parenting: income is often reduced dramatically; opportunities to present and process adult male and female roles, responsibilities, and skills to children is reduced; sharing of household maintenance with another adult is reduced; opportunities to see parents display affection and cooperation despite differences is reduced; both boys and girls will lack the cooperative presentation of adult male and adult female points of view regarding socialization fundamentals.
- Slow parenting – Encourages parents to plan and organise less for their children, instead allowing them to enjoy their childhood and explore the world at their own pace.
- Strict father model – An authoritarian approach, places a strong value on discipline as a means to survive and thrive in a harsh world.

Christian Parenting

In the United States, disparate models explicitly termed "Christian parenting" are popular among some parents who claim to apply biblical principles to parenting. Information on Christian parenting is found in publications, Christian parenting websites, and in seminars devoted to helping parents apply Christian principles to parenting. While some Christian parenting models are strict and authoritarian, others are "grace-based" and share methods advocated in attachment parenting and positive parenting theories. Particularly influential on opposite sides have been James Dobson and his book *Dare to Discipline*, and William Sears who has written several parenting books including *The Complete Book of Christian Parenting & Child Care' and 'The Discipline Book'.*

In a study of Christian parents done by *Christian Parenting Today* in 2000, 39% of the families surveyed have family devotions once a week or more, and 69% of parents consider Sunday school, youth and children's programs extremely important.

Other Models of Parenting

- Taking Children Seriously – Sees both praise and punishment as manipulative and harmful to children and advocates other methods to reach agreement with them.
- Parenting For Everyone – The philosophy of Parenting For Everyone, which stems from the book by the same name, considers parenting from the ethical point of view. It analyses parenting goals, conditions and means of childrearing. It offers to look at a child's internal world (emotions, intelligence and spirit) and derive the sources of parenting success from there. The concept of heart implies the child's sense of being loved and their ability to love others. The concept of intelligence implies the child's morals. And the concept of spirit implies the child's desire to do good actions, avoid bad behaviour, and avoid encroaching upon anybody's dignity. The core concept of the philosophy of Parenting For Everyone is the concept of dignity, the child's sense of worthiness and justice.
- One theory breaks down rules into four categories: safety rules, moral rules, rules of social convention, and regulation of personal areas (personal expression, choice of friends). This theory proposes that children tend to resist mostly only rules that they perceive to intrude on personal domains, and that parents should avoid such rules.

Parenting Practices

- Rules of traffic – an instructional approach to discipline where parents explain to their children how to behave, teaching the rules of behaviour as they would the rules of traffic, with little explanation or deeper moral and social implications.
- Fine gardening – parents believe that children have positive and negative qualities, the latter of which parents should "weed out" or "prune" into an appropriate shape.
- Rewards and punishments – a method of discipline based on logic: for a good behaviour the child receives a reward or praise, and for a bad or unwanted behaviour the child receives a punishment or reprimand. To teach a child by this logic may be very effective if it is done consistently.
- Concerted cultivation – fostering children's talents through organized leisure activities. Parents challenge their children to think critically and to speak properly and frequently, especially with other adults.

Parenting Across the Child's Lifespan

Planning and Pre-pregnancy

Family planning is the decision whether and when to become parents, including planning, preparing, and gathering resources. Parents should assess (amongst other matters) whether they have the required financial resources (the raising of a child costs around $16,198 yearly in the United States) and should also assess whether their family situation is stable enough and whether they themselves are responsible and qualified enough to raise a child. Reproductive health and preconceptional care affect pregnancy, reproductive success and maternal and child physical and mental health.

Pregnancy and Prenatal Parenting

During pregnancy the unborn child is affected by many decisions his or her parents make, particularly choices linked to their lifestyle. The health and diet decisions of the mother can have either a positive or negative impact on the child during prenatal parenting.

Many people believe that parenting begins with birth, but the mother begins raising and nurturing a child well before birth. Scientific evidence indicates that from the fifth month on, the unborn baby is able to hear sound, be aware of motion, and possibly exhibit short-term memory. Several studies (e.g. Kissilevsky et al., 2003) show evidence that the unborn baby can become familiar with his or her parents' voices. Other research indicates that by the seventh month, external schedule cues influence the unborn baby's sleep habits. Based on this evidence, parenting actually begins well before birth.

Depending on how many children the mother carries also determines the amount of care needed during prenatal and post-natal periods.

Newborns and Infants

Newborn parenting, up to one month of age, is where the responsibilities of parenthood begins. A newborn's basic needs are food, sleep, comfort and cleaning which the parent provides. An infant's only form of communication is crying, and attentive parents will begin to recognize different types of crying which represent different needs such as hunger, discomfort, boredom, or loneliness. Newborns and young infants require feedings every few hours which is disruptive to adult sleep cycles. They respond enthusiastically to soft stroking, cuddling and caressing. Gentle rocking back and forth often calms a crying infant, as do massages and warm baths. Newborns may comfort themselves by sucking their thumb or a pacifier. The need to suckle is instinctive and allows newborns to feed. Breastfeeding is the recommended method of feeding by all major infant health organizations. If breastfeeding is not possible or desired, bottle feeding is a common alternative. Other alternatives include feeding breastmilk or formula with a cup, spoon, feeding syringe, or nursing supplementer.

The forming of attachments is considered to be the foundation of the infant/child's capacity to form and conduct relationships throughout life. Attachment is not the same as love and/or affection although they often go together. Attachment and attachment behaviours tend to develop between the age of 6 months and 3 years. A lack of attachment or a seriously disrupted capacity for attachment could potentially amount to serious disorders.

Until infants learn to walk, between 10 and 14 months, they are carried in the arms, held in slings or baby carriers, or transported in baby carriages or strollers. Upon learning to walk the child is then known as a toddler.

Toddlers

Toddlers are much more active than infants and are challenged with learning how to do simple tasks by themselves. At this stage, parents are heavily involved in showing the child how to do things rather than just doing things for them, and the child will often mimic the parents. Toddlers need help to build their vocabulary, increase their communications skills, and manage their emotions. Toddlers will also begin to understand social etiquette such as being polite and taking turns.

Toddlers are very curious about the world around them and eager to explore it. They seek greater independence and responsibility and may become frustrated when things do not go the way they want or expect. Tantrums begin at this stage, which is sometimes referred to as the 'Terrible Twos'. Tantrums are often caused by the child's frustration over the particular situation, sometimes simply not being able to communicate properly. Parents of toddlers are expected to help guide and teach the child, establish basic routines (such as washing hands before meals or brushing teeth before bed), and increase the child's responsibilities.

Child

Younger children are becoming more independent and are beginning to build friendships. They are able to reason and can make their own decisions given hypothetical situations. Young children demand constant attention, but will learn how to deal with boredom and be able to play independently. They also enjoy helping and feeling useful and able. Parents may assist their child by encouraging social interactions and modelling proper social behaviours. A large part of learning in the early years comes from being involved in activities and household duties. Parents who observe their children in play or join with them in child-driven play have the opportunity to glimpse into their children's world, learn to communicate more effectively with their children and are given another setting to offer gentle, nurturing guidance. Parents are also teaching their children health, hygiene, and eating habits through instruction and by example.

Parents are expected to make decisions about their child's education. Parenting styles in this area diverge greatly at this stage with some parents becoming heavily involved in arranging organized activities and early learning programs. Other parents choose to let the child develop with few organized activities.

Children begin to learn responsibility, and consequences of their actions, with parental assistance. Some parents provide a small allowance that increases with age to help teach children the value of money and how to be responsible with it.

Parents who are consistent and fair with their discipline, who openly communicate and offer explanations to their children, and who do not neglect the needs of their children in some way often find they have fewer problems with their children as they mature.

Adolescents

During adolescence children are beginning to form their identity and are testing and developing the interpersonal and occupational roles that they will assume as adults. Although adolescents look to peers and adults outside of the family for guidance and models for how to behave, parents remain influential in their development.

Parents often feel isolated and alone in parenting adolescents, but they should still make efforts to be aware of their adolescents activities, provide guidance, direction, and consultation. Adolescence can be a time of high risk for children, where newfound freedoms can result in decisions that drastically open up or close off life opportunities. Parental issues at this stage of parenting include dealing with "rebellious" teenagers, who didn't know freedom while they were smaller.

Adults

- Young adults – as children become young adults their personalities show the result of successful or unsuccessful parenting. Especially it is noticeable when young adults make their independent life decisions about their education, work and choosing mates for friendship or marriage.
- Middle age and old age – Parenting doesn't stop when children grow up and age. Parents always remain to be parents for old children. Their relationship continues developing if both parties want to keep it or improve. The parenting issues may include the relationship with grandchildren and stepchildren.

Assistance

Traditionally, new mothers and fathers have received advice from older family members and other, experienced parents. Parents often ask pediatricians for advice about child development. In addition, informal mother's groups, playgroups, and online parenting communities provide new parents with opportunities for sharing advice and information.

Parenting books, magazines, and websites offer a wide range of advice and ideas. Parents magazine was started by George J. Hecht in 1926 and is the oldest parenting publication in the United States.

Dr. Benjamin Spock's book *The Common Sense Book of Baby and Child Care*, became a bestseller in 1946, and by 1998 it had sold more than 50 million copies.

Hundreds of books have been written on the topic, each with the author's own philosophy on how best to raise a child. Television documentaries such as The Trouble with Evan and programs such as Bringing Up Baby and Supernanny offer glimpses into the lives of other families and the effects of their parenting methods.

Physical Health

Further information: Childhood obesity, Childhood immunizations, and List of childhood diseases

Child Protection

Further information: Child labor, Child labor laws, Risk aversion, Child abuse, and Protection of Children Act

Childhood Play

Play is essential to the cognitive, physical, social, and emotional well-being of children. It offers children opportunities for physical (running, jumping, climbing, etc.), intellectual (social skills, community norms, ethics and general knowledge) and emotional development (empathy, compassion, and friendships). Unstructured play encourages creativity and imagination. Playing and interacting with other children, as well as some adults, provides opportunities for friendships, social interactions, conflicts and resolutions.

It is through play that children at a very early age engage and interact in the world around them. Play allows children to create and explore a world they can master, conquering their fears while practicing adult roles, sometimes in conjunction with other children or adult caregivers. Undirected play allows children to learn how to work in groups, to share, to negotiate, to resolve conflicts, and to learn self-advocacy skills. However when play is controlled by adults, children acquiesce to adult rules and concerns and lose some of the benefits play offers them, particularly in developing creativity, leadership, and group skills.

Play is considered to be so important to optimal child development that it has been recognized by the United Nations High Commission for Human Rights as a right of every child. Children who are being raised in a hurried and pressured style may limit the protective benefits they would gain from child-driven play.

Street Culture

Children's street culture refers to the cumulative culture created by young children and is sometimes referred to as their *secret world*. It is most common in children between the ages of seven and twelve. It is strongest in urban working class industrial districts where children are traditionally free to play out in the streets for long periods without supervision. It is invented and largely sustained by children themselves with little adult interference.

Young children's street culture usually takes place on quiet backstreets and pavements, and along routes that venture out into local parks, playgrounds, scrub and wasteland, and to local shops. It often imposes imaginative status on certain sections of the urban realm (local buildings, kerbs, street objects, etc). Children designate specific areas that serve as informal meeting and relaxation places. An urban area that looks faceless or neglected to an adult may have deep 'spirit of place' meanings in to children. Since the advent of indoor distractions such as video games, and television, concerns have been expressed about the vitality-or even the survival-of children's street culture.

Research in Social Sciences

In recent years there has been a rapid growth of interest in the sociological study of adulthood. Reaching on a large body of contemporary sociological and anthropological research, people have developed key links between the study of childhood and social theory, exploring its historical, political, and cultural dimensions in Ethiopia.

3

Physical Development during Adolescence

Adolescence is a transitional stage of physical and mental human development generally occurring between puberty and legal adulthood (age of majority), but largely characterized as beginning and ending with the teenage stage. According to Erik Erikson's stages of human development, for example, a young adult is generally a person between the ages of 20 and 40, whereas an adolescent is a person between the ages of 13 and 19. Historically, puberty has been heavily associated with teenagers and the onset of adolescent development. However, the start of puberty has had somewhat of an increase in preadolescence (particularly females, as seen with early and precocious puberty), and adolescence has had an occasional extension beyond the teenage years (typically males) compared to previous generations. These changes have made it more difficult to rigidly define the time frame in which adolescence occurs.

The end of adolescence and the beginning of adulthood varies by country and by function, and furthermore even within a single nation-state or culture there can be different ages at which an individual is considered to be (chronologically and legally) mature enough to be entrusted by society with certain tasks. Such milestones include, but are not limited to, driving a vehicle, having legal sexual relations, serving in the armed forces or on a jury, purchasing and drinking alcohol, voting, entering into contracts, completing certain levels of education, and marrying.

Adolescence is usually accompanied by an increased independence allowed by the parents or legal guardians and less supervision, contrary to the preadolescence stage.

Adolescence, the transitional stage of development between childhood and adulthood, represents the period of time during which a person experiences a variety of biological changes and encounters a number of emotional issues. The ages which are considered to be part of adolescence vary by culture, and ranges from preteens to 19 years. According to the World Health Organization (WHO), adolescence covers the period of life between 10 and 20 years of age. Adolescence is often divided by psychologists into three distinct phases: early, mid, and late adolescence.

Background

Adolescence can be a specifically turbulent as well as a dynamic period of one's life. It has been identified as a period in which young people develop abstract thinking abilities, become more aware of their sexuality, develop a clearer sense of psychological identity, and increase their independence from parents. G. Stanley Hall denoted this period as one of "Storm and Stress" and, according to him, conflict at this developmental stage is normal and not unusual. Margaret Mead, on the other hand, attributed the behaviour of adolescents to their culture and upbringing, as the majority of problems associated with adolescence in western society are not present in other cultures.

Several developmental stage models have placed adolescence in a period of human development. Sigmund Freud saw it as the "genital phase" of psychosexual development, where the child recaptures the sexual awareness of infancy. Jean Piaget focused on cognitive development, seeing adolescence as the "formal operative stage" where the young person develops the ability to think abstractly and draw conclusions from the information available. Erik Erikson's theory of psychosocial development identified the identity crisis as central to the notion of adolescence.

Adolescent psychology addresses the issues associated with adolescence, such as whether or not the aforementioned "storm and stress" is a normal part of this period. The American

Psychological Association has a separate division dedicated to adolescence, and the psychologists specializing in this topic attempt to answer questions dealing with the age group. One issue in adolescent psychology discusses whether adolescence is in fact a discrete developmental period, a point along a continuum of human development, or a social construction.

Social Behaviour Patterns

The social behaviour of mammals changes as they enter adolescence. In humans, adolescents typically increase the amount of time spent with their peers. Nearly eight hours are usually spent communicating with others, but only eight percent of this time is spent talking to adults. Adolescents report that they are far happier spending time with similarly-aged peers as compared to adults. Consequently, conflict between adolescents and their parents increase at this time as adolescents strive to create a separation and sense of independence. These interactions are not always positive; peer pressure is very prevalent during adolescence, leading to increases in cheating and misdemeanor crime. Young adolescents are particularly susceptible to conforming to the behaviour of their peers.

Early adolescence is a stage at which the peer group becomes increasingly important, with conformity to peers peaking at 11–13 years (Costanzo and Shaw 1966). 90% of adolescents identify themselves with a peer group (Palmonari, 1989). According to Judith Rich Harris's theory of group socialization, children and adolescents are shaped more by their peers than their parents (Harris 1997). Peers can encourage both pro-social behaviour, which peaks at 11–12 years, or anti-social behaviour, which peaks at 14–15 years (Bendt, 1979). Adolescents are less likely to feel depressed or anxious if the peer group provides emotional support (Buhrmester, 1992). Arguments between parents and children increase considerably during adolescence (Feeney, 1999). However, adolescents with few or no close friends are closer to their parents and are less likely to be subject to peer pressure.

Non-human mammals also exhibit changes in social attitude during adolescence. Adolescent rodents have also been observed spending more of their time with rodents of similar age. Conflicts between adolescents and parents have been noted in other primates, and overall increases in aggressiveness have been observed during this time period. Despite this, social bonding between adolescents and adults tends to improve due to reconciliatory behaviour. Allomaternal behaviour increases among females in several species, including humans, nonhuman primates, and rodents. However, males tend to exhibit less interest in infants during adolescence.

Puberty

Puberty is the process of physical changes by which a child's body becomes an adult body capable of reproduction. Puberty is initiated by hormone signals from the brain to the gonads (the ovaries and testes). In response, the gonads produce a variety of hormones that stimulate the growth, function, or transformation of brain, bones, muscle, blood, skin, hair, breasts, and reproductive organs. Growth accelerates in the first half of puberty and stops at the completion of puberty. Before puberty, body differences between boys and girls are almost entirely restricted to the genitalia. During puberty, major differences of size, shape, composition, and function develop in many body structures and systems. The most obvious of these are referred to as secondary sex characteristics.

In a strict sense, the term *puberty* (derived from the Latin word *puberatum* (age of maturity, manhood)) refers to the bodily changes of sexual maturation rather than the psychosocial and cultural aspects of adolescent development. Adolescence is the period of psychological and social transition between childhood and adulthood. Adolescence largely overlaps the period of puberty, but its boundaries are less precisely defined and it refers as much to the psychosocial and cultural characteristics of development during the teen years as to the physical changes of puberty.

Differences between Male and Female Puberty

Two of the most significant differences between puberty in girls and puberty in boys are the age at which it begins, and the major sex steroids involved. Although there is a wide range of normal ages, girls typically begin the process of puberty at age 10, boys at age 12. Girls usually complete puberty by ages 15–17, while boys usually complete puberty by ages 16–18. Any increase in height beyond these ages is uncommon. Girls attain reproductive maturity about 4 years after the first physical changes of puberty appear. In contrast, boys accelerate more slowly but continue to grow for about 6 years after the first visible pubertal changes.

For boys, an androgen called testosterone is the principal sex hormone. While testosterone produces all boys' changes characterized as virilization, a substantial product of testosterone metabolism in males is estradiol, though levels rise later and more slowly than in girls. The male "growth spurt" also begins later, accelerates more slowly, and lasts longer before the epiphyses fuse. Although boys are on average 2 cm shorter than girls before puberty begins, adult men are on average about 13 cm (5.2 inches) taller than women. Most of this sex difference in adult heights is attributable to a later onset of the growth spurt and a slower progression to completion, a direct result of the later rise and lower adult male levels of estradiol.

The hormone that dominates female development is an estrogen called estradiol. While estradiol promotes growth of breasts and uterus, it is also the principal hormone driving the pubertal growth spurt and epiphyseal maturation and closure. Estradiol levels rise earlier and reach higher levels in women than in men.

Puberty onset

The onset of puberty is associated with high GnRH pulsing, which precedes the rise in sex hormones, LH and FSH. Exogenous GnRH pulses cause the onset of puberty. Brain tumors which increase GnRH output may also lead to premature puberty

The cause of the GnRH rise is unknown. Leptin might be the cause of the GnRH rise. Leptin has receptors in the hypothalamus which synthesizes GnRH. Individuals who are deficient in leptin fail to initiate puberty. The levels of leptin increase with the onset of puberty, and then decline to adult levels when puberty is completed. The rise in GnRH might also be caused by genetics. A study discovered that a mutation in genes encoding both Neurokinin B as well as the Neurokinin B receptor can alter the timing of puberty. The researchers hypothesized that Neurokinin B might play a role in regulating the secretion of Kisspeptin, a compound responsible for triggering direct release of GnRH as well as indirect release of LH and FSH.

Physical Changes in Boys

Testicular Size, Function, and Fertility

In boys, testicular enlargement is the first physical manifestation of puberty (and is termed gonadarche). Testes in prepubertal boys change little in size from about 1 year of age to the onset of puberty, averaging about 2–3 cm in length and about 1.5–2 cm in width. Testicular size continues to increase throughout puberty, reaching maximal adult size about 6 years after the onset of puberty. After the boy's testicles have enlarged and developed for about one year, the length and then the breadth of the shaft of the penis will increase and the glans penis and corpora cavernosa will also start to enlarge to adult proportions. While 18–20 cc is an average adult size, there is wide variation in testicular size in the normal population.

The testes have two primary functions: to produce hormones and to produce sperm. The Leydig cells produce testosterone, which in turn produces most of the male pubertal changes. Most of the increasing bulk of testicular tissue is spermatogenic tissue (primarily Sertoli and Leydig cells). Sperm can be detected in the morning urine of most boys after the first year of pubertal changes, and occasionally earlier. On average, potential fertility in boys is reached at 13 years old, but full fertility will not be gained until 14–16 years of age.

During puberty, a male's scrotum will become larger and begin to dangle or hang below the body as opposed to being up tight, to accommodate the production of sperm whereby the testicles need a certain temperature to be fertile.

Pubic Hair

Pubic hair often appears on a boy shortly after the genitalia begin to grow. The pubic hairs are usually first visible at the dorsal (abdominal) base of the penis. The first few hairs are described as stage 2. Stage 3 is usually reached within another 6–12 months, when the hairs are too many to count. By stage 4, the pubic hairs densely fill the "pubic triangle." Stage 5 refers to the spread of pubic hair to the thighs and upward towards the navel as part of the developing abdominal hair.

Body and Facial Hair

In the months and years following the appearance of pubic hair, other areas of skin that respond to androgens may develop androgenic hair. The usual sequence is: underarm (axillary) hair, perianal hair, upper lip hair, sideburn (preauricular) hair, periareolar hair, and the beard area.

As with most human biological processes, this specific order may vary among some individuals. Arm, leg, chest, abdominal, and back hair become heavier more gradually. There is a large range in amount of body hair among adult men, and significant differences in timing and quantity of hair growth among different racial groups. Facial hair is often present in late adolescence, but may not appear until significantly later. Facial hair will continue to get coarser, darker and thicker for another 2–4 years after puberty. Some men do not develop full facial hair for up to 10 years after the completion of puberty. Chest hair may appear during puberty or years after. Not all men have chest hair.

Voice Change

Under the influence of androgens, the voice box, or larynx, grows in both sexes. This growth is far more prominent in boys, causing the male voice to drop and deepen, sometimes abruptly but rarely "over night," about one octave, because the longer and thicker vocal folds have a lower fundamental frequency. Before puberty, the larynx of boys and girls is about equally small. Occasionally, voice change is accompanied by unsteadiness of vocalization in the early stages of untrained voices. Most of the voice change happens during stage 3-4 of male puberty around the time of peak growth. Full adult pitch is attained at an average age of 15 years. It usually precedes the development of significant facial hair by several months to years.

Male Musculature and Body Shape

By the end of puberty, adult men have heavier bones and nearly twice as much skeletal muscle. Some of the bone growth (e.g. shoulder width and jaw) is disproportionately greater, resulting in noticeably different male and female skeletal shapes. The average adult male has about 150% of the lean body mass of an average female, and about 50% of the body fat.

This muscle develops mainly during the later stages of puberty, and muscle growth can continue even after boys are biologically adult. The peak of the so-called "strength spurt", the rate of muscle growth, is attained about one year after a male experiences his peak growth rate.

Often, the fat pads of the male breast tissue and the male nipples will develop during puberty; sometimes, especially in one breast, this becomes more apparent and is termed gynecomastia. It is usually not a permanent phenomenon.

Body Odor and Acne

Rising levels of androgens can change the fatty acid composition of perspiration, resulting in a more "adult" body odor. As in girls, another androgen effect is increased secretion of oil (sebum) from the skin and the resultant variable amounts of acne. Acne can not be prevented or diminished easily, but it typically fully diminishes at the end of puberty. However, it is not unusual for a fully grown adult to suffer the occasional bout of acne, though it is normally less severe than in adolescents. Some may desire using prescription topical creams or ointments to keep acne from getting worse, or even oral medication, due to the fact that acne is emotionally difficult and can cause scarring.

Physical Changes in Girls

Breast Development

The first physical sign of puberty in girls is usually a firm, tender lump under the center of the areola of one or both breasts, occurring on average at about 10.5 years of age. This is referred to as thelarche. By the widely used Tanner staging of puberty, this is stage 2 of breast development (stage 1 is a flat, prepubertal breast). Within six to 12 months, the swelling has clearly begun in both sides, softened, and can be felt and seen extending beyond the edges of the areolae. This is stage 3 of breast development. By another 12 months (stage 4), the breasts are approaching mature size and shape, with areolae and papillae forming a secondary mound. In most young women, this mound disappears into the contour of the mature breast (stage 5), although there is so much variation in sizes and shapes of adult breasts that stages 4 and 5 are not always separately identifiable.

Pubic Hair

Pubic hair is often the second noticeable change in puberty, usually within a few months of thelarche. It is referred to as pubarche. The pubic hairs are usually visible first along the labia. The first few hairs are described as Tanner stage 2. Stage 3 is usually reached within another 6–12 months, when the hairs are too numerous to count and appear on the pubic mound as well. By stage 4, the pubic hairs densely fill the "pubic triangle." Stage 5 refers to spread of pubic hair to the thighs and sometimes as abdominal hair upward towards the navel. In about 15% of girls, the earliest pubic hair appears before breast development begins.

Vagina, Uterus, Ovaries

The mucosal surface of the vagina also changes in response to increasing levels of estrogen, becoming thicker and duller pink in color (in contrast to the brighter red of the prepubertal vaginal mucosa). Whitish secretions (physiologic leukorrhea) are a normal effect of estrogen as well. In the two years following thelarche, the uterus, ovaries, and the follicles in the ovaries increase in size. The ovaries usually contain small follicular cysts visible by ultrasound.

Menstruation and Fertility

The first menstrual bleeding is referred to as menarche, and typically occurs about two years after thelarche. The average age of menarche in girls is 11.75 years. The time between menstrual periods (menses) is not always regular in the first two years after menarche. Ovulation is necessary for fertility, but may or may not accompany the earliest menses. In postmenarchal girls, about 80% of the cycles were anovulatory in the first year after menarche, 50% in the third year and 10% in the sixth year. Initiation of ovulation after menarche is not inevitable. A high proportion of girls with continued irregularity in the menstrual cycle several years from menarche will continue to have prolonged irregularity and anovulation, and are at higher risk for reduced fertility. Nubility is used to designate achievement of fertility.

Body Shape, Fat Distribution, and Body Composition

During this period, also in response to rising levels of estrogen, the lower half of the pelvis and thus hips widen (providing a larger birth canal). Fat tissue increases to a greater percentage of the body composition than in males, especially in the typical female distribution of breasts, hips, buttocks, thighs, upper arms, and pubis. Progressive differences in fat distribution as well as sex differences in local skeletal growth contribute to the typical female body shape by the end of puberty. On average, at 10 years, girls have 6% more body fat than boys.

Body odor and Acne

Rising levels of androgens can change the fatty acid composition of perspiration, resulting in a more "adult" body odor. This often precedes thelarche and pubarche by one or more years. Another androgen effect is increased secretion of oil (sebum) from the skin. This change increases the susceptibility to acne, a skin condition that is characteristic of puberty. Acne varies greatly in its severity.

Variations

Timing of the Onset of Puberty

The definition of the onset of puberty depends on perspective (e.g., hormonal versus physical) and purpose (establishing population normal standards, clinical care of early or late pubescent individuals, etc.) The most commonly used definition of the onset of puberty is physical changes to a person's body. These physical changes are the first visible signs of neural, hormonal, and gonadal function changes.

The age at which puberty begins varies between individuals usually, puberty begins between 10-13. The age at which puberty begins is affected by both genetic factors and by environmental factors such as nutritional state and social circumstances. An example of social circumstances is the Vandenbergh effect; a juvenile female who has significant interaction with adult males will enter puberty earlier than juvenile females who are not socially overexposed to adult males.

The average age at which puberty begins may be affected by race as well. For example, the average age of menarche in various populations surveyed has ranged from 12 to 18 years. The earliest average onset of puberty is for African-American girls and the latest average onset for high altitude subsistence populations in Asia. However, much of the higher age averages reflect nutritional limitations more than genetic differences and can change within a few generations with a substantial change in diet. The median age of menarche for a population may be an index of the proportion of undernourished girls in the population, and the width of the spread may reflect unevenness of wealth and food distribution in a population.

Researchers have identified an earlier age of the onset of puberty. However, they have based their conclusions on a comparison of data from 1999 with data from 1969. In the earlier example, the sample population was based on a small sample of white girls (200, from Britain). The later study identified as puberty as occurring in 48% of African-American girls by age nine, and 12% of white girls by that age.

Historical Shift

The average age at which the onset of puberty occurs has dropped significantly since the 1840s. Researchers refer to this drop as the 'secular trend'. In every decade from 1840 to 1950 there was a drop of four months in the average age of menarche among Western European females. In Norway, girls born in 1840 had their menarche at an average age of 17 years. In France the average in 1840 was 15.3 years. In England the average in 1840 was 16.5 years. In Japan the decline happened later and was then more rapid: from 1945 to 1975 in Japan there was a drop of 11 months per decade. A 2006 study in Denmark found that puberty, as evidenced by breast development, started at an average age of 9 years and 10 months, a year earlier than when a similar study was done in 1991. Scientists believe the phenomenon could be linked to obesity or exposure to chemicals in the food chain, and is putting girls at greater long-term risk of breast cancer.

Genetic Influence and Environmental Factors

Various studies have found direct genetic effects to account for at least 46% of the variation of timing of puberty in well-nourished populations. The genetic association of timing is strongest between mothers and daughters. The specific genes affecting timing are not yet known. Among the candidates is an androgen receptor gene.

Researchers have hypothesized that early puberty onset may be caused by certain hair care products containing estrogen or placenta, and by certain chemicals, namely phthalates, which are used in many cosmetics, toys, and plastic food containers.

If genetic factors account for half of the variation of pubertal timing, environment factors are clearly important as well. One of the first observed environmental effects is that puberty occurs later in children raised at higher altitudes. The most important of the environmental influences is clearly nutrition, but a number of others have been identified, all which affect timing of female puberty and menarche more clearly than male puberty.

Hormones and Steroids

There is theoretical concern, and animal evidence, that environmental hormones and chemicals may affect aspects of prenatal or postnatal sexual development in humans. Large amounts of incompletely metabolized estrogens and progestagens from pharmaceutical products are excreted into the sewage systems of large cities, and are sometimes detectable in the environment. Sex steroids are sometimes used in cattle farming but have been banned in chicken meat production for 40 years. Although agricultural laws regulate use to minimize accidental human consumption, the rules are largely self-enforced in the United States. Significant exposure of a child to hormones or other substances that activate estrogen or androgen receptors could produce some or all of the changes of puberty. Harder to detect as an influence on puberty are the more diffusely distributed environmental chemicals like PCBs (polychlorinated biphenyl), which can bind and trigger estrogen receptors.

More obvious degrees of partial puberty from direct exposure of young children to small but significant amounts of pharmaceutical sex steroids from exposure at home may be detected during medical evaluation for precocious puberty, but mild effects and the other potential exposures outlined above would not.

Bisphenol A (BPA) is a chemical used to make plastics, and is frequently used to make baby bottles, water bottles, sports equipment, medical devices, and as a coating in food and beverage cans. Scientists are concerned about BPA's behavioral effects on fetuses, infants, and children at current exposure levels because it can affect the prostate gland, mammary gland, and lead to early puberty in girls. BPA mimics and interferes with the action of estrogen-an important reproduction and development regulator. It leaches out of plastic into liquids and foods, and the Centres for Disease Control and Prevention (CDC) found measurable amounts of BPA in the bodies of more than 90 percent of the U.S. population studied. The highest estimated daily intakes of BPA occur in infants and children. Many plastic baby bottles contain BPA, and BPA is more likely to leach out of plastic when its temperature is increased, as when one warms a baby bottle or warms up food in the microwave.

Nutritional Influence

Nutritional factors are the strongest and most obvious environmental factors affecting timing of puberty. Girls are especially sensitive to nutritional regulation because they must contribute all of the nutritional support to a growing fetus. Surplus calories (beyond growth and activity requirements) are reflected in the amount of body fat, which signals to the brain the availability of resources for initiation of puberty and fertility.

Much evidence suggests that for most of the last few centuries, nutritional differences accounted for majority of variation of pubertal timing in different populations, and even among social classes in the same population. Recent worldwide increased consumption of animal protein, other changes in nutrition, and increases in childhood obesity have resulted in falling ages of puberty, mainly in those populations with the higher previous ages. In many populations the amount of variation attributable to nutrition is shrinking.

Although available dietary energy (simple calories) is the most important dietary influence on timing of puberty, quality of the diet plays a role as well. Lower protein intakes and higher dietary fiber intakes, as occur with typical vegetarian diets, are associated with later onset and slower progression of female puberty.

Obesity Influence and Exercise

Scientific researchers have linked early obesity with an earlier onset of puberty in girls. They have cited obesity as a cause of breast development before nine years and menarche before twelve years. Early puberty in girls can be a harbinger of later health problems.

The average level of daily physical activity has also been shown to affect timing of puberty, especially in females. A high level of exercise, whether for athletic or body image purposes, or for daily subsistence, reduces energy calories available for reproduction and slows puberty. The exercise effect is often amplified by a lower body fat mass and cholesterol.

Physical and Mental Illness

Chronic diseases can delay puberty in both boys and girls. Those that involve chronic inflammation or interfere with nutrition have the strongest effect. In the western world, inflammatory bowel disease and tuberculosis have been notorious for such an effect in the last century, while in areas of the underdeveloped world, chronic parasite infections are widespread. Mental illnesses occur in puberty. The brain undergoes significant development by hormones which can contribute to mood disorders such as Major depressive disorder, bipolar disorder, dysthymia and schizophrenia. Girls aged between 15 and 19 make up 40% of anorexia nervosa cases.

Stress and Social Factors

Some of the least understood environmental influences on timing of puberty are social and psychological. In comparison with the effects of genetics, nutrition, and general health, social influences are small, shifting timing by a few months rather than years. Mechanisms of these social effects are unknown, though a variety of physiological processes, including pheromones, have been suggested based on animal research.

The most important part of a child's psychosocial environment is the family, and most of the social influence research has investigated features of family structure and function in relation to earlier or later female puberty. Most of the studies have reported that menarche may occur a few months earlier in girls in high-stress households, whose fathers are absent during their early childhood, who have a stepfather in the home, who are subjected to prolonged sexual abuse in childhood, or who are adopted from a developing country at a young age. Conversely, menarche may be slightly later when a girl grows up in a large family with a biological father present.

More extreme degrees of environmental stress, such as wartime refugee status with threat to physical survival, have been found to be associated with delay of maturation, an effect that may be compounded by dietary inadequacy.

Most of these reported social effects are small and our understanding is incomplete. Most of these "effects" are statistical associations revealed by epidemiologic surveys. Statistical associations are not necessarily causal, and a variety of covariables and alternative explanations can be imagined. Effects of such small size can never be confirmed or refuted for any individual child. Furthermore, interpretations of the data are politically controversial because of the ease with which this type of research can be used for political advocacy. Accusations of bias based on political agenda sometimes accompany scientific criticism.

Another limitation of the social research is that nearly all of it has concerned girls, partly because female puberty requires greater physiologic resources and partly because it involves a unique event (menarche) that makes survey research into female puberty much simpler than male. More detail is provided in the menarche article.

Variations of Sequence

The sequence of events of pubertal development can occasionally vary. For example, in about 15% of boys and girls, pubarche (the first pubic hairs) can precede, respectively, gonadarche and thelarche by a few months. Rarely, menarche can occur before other signs of puberty in a few girls. These variations deserve medical evaluation because they can occasionally signal a disease.

In a general sense, the conclusion of puberty is reproductive maturity. Criteria for defining the conclusion may differ for different purposes: attainment of the ability to reproduce, achievement of maximal adult height, maximal gonadal size, or adult sex hormone levels. Maximal adult height is achieved at an average age of 15 years for an average girl and 18 years for an average boy. Potential fertility (sometimes termed *nubility*) usually precedes completion of growth by 1–2 years in girls and 3–4 years in boys. Stage 5 typically represents maximal gonadal growth and adult hormone levels.

Neurohormonal Process

The endocrine reproductive system consists of the hypothalamus, the pituitary, the gonads, and the adrenal glands, with input and regulation from many other body systems. True puberty is often termed "central puberty" because it begins as a process of the central nervous system. A simple description of hormonal puberty is as follows:

1. The brain's hypothalamus begins to release pulses of GnRH.
2. Cells in the anterior pituitary respond by secreting LH and FSH into the circulation.
3. The ovaries or testes respond to the rising amounts of LH and FSH by growing and beginning to produce estradiol and testosterone.
4. Rising levels of estradiol and testosterone produce the body changes of female and male puberty.

The onset of this neurohormonal process may precede the first visible body changes by 1–2 years.

Components of the Endocrine Reproductive System

The arcuate nucleus of the hypothalamus is the driver of the reproductive system. It has neurons which generate and release pulses of GnRH into the portal venous system of the pituitary gland. The arcuate nucleus is affected and controlled by neuronal input from other areas of the brain and hormonal input from the gonads, adipose tissue and a variety of other systems. The pituitary gland responds to the pulsed GnRH signals by releasing LH and FSH into the blood of the general circulation, also in a pulsatile pattern.

The gonads (testes and ovaries) respond to rising levels of LH and FSH by producing the steroid sex hormones, testosterone and estrogen.

The adrenal glands are a second source for steroid hormones. Adrenal maturation, termed adrenarche, typically precedes gonadarche in mid-childhood.

Major Hormones

- Neurokinin B (a tachykinin peptide) and kisspeptin (a neuropeptide), both present in the same hypothalamic neurons, are critical parts of the control system that switches on the release of GnRH at the start of puberty.
- GnRH (gonadotropin-releasing hormone) is a peptide hormone released from the hypothalamus which stimulates gonadotrope cells of the anterior pituitary.
- LH (luteinizing hormone) is a larger protein hormone secreted into the general circulation by gonadotrope cells of the anterior pituitary gland. The main target cells of LH are the Leydig cells of testes and the theca cells of the ovaries. LH secretion changes more dramatically with the initiation of puberty than FSH, as LH levels increase about 25-fold with the onset of puberty, compared with the 2.5-fold increase of FSH.
- FSH (follicle stimulating hormone) is another protein hormone secreted into the general circulation by the gonadotrope cells of the anterior pituitary. The main

target cells of FSH are the ovarian follicles and the Sertoli cells and spermatogenic tissue of the testes.

- Testosterone is a steroid hormone produced primarily by the Leydig cells of the testes, and in lesser amounts by the theca cells of the ovaries and the adrenal cortex. Testosterone is the primary mammalian androgen and the "original" anabolic steroid. It acts on androgen receptors in responsive tissue throughout the body.
- Estradiol is a steroid hormone produced by aromatization of testosterone. Estradiol is the principal human estrogen and acts on estrogen receptors throughout the body. The largest amounts of estradiol are produced by the granulosa cells of the ovaries, but lesser amounts are derived from testicular and adrenal testosterone.
- Adrenal androgens are steroids produced by the zona reticulosa of the adrenal cortex in both sexes. The major adrenal androgens are dehydroepiandrosterone, androstenedione (which are precursors of testosterone), and dehydroepiandrosterone sulfate which is present in large amounts in the blood. Adrenal androgens contribute to the androgenic events of early puberty in girls.
- IGF1 (insulin-like growth factor 1) rises substantially during puberty in response to rising levels of growth hormone and may be the principal mediator of the pubertal growth spurt.
- Leptin is a protein hormone produced by adipose tissue. Its primary target organ is the hypothalamus. The leptin level seems to provide the brain a rough indicator of adipose mass for purposes of regulation of appetite and energy metabolism. It also plays a permissive role in female puberty, which usually will not proceed until an adequate body mass has been achieved.

Endocrine Perspective

The endocrine reproductive system becomes functional by the end of the first trimester of fetal life. The testes and ovaries become briefly inactive around the time of birth but resume hormonal activity until several months after birth, when incompletely understood mechanisms in the brain begin to suppress the activity of the arcuate nucleus. This has been referred to as maturation of the prepubertal "gonadostat," which becomes sensitive to negative feedback by sex steroids. The period of hormonal activity until several months after birth, followed by suppression of activity, may correspond to the period of infant sexuality, followed by a latency stage, which Sigmund Freud described.

Gonadotropin and sex steroid levels fall to low levels (nearly undetectable by current clinical assays) for approximately another 8 to 10 years of childhood. Evidence is accumulating that the reproductive system is not totally inactive during the childhood years. Subtle increases in gonadotropin pulses occur, and ovarian follicles surrounding germ cells (future eggs) double in number.

Normal puberty is initiated in the hypothalamus, with de-inhibition of the pulse generator in the arcuate nucleus. This inhibition of the arcuate nucleus is an ongoing active suppression by other areas of the brain. The signal and mechanism releasing the arcuate nucleus from inhibition have been the subject of investigation for decades and remain incompletely understood. Leptin levels rise throughout childhood and play a part in allowing the arcuate nucleus to resume operation. If the childhood inhibition of the arcuate nucleus is interrupted prematurely by injury to the brain, it may resume pulsatile gonadotropin release and puberty will begin at an early age.

Neurons of the arcuate nucleus secrete gonadotropin releasing hormone (GnRH) into the blood of the pituitary portal system. An American physiologist, Ernst Knobil, found that the GnRH signals from the hypothalamus induce pulsed secretion of LH (and to a lesser degree, FSH) at roughly 1-2 hour intervals. The LH pulses are the consequence of pulsatile GnRH secretion by the arcuate nucleus that, in turn, is the result of an oscillator or signal generator in the central nervous system ("GnRH pulse generator"). In the years preceding physical puberty, Robert M. Boyar discovered that the gonadotropin pulses occur only during sleep, but as puberty progresses they can be detected during the day. By the end of puberty, there is little day-night difference in the amplitude and frequency of gonadotropin pulses.

Some investigators have attributed the onset of puberty to a resonance of oscillators in the brain. By this mechanism, the gonadotropin pulses that occur primarily at night just before puberty represent beats.

An array of "autoamplification processes" increases the production of all of the pubertal hormones of the hypothalamus, pituitary, and gonads.

Regulation of adrenarche and its relationship to maturation of the hypothalamic-gonadal axis is not fully understood, and some evidence suggests it is a parallel but largely independent process coincident with or even preceding central puberty. Rising levels of adrenal androgens (termed adrenarche) can usually be detected between 6 and 11 years of age, even before the increasing gonadotropin pulses of hypothalamic puberty. Adrenal androgens contribute to the development of pubic hair (pubarche), adult body odor, and other androgenic changes in both sexes. The primary clinical significance of the distinction between adrenarche and gonadarche is that pubic hair and body odor changes by themselves do not prove that central puberty is underway for an individual child.

Hormonal Changes in Boys

Early stages of male hypothalamic maturation seem to be very similar to the early stages of female puberty, though occurring about 1–2 years later.

LH stimulates the Leydig cells of the testes to make testosterone and blood levels begin to rise. For much of puberty, nighttime levels of testosterone are higher than daytime. Regularity of frequency and amplitude of gonadotropin pulses seems to be less necessary for progression of male than female puberty.

However, a significant portion of testosterone in adolescent boys is converted to estradiol. Estradiol mediates the growth spurt, bone maturation, and epiphyseal closure in boys just as in girls. Estradiol also induces at least modest development of breast tissue (gynecomastia) in a large proportion of boys. Boys who develop mild gynecomastia or even developing swellings under nipples during puberty are told the effects are temporary in some male teenagers due to high levels of estradiol.

Another hormonal change in males takes place during the teenage years for most young men. At this point in a males life the testosterone levels slowly rise, and most of the effects are mediated through the androgen receptors by way of conversion dihydrotestosterone in target organs (especially that of the bowels).

Hormonal Changes in Girls

As the amplitude of LH pulses increases, the theca cells of the ovaries begin to produce testosterone and smaller amounts of progesterone. Much of the testosterone moves into nearby cells called granulosa cells. Smaller increases of FSH induce an increase in the aromatase activity of these granulosa cells, which converts most of the testosterone to estradiol for secretion into the circulation.

Rising levels of estradiol produce the characteristic estrogenic body changes of female puberty: growth spurt, acceleration of bone maturation and closure, breast growth, increased fat composition, growth of the uterus, increased thickness of the endometrium and the vaginal mucosa, and widening of the lower pelvis.

As the estradiol levels gradually rise and the other autoamplification processes occur, a point of maturation is reached when the feedback sensitivity of the hypothalamic "gonadostat" becomes positive. This attainment of positive feedback is the hallmark of female sexual maturity, as it allows the mid cycle LH surge necessary for ovulation.

Levels of adrenal androgens and testosterone also increase during puberty, producing the typical androgenic changes of female puberty: pubic hair, other androgenic hair as outlined above, body odor, acne.

Growth hormone levels rise steadily throughout puberty. IGF1 levels rise and then decline as puberty ends. Growth finishes and adult height is attained as the estradiol levels complete closure of the epiphyses.

Stages

- adrenarche (approximately age 7)
- gonadarche (approximately age 8)
- thelarche (approximately age 11 in females)
- pubarche (approximately age 12)
- menarche (approximately age 12.5 in females)
- spermarche (in males).

Psychological Issues

Adolescents are widely considered by the psychological establishment to be prone to recklessness and risk-taking behaviours, which can lead to substance abuse, car accidents, unsafe sex, and youth crime. There is some evidence that this risk-taking is biologically driven, caused by the social and emotional part of the brain (amygdala) developing faster than the cognitive-control part of the brain (frontal cortex).

Although most adolescents are psychologically healthy, they can (like adults) exhibit signs of mental illness. Late adolescence and early adulthood are peak years for the onset of schizophrenia. Mood disorders such as clinical depression, bipolar disorder, and anxiety disorders can initially show in adolescence. For example, girls aged between 15 and 19 make up 40% of anorexia nervosa cases.

4

Dynamics of Human Behaviour

Human behaviour is the population of behaviours exhibited by humans and influenced by culture, attitudes, emotions, values, ethics, authority, rapport, hypnosis, persuasion, coercion and/or genetics.

The behaviour of people (and other organisms or even mechanisms) falls within a range with some behaviour being common, some unusual, some acceptable, and some outside acceptable limits. In sociology, behaviour is considered as having no meaning, being not directed at other people and thus is the most basic human action.

Behaviour should not be mistaken with social behaviour, which is more advanced action, as social behaviour is behaviour specifically directed at other people. The acceptability of behaviour is evaluated relative to social norms and regulated by various means of social control.

The behaviour of people is studied by the academic disciplines of psychiatry, psychology, social work, sociology, economics, and anthropology.

Factors Affecting Human Behaviour

- Genetics
- Attitude – the degree to which the person has a favorable or unfavorable evaluation of the behaviour in question.
- Social norms – the influence of social pressure that is perceived by the individual (normative beliefs) to perform or not perform a certain behaviour.

- Perceived behavioral control – the individual's belief concerning how easy or difficult performing the behaviour will be.

Human Nature

Human nature is the concept that there is a set of inherent distinguishing characteristics, including ways of thinking, feeling and acting, that all humans tend to have.

The questions of what causes these distinguishing characteristics of humanity and in turn how fixed human nature is, are amongst the oldest and most important questions in western philosophy. They have particularly important implications in ethics, politics and theology because human nature is seen as providing standards or norms that humans can use when judging how best to live either as individuals, or members of a community. The complex implications of such discussion are also often themes which are dealt with in art.

For example the so-called "nature versus nurture" debate is a specific contemporary discussion topic within this theme. The branches of contemporary science associated with the study of human nature include sociology, sociobiology and psychology, particularly evolutionary psychology and developmental psychology.

In pre-modern scientific understandings of nature, human nature is understood with reference to final and formal causes. Such understandings imply the existence of an ideal, "idea," or "form" of a human which exists independently of individual humans. This in turn is sometimes understood to imply the existence of a divine interest in human nature, and indeed the concepts of formal and final cause are today often associated with attempts to reconcile religious and scientific understandings of nature.

The existence of an invariable human nature is a subject of much historical debate, continuing into modern times. Against this idea of a fixed human nature, the relative malleability of man has been argued especially strongly in recent centuries-firstly by early modernists such as Thomas Hobbes and Jean-Jacques Rousseau, and since the mid-19th century, by thinkers such as Hegel, Marx, Nietzsche, Sartre, structuralists and postmodernists. Still more recent scientific perspectives such as behaviourism, determinism, and the chemical model within modern psychiatry and psychology, claim to be neutral regarding human nature. (As in all modern science they seek to explain without recourse to metaphysical causation.) They can be offered to explain its origins and underlying mechanisms, or to demonstrate capacities for change and diversity which would arguably violate the concept of a fixed human nature.

Socratic Philosophy

Philosophy in classical Greece is the ultimate origin of the western conception of the nature of a thing. The study of human nature itself originated, according to Aristotle at least, with Socrates, who turned philosophy from study of the heavens to study of the human things. Socrates is said to have studied the question of how a person should best live, but he left no written works. It is clear from the works of his students Plato and Xenophon, and also what was said by Aristotle about him, that Socrates was a rationalist and believed that an the best life and the life most suited to human nature involved reasoning. The Socratic school was the dominant surviving influence in philosophical discussion in the Middle Ages, amongst Islamic, Christian and Jewish philosophers.

Plato's main surviving writings are dialogues wherein Scorates, or some other wise person, appears as a character discussing questions such as the question of how humans should best live. The human soul was said by Plato to have a divided nature, divided in a specifically human way. For example, in the Timaeus it consisted of a rational part, resident in the human head, a spirited tendency, resident in the heart, and an appetitive beast, resident in the belly and genitals. The proper function of the 'rational' was to keep the other parts of the soul.

Aristotle, Plato's most famous student made some of the most famous and influential statements about human nature. His approach and understanding overlaps with Plato's but he wrote treatises, and not dialogues. In his works, some clear statements about human nature are made:-

- Man is a conjugal animal, meaning an animal which is born to couple when an adult, thus building a household (*oikos*) and in more successful cases, a clan or small village still run upon patriarchal lines.

- Man is a political animal, meaning an animal with an innate propensity to develop complex communities the size of a city or town. As a political animal, in contrast to his family and clan life, man thrives in his rationality-most fully in the making of laws and traditions.
- Man is a mimetic animal. Man loves to use his imagination, and not only to make laws and run town councils.

For Aristotle, reason is not only what is most special about humanity compared to other animals, but it is also what we were meant to achieve at his or her best. Much of Aristotle's position concerning human nature is still influential today, but the particular teleological idea that humans are "meant" or intended to be something, has become much less popular in modern times.

For the Socratics, human nature, and all natures, are metaphysical concepts. Aristotle developed the standard presentation of this approach with his theory of four causes. Human nature is an example of a formal cause according to Aristotle.

Modernism

One of the defining changes occurring at the end of the Middle Ages, is the end of the dominance of Aristotelian philosophy, and its replacement by a new approach to the study of nature, including human nature. In this approach, all attempts at conjecture about formal and final causes was rejected as useless. Under this approach a laws of nature is any regular and predictable pattern in nature, not literally a law, and in the same way "human nature" becomes not a special metaphysical cause, but simply whatever can be said to be typical tendencies of humans.

Although this new realism applied to the study of human life from the beginning, for example in Machiavelli's works, the definitive argument for the final rejection of Aristotle was associated especially with Francis Bacon, whose prime examples of the new approach returned philosophy or science to its pre-

Socratic focus upon non-human things. David Hume, some centuries later, explicitly compared the time between Bacon and himself, with the time between the first Greek philosophers such as Thales and Socrates.

In fact, Thomas Hobbes, the generation following Bacon, already claimed to be the first to use the approach of Bacon and Descartes in the study of human things. His controversial works, such as *Leviathan*, were accused of political and religious inappropriateness, but were very influential upon writers such as John Locke, Jean-Jacques Rousseau, and David Hume. In them, Hobbes famously described humanity as matter in motion, just like machines, and he described man's natural state (without science and artifice) as one where life would be nasty, short and brutish.

Jean Jacques Rousseau, was a contemporary and acquaintance of Hume, writing before the French Revolution, and long before Darwin. He shocked Western Civilization with his Second Discourse by proposing, building upon Hobbes, that humans had once been solitary animals, and had learned to be political. The important point about this was the idea that human nature was not fixed, or at least not anywhere near the extent previously suggested by philosophers. Humans are political, and rational, and have language now, but originally they had none of these things.

Rousseau still saw himself as a student of nature, and did not deny the existence of a human nature, but it was only now to be defined in terms of the instinctive passions of the original irrational and amoral human, such as those associated with self preservation. This has been seen as breaking ground for shocking political developments of the 19th and 20th centuries, such as totalitarianism and brain washing.

He was an important influence upon Kant, Hegel and Marx, but he himself made it clear that he was partly developing ideas based on the description of the "state of nature" in the *Leviathan* by Thomas Hobbes.

David Hume in Britain whose major works include *A Treatise of Human Nature* (1739-1740), and the two volumes developed to present the same material in a more popular way, *An Enquiry Concerning Human Understanding* (1748) and An

Enquiry Concerning the Principles of Morals (1751). As a major figure in British empiricism and the development of modern economics, his influence on contemporary thinking is large. Despite treating this subject in a similar way to Rousseau, developing from the "state of nature" idea in Hobbes and Locke, Hume is often treated as a political conservative, and was in any case much less influential in inspiring violent political revolution.

Like Rousseau, he did not reject the idea that there were basic consistencies in humanity which tended to cause what we think of as human nature. He wrote of "human nature" itself, meaning the social aspects of it as it is often conceived, as something which humans did not even necessarily have, but rather something developed during the lifetime of individuals. It could be destroyed, for example if people did not associate in just societies. Nevertheless, like Rousseau he did not reject the concept of human nature entirely and rejected what he called the "paradox of the sceptics" saying that no politician could have invented words like "'honourable' and 'shameful', 'lovely' and 'odious' 'noble' and 'despicable'", unless there was not some natural "original constitution of the mind".

Hume was controversial in his own time for his modernist approach, following the example of Francis Bacon and Thomas Hobbes, of avoiding even considering metaphysical explanations for any type of cause and effect. He was accused of being an atheist. Concerning human nature also, he wrote for example:

We needn't push our researches so far as to ask 'Why do we have humanity, i.e. a fellow-feeling with others?' It's enough that we experience this as a force in human nature. Our examination of causes must stop somewhere

After Rousseau and Hume, the nature of philosophy and science changes, branching into different disciplines and approaches, and the study of human nature changes accordingly.

Karl Marx

Karl Marx's conception of human nature has been the subject of much misunderstanding. It is often believed that Marx, like Rousseau, denied that there was any human nature, and said that human beings are simply a blank slate, whose character will depend wholly upon their socialization and experience. It is true that Marx placed enormous importance on the view that people are influenced and, in part, determined by their environments. But at least in one stage of his development he had a very strong concept of human nature.

In that stage, Marx discussed the concept of 'species-essence' (from the German *Gattungswesen*, sometimes also translated as 'species being'). He believed that under capitalism, we are alienated-that is, divorced from aspects of our human nature. He envisaged the possibility of a society following capitalism which would allow human beings to fully exercise their human nature and individuality. His name for this society was 'communism'. However, it is worth bearing in mind that, since Marx's day, this term has been used with several different meanings, not all of which have been compatible with Marx's original usage.

Marx's understanding of human nature did not only play a role in his critique of capitalism, and in his belief that a better society would be possible (as already indicated). It also informed his theory of history. The underlying dynamic of history, for Marx, is the expansion of the productive forces. In *The German Ideology*, Marx says that two of the three aspects of social activity which ground history is the tendency of humans to act to fulfil their needs, and thereafter, the tendency to generate new needs. This human tendency, for Marx, is what drives the continuing expansion of productive power in human civilization.

After *The German Ideology*, however, mention of 'species-essence' as such is virtually absent from Marx's writings. Some major interpreters of Marx, such as Louis Althusser, dismiss 'species-essence' as irrelevant to Marx's "later" writings, while others, such as Terry Eagleton and Andrew Chitty, believe it continues to be an important concept in understanding Marx.

Natural Science

As the sciences concerned with humanity split up into more specialized branches, many of the key figures of this evolution expressed influential understandings about human nature.

Darwin gave a widely accepted scientific argument for what Rousseau had already argued from a different direction, that humans and other animal species have no truly fixed nature, at least in the long term.

Sigmund Freud, the founder of psychoanalysis, famously referred to the hidden pathological character of typical human behaviour. He believed that the Marxists were right to focus on what he called "the decisive influence which the economic circumstances of men have upon their intellectual, ethical and artistic attitudes." But he thought that the Marxist view of the class struggle was a too shallow one, assigning to recent centuries conflicts that were, rather, primordial. Behind the class struggle, according to Freud, there stands the struggle between father and son, between established clan leader and rebellious challenger. Freud also popularized his notions of the id and the desires associated with each supposed aspect of personality.

In his book, *Consilience: The Unity of Knowledge* (1998), Edward O. Wilson claimed that it was time for a cooperation of all the sciences to explore human nature. He defined human nature as a collection of epigenetic rules: the genetic patterns of mental development. Cultural phenomena, rituals etc. are products, not part of human nature. Artworks, for example are not part of human nature, but our appreciation of art is. And this art appreciation, or our fear for snakes, or incest taboo (Westermarck effect) can be studied by the methods of reductionism. Until now these phenomena were only part of psychological, sociological and anthropological studies. Wilson proposes it can be part of interdisciplinary research.

An example of this fear is discussed in the book *An Instinct for Dragons*, where anthropologist David E. Jones suggests a hypothesis that humans, just like monkeys, have inherited instinctive reactions to snakes, large cats and birds of prey. Folklore dragons have features that are combinations of these three, which would explain why dragons with similar features occur in stories from independent cultures on all continents. Other authors have suggested that especially under the influence of drugs or in children's dreams, this instinct may give raise to fantasies and nightmares about dragons, snakes, spiders, etc., which makes these symbols popular in drug culture and in fairy tales for children. The traditional mainstream explanation to the folklore dragons does however not rely on human instinct, but on the assumption that fossils of, for example, dinosaurs gave raise to similar fantasies all over the world.

Metaphysics and Ethics

There are a number of perspectives regarding the fundamental nature and substance of humans. These are by no means mutually exclusive, and the following list is by no means exhaustive:

- Philosophical naturalism (which includes materialism and rationalism) encompasses a set of views that humans are purely natural phenomena; sophisticated beings that evolved to our present state through natural mechanisms such as evolution. Humanist philosophers determine good and evil by appeal to universal human qualities, but other naturalists regard these terms as mere labels placed on how well individual behaviour conforms to societal expectations, and is the result of our psychology and socialization.
- Abrahamic religions (most notably Judaism, Christianity and Islam) hold that a human is a spiritual being which was deliberately created (ex nihilo) by a single God in his image (according to the former two), and exists in continued relationship with God. Good and evil are defined in terms of how well humans conform to God's character or God's law.
- Polytheistic or animistic notions vary, but generally regard humans as citizens in a world populated by other intelligent spiritual or mythological beings, such as gods, demons, ghosts, etc. In these cases, human evil is often regarded as the result of supernatural influences or mischief (although it may have many other causes as well).
- Holistic, pantheistic, and panentheistic spiritual traditions regard humanity as existing within God or as a part of the divine cosmos. In this case, human "evil" is usually regarded as the result of ignorance of this universal Divine nature. Traditions of this kind

include the Indian religions such as Buddhism and Hinduism and other forms of Eastern philosophy, as also schools of western philosophy such as Stoicism, Neoplatonism, or Spinoza's pantheistic cosmology. Certain kinds of polytheism, animism, and monism have similar interpretations.

- Some astrologers believe that a person's personality and many of the challenges they will face in life are determined by the placements of the planets, each represents different aspects of their mental and physical nature. At the time of birth they may use many different techniques to 'guesstimate' the issues that will unfold throughout their lives and the actions that can be taken to gain the best results.

Free will and Determinism

The issue of free will and determinism underlies much of the debate about human nature. Free will, or agency, refers to the ability of humans to make genuinely free choices (in some sense).

As it relates to humans, the thesis of determinism implies that human choices are fully caused by internal and external forces.

1. Incompatibilism holds that determinism and free will are contradictory (i.e. both cannot be true). Incompatibilist views can either deny or accept free will.
   - Incompatibilist views holding to free will include:
     * Libertarianism holds that the human perception of free choice in action is genuine, rather than seemingly genuine, so that some of our actions are performed without there being any compulsion by internal or external forces to do so (i.e., indeterminism).
     * Thomism holds that humans have a genuine experience of free will, and this experience of free will is evidence of a soul that transcends the mere physical components of the human being.

* Incompatibilist views that deny free will include:
    * Determinism refers to the logic that humans, like all physical phenomena, are subject to cause and effect. Determinism also holds that our actions stem from environmental, biological, or theological factors. A common misconception is that all determinists are fatalists, who believe that deliberation is pointless as the future is already caused; when in fact most determinists hold the idea that we should deliberate on our actions and that deliberating on our actions is part of the complex interplay between cause and effect.
    * Predestination is the position that God orchestrates all the events in the universe, human and otherwise, according to his will; however he does it in a way that includes the free choices of humans.
    * Biological determinism and social determinism are the views that human actions are determined by their biology and social interaction, respectively. The debate between these two positions is known as nature versus nurture.

2. Compatibilism is the view that free will and determinism can conceptually coexist. Compatibilist views include:
    - Human compatibilitism is the view that they are compatible because free will is merely the hypothetical ability to choose differently if one were differently disposed according to the physical factors of determinism.
    - Molinism is the view that God is able to predestine all events on Earth because he knows in advance what people will freely choose.
    - Contemporary compatibilists seek definitions of free will that permit determinism.

Spiritual Versus Natural

Another often-discussed aspect of human nature is the existence and relationship of the physical body with a spirit or soul that transcends the human's physical attributes, as well as the existence of any transcendent purpose. In this area, there are three dominant views:

- The philosophical naturalist position is that humans are entirely natural, with no spiritual component or transcendent purpose. Subsets of the naturalist view include the materialist and physicalist positions, which hold that humans are entirely physical. However, some naturalists are also dualists about mind and body. Naturalism, combined with the natural and social sciences, views humans as the unplanned product of evolution, which operated in part by natural selection on random mutations. Philosophical naturalists do not believe in a supernatural afterlife. While philosophical naturalism is often assailed as an unacceptable view of human nature, it is promoted by many prominent philosophers and thinkers. The philosophical naturalist often will view religious belief as similar to superstition and as the product of unsound or magical thinking.
- In contrast to materialism, there is the Platonic or idealist position. It can be expressed in many ways, but in essence it is the view that there is a distinction between appearance and reality, and that the world we see around us is simply a reflection of some higher, divine existence, of which the human (and perhaps also the animal) soul/mind or spirit may be part. In his *Republic*, Book VII, Plato represents humankind as prisoners chained from birth inside an underground cave, unable to move their heads, and therefore able to see only the shadows on the walls created by a fire outside the cave, shadows that, in their ignorance, the cave dwellers mistake for reality. For Plato, therefore, the soul is a spirit that uses the body. It is in a non-natural state of union, and longs to be freed from its bodily prison.
- Between materialism and idealism lies the thought of St. Thomas Aquinas, whose system of thought is known as Thomism. His thought is, in essence, a synthesis of Christian theology and the philosophy of Aristotle.

> Aristotle describes man as a "rational animal," i.e., a single, undivided being that is at once animal (material) and rational (intellectual soul). Drawing from Aristotelian hylomorphism, the soul is seen as the substantial form of the body (matter). The soul, as the substantial form, is what is universal, or common, to all humanity, and therefore, is indicative of human nature; that which differentiates one person from another is matter, which Aquinas refers to as the principle of individuation. The human soul is characterized as spiritual, immortal, substantial, and subsistent: it is the spiritual and vital principle of the human being, but is also dependent on the body in a variety of ways in order to possess these characteristics. Thus, no *division* is made between the "physical" and the "spiritual," though they are in fact *distinct*. This position differentiates Thomism from both materialism and idealism. Unlike idealism, it holds that the visible universe is not a mere shadow of a transcendent reality, but instead is fully real in and of itself. However, unlike materialism, Thomism holds that empiricism and philosophy, when properly exercised, lead inevitably to reasonable belief in God, the human soul, and moral objectivism. Thus, to a Thomist, it is obvious from the evidence that there is a God and an eternal soul.

In addition to these traditional philosophical distinctions between the soul and body, recent adaptations in humanistic psychology attempt to explain the natural transcendent purpose of human life. Richard Shweder of the University of Chicago separated human morality into three components: the ethic of autonomy, the ethic of community, and the ethic of divinity. The idea of religious fundamentalist countries is to uphold the ethic of divinity, which consists of protecting the divinity that exists in each person, even if that means imposing religious and moral laws on people of other faiths. Abraham Maslow, one of the founders of humanistic psychology attempted to demonstrate that spiritual life can be rationally explained as a naturalistic meaning. He claims that 'peak experiences'- moments of extreme self-transcendence, are the same amongst religious and secular people alike. Peak experiences make people see beyond the two dimensional world of self-advancement and try live a nobler life. Religions can thus be explained in a naturalistic sense as the coordination of transcendent ideas in order to maximize 'peak experiences'.

State of Nature

State of nature refers to philosophical assertions regarding the condition of humans before social factors are imposed, thus attempting to describe the "natural essence" of human nature.

- Views which see humans as inherently good:
    - According to John Locke, humans in the state of nature have perfect freedom to order their actions according to the laws of nature. Locke agreed with Thomas Hobbes, that people could do so without having to ask permission to act from any other person, because people are of equal value. People only leave the state of nature when they consent to take part in a community in order to protect their property rights.
    - According to Pelagius, humans in the state of nature are not tainted by original sin, but are instead fully capable of choosing good or evil.
    - According to social determinism and biological determinism, human behaviour is determined by biological and social factors, so people are never truly to blame for actions generally considered "bad" nor truly credited with actions generally considered "good."
- Views which see humans as inherently bad:
    - According to Hobbes, humans in the state of nature are inherently in a "war of all against all," and life in that state is ultimately "solitary, poor, nasty, brutish, and short." To Hobbes, this state of nature is remedied by a strong government. According to Locke, human nature is rather the law of reason. What is reasonable is natural, what is natural is good. When humans do the illogical bad happens. According to Rousseau, humans are born natural, contain the urge to survive and natural pity.

  * According to the Protestant doctrine of original sin, humans are inherently corrupt creatures stained by the sin of Adam, and can only be redeemed by the grace of God through faith in the righteousness of Jesus Christ, whom they believe to be His morally perfect Son. Who will in turn save us all from sin. In Christian theology, the virgin birth of Jesus is believed to make this possible, as original sin is thought to pass from the seed of man. Catholicism, however, holds that the natures of both Jesus and His mother Mary, as a holy vessel for the Messiah, were uncorrupted by original sin.
  * According to Bertrand Russell moral evil or sin is derived from the instincts that have been transmitted to us from our ancestry of beasts of prey. This ancestry originated when certain animals became omnivorous and employed predation (killing and thievery) in order periodically to ingurgitate the flesh as well as the fruit and produce of other once-living things to support metabolism in competition with other animals for scarce food-animal and food-plant sources in the predatory environment in which we evolved. Thus, the simple fact that we humans must eat other life or else starve, die and rot is the probable primordial origin of contemporary and historical moral evil; i.e., the bad things we do to each other by lying, cheating, slandering, thieving and slaughtering.
- View which sees humans as having a "wounded human nature"
  * According to the Catholic Church, humans were created good but were wounded by their own free decision to sin. Humans were in a state of "original holiness and justice," but lost these due to original sin, committed by Adam and passed on by him as a state of nature to his descendants. According to its Catechism of the Catholic Church, "human nature has not been totally corrupted: it is wounded in the natural powers proper to it, subject to ignorance, suffering and the dominion of death,

> and inclined to sin-an inclination to evil that is called concupiscence. Baptism, by imparting the life of Christ's grace, erases original sin and turns a man back towards God, but the consequences for nature, weakened and inclined to evil, persist in man and summon him to spiritual battle."

Morality

There are a number of views regarding the origin and nature of human morality

- Moral realism or moral objectivism holds that moral codes exist outside of human opinion—that certain things are right or wrong regardless of human opinion on the topic. Objective morality may be seen as stemming from the inherent nature of humanity, divine command, or both.
- Moral subjectivism holds that moral codes depend on human opinion.
- Moral relativism holds that moral codes are a function of human values and social structures, and hold no meaning outside social convention.
- Moral absolutism is the view that certain acts are right or wrong regardless of context.
- Moral universalism compromises between moral relativism and moral absolutism and holds that there is, or should be, a common universal core of morality.
- Moral nihilism is the view that no morality exists.
- Amoralism is the view that the concepts of moral right and wrong do not have meaning.

Purpose

- Materialism and philosophical naturalism hold that there is no external purpose to human life. Proponents of this view often adopt the philosophy of secular humanism.
- Teleology holds that there is inherent purpose to human existence. This purpose may arise from the inherent nature of humanity itself (what a human is "supposed

to be," as in the case of objectivist philosophy), from mankind's relationship to the divine (what God *wants* humanity to be, as in the case of religion), or from both (as when the divine commands are seen as being in accord with the inherent nature of humanity and humanity's best interests).

- Nihilism argues that existence is without objective meaning, purpose, or intrinsic value.

Psychology and Biology

A long standing question in philosophy and science is whether there exists an invariant human nature. For those who believe there is a human nature, further questions include:

- What determines/constrains human nature?
- To what extent is human nature malleable?
- How does it vary between people and populations?

Since human behaviour is so diverse, it can be difficult to find absolutely invariant human behaviours that are of interest to philosophers. A lesser (but still scientifically valid) standard for evidence pertaining to "human nature" is used by scientists who study behaviour. Biologists look for evidence of genetic predisposition to behavioral patterns. Human behaviour can be influenced by the environment, so penetrance of genetically predisposed behavioral traits is not expected to reach 100 percent. A type of human behaviour for which there is a strong genetic predisposition can be considered to be part of human nature. In other words, human nature is not seen as something that *forces* individuals to behave in a certain way, but as something that makes individuals more inclined to act in a certain way than in another.

An enduring evolutionary psychology controversy often revolves around "human nature". Common evolutionary psychology explanations posit that the mind is made up of a massive number of interacting adaptations or "mental modules", the genes for which are a common human inheritance and result in a common human phenotype in the typical environments in which humans find themselves, and which constitute "human nature". This view has been critiqued as essentialist, as neglecting "natural" genetic, environmental and individual variation (and that the closest you can come is norms of reaction), and as equivocating between the levels of genes, developmental programs, and actual human psychology/culture, and between individuals and population averages.

Tabula Rasa

John Locke's philosophy of empiricism saw human nature as a *tabula rasa*. In this view, the mind is at birth a "blank slate" without rules, so data is added, and rules for processing them are formed solely by our sensory experiences.

The contrary view is seen in E. O. Wilson's sociobiology and the closely related theory of evolutionary psychology.

Behavioral Genetics

The nature versus nurture debate. Behavioral genetics

Human Genetic Variation

Human genetic variation is the genetic diversity of humans and represents the total amount of genetic characteristics observed within the human species. No two humans are genetically identical, even monozygotic twins, who develop from a single zygote, have infrequent genetic differences due to mutations occurring during development and gene copy number variation has been observed. Differences between individuals, even closely related individuals, are the key to techniques such as genetic fingerprinting. Alleles occur at different frequencies in different human populations, with populations that are more geographically and ancestrally remote tending to differ more.

Arguments for Invariance

All individuals and all societies have a similar facial grammar. Everyone smiles the same, and the way we use our eyes to convey cognition or flirtatiousness is the same. Evaluations of facial attractiveness are consistent across races and cultures with a preference for symmetry and proportion which are explained by scientists as markers of health during physical development attributable to good genes or a good environment. Human females find male faces that are rated more masculine and aggressive, less feminine and sensitive, more attractive during ovulation, the stage of their menstrual cycle when women are most fertile.

No success has ever been scientifically demonstrated in re-assigning an individual's handedness. Although individuals may change their external behaviour (picking up scissors with their right hand instead of the left, for instance), their internal inclination never changes. Even people who lose a limb, who physically do not possess the ability to pick up scissors with their left hand, will try to do so if they are 'left-handed.' The percentage of left-handers in all cultures at all times remains constant (because left-handedness is a recessive trait).

Newborn babies, far too young to have been acculturated to do so, have measurable behaviours such as being more attracted to human faces than other shapes and having a preference for their mother's voice over any other voice.

In his book *Human Universals*, Donald E Brown presents his case and identifies approximately 400 specific behaviours that are essentially invariant among all humans.

Arguments for Social Malleability

The Duke of Wellington is said to have become indignant upon hearing someone refer to habit as "second nature." He replied, "It is ten times nature!"

William James likewise referred to habit as the fly-wheel of society. Habits, though, are by definition acquired, and different habits will be both the effect and the cause of very different societies.

Different human societies have held very different moral codes. Thus, regardless of whether objective morality exists or not, humans are clearly *capable* of imposing a wide variety of different moral codes on themselves.

Some have argued that the role for nurture comes not from the absence of impulses in human nature but from the plethora of such impulses—so many, and so contradictory, that nurture must sort them out and put them into a hierarchy.

Some believe there is no single universal law of behaviour that holds true for all human beings. There are many such laws that apply to the *majority* of individuals (for example, the majority of individuals try to avoid dying), but there are always exceptions (some individuals commit suicide). Most animals, including humans, have an innate self-preservation instinct (fear of injury and death). The fact that humans may override this basic instinct is seen as evidence that human nature is subordinate to the human mind, and/or various outside factors. However, this may not be entirely unique to the human mind, as certain animals are observed to wilfully commit suicide.

Finally, it has been noted that recent advancements in biology have opened the door to genetic manipulation. This means that we may soon have the possibility of altering our genes and therefore changing the instincts that are coded in those genes.

5

Home and Community Influences in Social Development

Community, home, school, peers, and media exert a greater or lesser influence on children's learning, depending on the age of the children concerned. Many theorists have described the stages in children's development from dependency to independence and have theorized how children learn. In practice, parents, teachers, and community people rarely subscribe to one particular theory, but the decisions they make about children's learning will reflect a stronger belief in one viewpoint. As you develop strategies to promote partnerships for children's education, it is helpful to keep in mind that the perspective others may have on development may differ from your own.

The Early Years-Strong Home Influence

Early researchers such as Maslow (1970), Erikson (1963), and Piaget (1967) all emphasize the strong need for attachment and environmental support of infants and toddlers. Developing children require a physically and emotionally supportive environment in which their basic needs can be met. Infants must first develop trust in others so that they can explore their surroundings. According to Piaget, it is this exploration that enables them to construct knowledge about themselves and their world (Piaget, 1967).

Neuroscientists have discovered links between brain structure and brain activity, and brain research substantiates the notion that a child's knowledge develops because of an interactive process, beginning even as the brain develops before birth. Heredity may determine the framework of a developing child's brain, but researchers point out the many ways in which genes, environment, and infant responses interact to develop the connections between the brain cells that account for learning.

Because of this brain–environment interactive development, we can see that myriad events will affect growth, some positively and some negatively.

Type of housing, presence of caregivers, and lifestyles associated with different homes influence children's lives in profound and dramatic ways. Some environments are extremely supportive and nurturing, whereas others are dominating, negligent, and even dysfunctional.

For example, affectionate interactions, consistent practices, organized schedules, and high-quality nourishment bring support and security to young children. Such nurturing environments have secure caregivers who respond to their children by touching, cuddling, talking to, and reading with them.

Most authorities agree that emotional support and interactions with the child provide building blocks for intellectual competence and language comprehension.

On the other hand, the trials of homelessness, highly mobile families, absentee parents, and poverty often mean that parents are unable to provide positive and secure environments. The lack of a responsive environment, which stems from the parents' own life experience, will affect a child's intellectual, social, and emotional competence. The young brain is quite resilient, however, and later stimulation or strong emotional bonds can help many children overcome some of the negative results of early deprivation.

Regardless of family configuration, American society expects all families to provide economic and emotional support for infants and toddlers. With more single-parent and dual-income parents, and fewer extended family members available to support them, families face many challenges in providing optimal care for their children.

Preschool and Kindergarten Years-Increasing School Influence

As children develop a sense of autonomy, they need to learn the boundaries within which they can operate, and they must learn to identify new ones they will encounter as they separate from home. Bronfenbrenner's (1979, 1993) bioecological model accurately explains the transitions from the intimate microsystem of home to the mesosystem of outer linkages that come to bear on the developing child's perceptions and behaviour. As parents give their children necessary support, they must also give them freedom to try things on their own.

As we noted, one's sense of self first develops in the home and then extends into the neighbourhood, child-care center, and larger community. At school, the teacher and the children's peers begin to alter or reinforce this sense. Children modify their behaviour in school in response to various rules and regulations and to perceived teacher and peer expectations. At the same time, significant others in the home setting continue to influence development as the early schoolers move from basic trust to autonomy and independence.

Many children have school-like experiences in their preschool years. For other children, school as a culture first comes into focus when they enter formal public or private elementary school. In the preschool years, children may encounter several different types of school-like experiences. Head Start programs, child-care centres, and nursery schools all demonstrate somewhat different philosophical orientations.

Some programs seek to introduce children to school through a more structured curriculum, others try to extend the nurturance of the home, and still others combine facets of both. The current movement toward universal preschool for children is an indication of the growing awareness of the importance of this developmental stage.

Although it is difficult to conduct rigorous studies to determine the influence of different programs on developing children, we have evidence that quality preschool programs do have a lasting, positive effect on children's academic growth and on subsequent life-skill development.

Primary Years-Growing Community Influence

Community influence appears early in children's lives and progresses steadily as children mature. The effect of community depends, however, on how families use neighbourhood resources. The nature of that effect is not simple; it derives from the many subsystems within the community. For example, the family may live in a neighbourhood that provides positive social and physical support or in an area where parents are afraid to take their children outside.

As children expand their horizons, the living conditions of the neighbourhood and community give them experiences on which to build their linguistic, kinesthetic, artistic, spatial, and interpersonal skills. Children who can visit zoos, museums, libraries, business establishments, parks, and other natural settings are better equipped to deal with the many mathematical, scientific, social, and language concepts discussed in schools than are children who can't. Recent decades have produced a rich mix of cultural and ethnic diversity in many American communities which contrasts starkly with the situation that existed in the mid-20th century. Inclusive schools, ethnically diverse neighborhoods, and transcultural events in most vicinities all produce a positive effect on young children.

Traditions, cultural values, community mores, opportunities for recreation, and other social and cultural activities all play a part in children's development. Experiences interacting with adults in clubs, sports, and art and music activities open up children to differences in communication styles and offer them a range of experiences. Coleman (1991) called this type of involvement with adults a child's social capital and stressed that this capital is as important as financial capital in determining school performance. Maeroff (1999) pointed out how childrern living in poverty may have fewer opportunities to participate in interactive incidents with different adults than those children who do not. Although socialization practices are learned at home, children who participate in community activities have greater opportunities to practice their negotiating, problem-solving, and intellectual skills.

Positive interactions between community and family give a sense of security and well-being to all. This situation helps families provide the kind of nurturing that children need. Regrettably, not all communities provide healthy conditions for children. Community tolerance for gangs, illicit activities, or establishments with erotic content will have unhealthy and negative influences on children's growth and the experiences they have. Violence in the streets limits everyone's sense of security. Yet, even in neighborhoods besieged by poverty, extended family, churches, social and service organizations, and neighbourhood groups can make a positive difference in children's lives and support and extend the work of families and schools

Emotional Development

Emotion is the complex psychophysiological experience of an individual's state of mind as interacting with biochemical and environmental influences. In humans, emotion fundamentally involves "physiological arousal, expressive behaviours, and conscious experience". Emotion is associated with mood, temperament, personality and disposition, and motivation. The English word 'emotion' is derived from the French word *émouvoir*. This is based on the Latin *emovere*, where *e*-(variant of *ex*-) means 'out' and *movere* means 'move'. The related term "motivation" is also derived from the word *movere*.

No definitive taxonomy of emotions exists, though numerous taxonomies have been proposed. Some categorizations include:

- 'Cognitive' versus 'non-cognitive' emotions
- Instinctual emotions (from the amygdala), versus cognitive emotions (from the prefrontal cortex).
- Categorization based on duration: Some emotions occur over a period of seconds (for example, surprise), whereas others can last years (for example, love).

A related distinction is between the emotion and the results of the emotion, principally behaviours and emotional expressions. People often behave in certain ways as a direct result of their emotional state, such as crying, fighting or fleeing. If one can have the emotion without the corresponding behaviour, then we may consider the behaviour not to be essential to the emotion. Neuroscientific research suggests there is a "magic quarter second" during which it's possible to catch a thought before it becomes an emotional reaction. In that instant, one can catch a feeling before allowing it to take hold.

The James-Lange theory posits that emotional experience is largely due to the experience of bodily changes. The functionalist approach to emotions (for example, Nico Frijda and Freitas-Magalhaes) holds that emotions have evolved for a particular function, such as to keep the subject safe.

Classification

There are basic and complex categories, where some basic emotions can be modified in some way to form complex emotions (for example, Paul Ekman). In one model, the complex emotions could arise from cultural conditioning or association combined with the basic emotions. Alternatively, analogous to the way primary colors combine, *primary emotions* could blend to form the full spectrum of human emotional experience. For example interpersonal anger and disgust could blend to form contempt.

Robert Plutchik proposed a three-dimensional "circumplex model" which describes the relations among emotions. This model is similar to a color wheel. The vertical dimension represents intensity, and the circle represents degrees of similarity among the emotions. He posited eight primary emotion dimensions arranged as four pairs of opposites. Some have also argued for the existence of meta-emotions which are emotions about emotions.

Another important means of distinguishing emotions concerns their occurrence in time. Some emotions occur over a period of seconds (for example, surprise), whereas others can last years (for example, love). The latter could be regarded as a long term *tendency* to have an emotion regarding a certain object rather than an emotion proper (though this is disputed). A distinction is then made between emotion episodes and emotional dispositions. Dispositions are also comparable to character traits, where someone may be said to be generally disposed to experience certain emotions, though about different objects. For example an irritable person is generally disposed to feel irritation more easily or quickly than others do. Finally, some theorists (for example, Klaus Scherer, 2005) place emotions within a more general category of 'affective states' where affective states can also include emotion-related phenomena such as pleasure and pain, motivational states (for example, hunger or curiosity), moods, dispositions and traits.

The neural correlates of hate have been investigated with an fMRI procedure. In this experiment, people had their brains scanned while viewing pictures of people they hated. The results showed increased activity in the medial frontal gyrus, right putamen, bilaterally in the premotor cortex, in the frontal pole, and bilaterally in the medial insula of the human brain. The researchers concluded that there is a distinct pattern of brain activity that occurs when people are experiencing hatred.

Theories

Theories about emotions stretch back at least as far as the Ancient Greek Stoics, as well as Plato and Aristotle. We also see sophisticated theories in the works of philosophers such as René Descartes, Baruch Spinoza and David Hume. Later theories of emotions tend to be informed by advances in empirical research. Often theories are not mutually exclusive and many researchers incorporate multiple perspectives in their work.

Somatic Theories

Somatic theories of emotion claim that bodily responses rather than judgements are essential to emotions. The first modern version of such theories comes from William James in the 1880s. The theory lost favour in the 20th century, but has regained popularity more recently due largely to theorists such as John Cacioppo, António Damásio, Joseph E. LeDoux and Robert Zajonc who are able to appeal to neurological evidence.

James-Lange Theory

William James, in the article 'What is an Emotion?' (*Mind*, 9, 1884: 188-205), argued that emotional experience is largely due to the experience of bodily changes. The Danish psychologist Carl Lange also proposed a similar theory at around the same time, so this position is known as the James-Lange theory. This theory and its derivatives state that a changed situation leads to a changed bodily state. As James says "the perception of bodily changes as they occur *is* the emotion." James further claims that "we feel sad because we cry, angry because we strike, afraid because we tremble, and neither we cry, strike, nor tremble because we are sorry, angry, or fearful, as the case may be."

This theory is supported by experiments in which by manipulating the bodily state, a desired emotion is induced. Such experiments also have therapeutic implications (for example, in laughter therapy, dance therapy). The James-Lange theory is often misunderstood because it seems counter-intuitive. Most people believe that emotions give rise to emotion-specific actions: e.g. "I'm crying because I'm sad", or "I ran away because I was scared". The James-Lange theory, conversely, asserts that *first* we react to a situation (running away and crying happen before the emotion), and *then* we interpret our actions into an emotional response. In this way, emotions serve to explain and organize our own actions to us.

The James-Lange theory has now been all but abandoned by most scholars.

Tim Dalgleish (2004) states the following:

> *"The James-Lange theory has remained influential. Its main contribution is the emphasis it places on the embodiment of emotions, especially the argument that changes in the bodily concomitants of emotions can alter their experienced intensity. Most contemporary neuroscientists would endorse a modified James-Lange view in which bodily feedback modulates the experience of emotion."*

The issue with James-Lange theory is that of causation (bodily states causing emotions and being a priori), not that of the bodily influences on emotional experience (which I would argue is still quite prevalent today in biofeedback studies and embodiment theory).

Neurobiological Theories

Based on discoveries made through neural mapping of the limbic system, the neurobiological explanation of human emotion is that emotion is a pleasant or unpleasant mental state organized in the limbic system of the mammalian brain. If distinguished from reactive responses of reptiles, emotions would then be mammalian elaborations of general vertebrate arousal patterns, in which neurochemicals (for example, dopamine, noradrenaline, and serotonin) step-up or step-down the brain's activity level, as visible in body movements, gestures, and postures. For example, the emotion of love is proposed to be the expression of paleocircuits of the mammalian brain (specifically, modules of the cingulate gyrus) which facilitate the care, feeding, and grooming of offspring. Paleocircuits are neural platforms for bodily expression configured before the advent of cortical circuits for speech. They consist of pre-configured pathways or networks of nerve cells in the forebrain, brain stem and spinal cord.

The motor centres of reptiles react to sensory cues of vision, sound, touch, chemical, gravity, and motion with pre-set body movements and programmed postures. With the arrival of night-active mammals, smell replaced vision as the dominant sense, and a different way of responding arose from the olfactory sense, which is proposed to have developed into mammalian emotion and emotional memory. The mammalian brain invested heavily in olfaction to succeed at night as reptiles slept—one explanation for why olfactory lobes in mammalian brains are proportionally larger than in the reptiles. These odor pathways gradually formed the neural blueprint for what was later to become our limbic brain.

Emotions are thought to be related to activity in brain areas that direct our attention, motivate our behaviour, and determine the significance of what is going on around us. Pioneering work by Broca (1878), Papez (1937), and MacLean (1952) suggested that emotion is related to a group of structures in the center of the brain called the limbic system, which includes the hypothalamus, cingulate cortex, hippocampi, and other structures. More recent research has shown that some of these limbic structures are not as directly related to emotion as others are, while some non-limbic structures have been found to be of greater emotional relevance.

Prefrontal Cortex

There is ample evidence that the left prefrontal cortex is activated by stimuli that cause positive approach. If attractive stimuli can selectively activate a region of the brain, then logically the converse should hold, that selective activation of that region of the brain should cause a stimulus to be judged more positively. This was demonstrated for moderately attractive visual stimuli and replicated and extended to include negative stimuli.

Two neurobiological models of emotion in the prefrontal cortex made opposing predictions. The Valence Model predicted that anger, a negative emotion, would activate the right prefrontal cortex. The Direction Model predicted that anger, an approach emotion, would activate the left prefrontal cortex. The second model was supported.

This still left open the question of whether the opposite of approach in the prefrontal cortex is better described as moving away (Direction Model), as unmoving but with strength and resistance (Movement Model), or as unmoving with passive yielding (Action Tendency Model). Support for the Action Tendency Model (passivity related to right prefrontal activity) comes from research on shyness and research on behavioral inhibition. Research that tested the competing hypotheses generated by all four models also supported the Action Tendency Model.

Homeostatic Emotion

Another neurological approach, described by Bud Craig in 2003, distinguishes between two classes of emotion. "Classical emotions" include lust, anger and fear, and they are feelings evoked by *environmental stimuli*, which motivate us (in these examples, respectively, to copulate/fight/flee). "Homeostatic emotions" are feelings evoked by *internal body states*, which modulate our behaviour. Thirst, hunger, feeling hot or cold (core temperature), feeling sleep deprived, salt hunger and air hunger are all examples of homeostatic emotion; each is a signal from a body system saying "Things aren't right down here. Drink/eat/move into the shade/put on something warm/ sleep/lick salty rocks/breathe." We begin to feel a homeostatic emotion when one of these systems drifts out of balance, and the feeling prompts us to do what is necessary to restore that system to balance. Pain is a homeostatic emotion telling us "Things aren't right here. Withdraw and protect."

Cognitive Theories

There are some theories arguing that cognitive activity—in the form of judgments, evaluations, or thoughts—is necessary for an emotion to occur. This, argued by Richard Lazarus, is necessary to capture the fact that emotions are about something or have intentionality. Such cognitive activity may be conscious or unconscious and may or may not take the form of conceptual processing.

An influential theory here is that of Lazarus: emotion is a disturbance that occurs in the following order: 1.) Cognitive appraisal—The individual assess the event cognitively, which cues the emotion. 2.) Physiological changes—The cognitive reaction starts biological changes such as increased heart rate or pituitary adrenal response. 3.) Action—The individual feels the emotion and chooses how to react.) Jenny cognitively assesses the snake in her presence, which triggers fear. 2.) Her heart begins to race faster. Adrenaline pumps through her blood stream. 3.) Jenny screams and runs away. Lazarus stressed that the quality and intensity of emotions are controlled through cognitive processes. These processes underlie coping strategies that form the emotional reaction by altering the relationship between the person and the environment.

There are some theories on emotions arguing that cognitive activity in the form of judgements, evaluations, or thoughts is necessary in order for an emotion to occur. A prominent philosophical exponent is Robert C. Solomon (for example, *The Passions, Emotions and the Meaning of Life*, 1993). The theory proposed by Nico Frijda where appraisal leads to action tendencies is another example.

It has also been suggested that emotions (affect heuristics, feelings and gut-feeling reactions) are often used as shortcuts to process information and influence behaviour. The Affect infusion model (AIM) is a theoretical model developed by Joseph Forgas in the early 1990s that attempts to explain how emotion and mood interact with one's ability to process information.

Perceptual Theory

A recent hybrid of the somatic and cognitive theories of emotion is the perceptual theory. This theory is neo-Jamesian in arguing that bodily responses are central to emotions, yet it emphasises the meaningfulness of emotions or the idea that emotions are about something, as is recognised by cognitive theories.

The novel claim of this theory is that conceptually based cognition is unnecessary for such meaning. Rather the bodily changes themselves *perceive* the meaningful content of the emotion because of being causally triggered by certain situations. In this respect, emotions are held to be analogous to faculties such as vision or touch, which provide information about the relation between the subject and the world in various ways. A sophisticated defence of this view is found in philosopher Jesse Prinz's book *Gut Reactions* and psychologist James Laird's book *Feelings.*

Affective Events Theory

This a communication-based theory developed by Howard M. Weiss and Russell Cropanzano (1996), that looks at the causes, structures, and consequences of emotional experience (especially in work contexts). This theory suggests that emotions are influenced and caused by events which in turn influence attitudes and behaviours.

This theoretical frame also emphasizes *time* in that human beings experience what they call emotion episodes—a "series of emotional states extended over time and organized around an underlying theme". This theory has been utilized by numerous researchers to better understand emotion from a communicative lens, and was reviewed further by Howard M. Weiss and Daniel J. Beal in their article, *Reflections on Affective Events Theory* published in *Research on Emotion in Organizations* in 2005.

Cannon-Bard Theory

In the Cannon-Bard theory, Walter Bradford Cannon argued against the dominance of the James-Lange theory regarding the physiological aspects of emotions in the second edition of *Bodily Changes in Pain, Hunger, Fear and Rage*. Where James argued that emotional behaviour often precedes or defines the emotion, Cannon and Bard argued that the emotion arises first and then stimulates typical behaviour.

Two-factor Theory

Another cognitive theory is the Singer-Schachter theory. This is based on experiments purportedly showing that subjects can have different emotional reactions despite being placed into the same physiological state with an injection of adrenaline. Subjects were observed to express either anger or amusement depending on whether another person in the situation displayed that emotion. Hence, the combination of the appraisal of the situation (cognitive) and the participants' reception of adrenaline or a placebo together determined the response. This experiment has been criticized in Jesse Prinz's (2004) *Gut Reactions*.

Component Process Model

A recent version of the cognitive theory regards emotions more broadly as the synchronization of many different bodily and cognitive components. Emotions are identified with the overall process whereby low-level cognitive appraisals, in particular the processing of relevance, trigger bodily reactions, behaviours, feelings, and actions.

Disciplinary Approaches

Many different disciplines have produced work on the emotions. Human sciences study the role of emotions in mental processes, disorders, and neural mechanisms. In psychiatry, emotions are examined as part of the discipline's study and treatment of mental disorders in humans. Psychology examines emotions from a scientific perspective by treating them as mental processes and behaviour and they explore the underlying physiological and neurological processes. In neuroscience sub-fields such as social neuroscience and affective neuroscience, scientists study the neural mechanisms of emotion by combining neuroscience with the psychological study of personality, emotion, and mood. In linguistics, the expression of emotion may change to the meaning of sounds. In education, the role of emotions in relation to learning are examined.

Social sciences often examine emotion for the role that it plays in human culture and social interactions. In sociology, emotions are examined for the role they play in human society, social patterns and interactions, and culture. In anthropology, the study of humanity, scholars use ethnography to undertake contextual analyses and cross-cultural comparisons of a range of human activities; some anthropology studies examine the role of emotions in human activities. In the field of communication sciences, critical organizational scholars have examined the role of emotions in organizations, from the perspectives of managers, employees, and even customers. A focus on emotions in organizations can be credited to Arlie Russell Hochschild's concept of emotional labor. The University of Queensland hosts EmoNet, an email distribution list representing a network of academics that facilitates scholarly discussion of all matters relating to the study of emotion in organizational settings. The list was established in January, 1997 and has over 700 members from across the globe.

In economics, the social science that studies the production, distribution, and consumption of goods and services, emotions are analysed in some sub-fields of microeconomics, in order to assess the role of emotions on purchase decision-making and risk perception. In criminology, a social science approach to the study of crime, scholars often draw on behavioral sciences, sociology, and psychology; emotions are examined in criminology issues such as anomie theory and studies of "toughness", aggressive behaviour, and hooliganism. In law, which underpins civil obedience, politics, economics and society, evidence about people's emotions is often raised in tort law claims for compensation and in criminal law prosecutions against alleged lawbreakers (as evidence of the defendant's state of mind during trials, sentencing, and parole hearings). In political science, emotions are examined in a number of sub-fields, such as the analysis of voter decision-making.

In philosophy, emotions are studied in sub-fields such as ethics, the philosophy of art (for example, sensory-emotional values, and matters of taste and sentimentality), and the philosophy of music. In history, scholars examine documents and other sources to interpret and analyze past activities; speculation on the emotional state of the authors of historical documents is one of the tools of interpretation. In literature and film-making, the expression of emotion is the cornerstone of genres such as drama, melodrama, and romance. Ir communication studies, scholars study the role that emotion plays in the dissemination of ideas and messages. Emotion is also studied in non-human animals in ethology, a branch of zoology which focuses on the scientific study of animal behaviour. Ethology is a combination of laboratory and field science, with strong ties to ecology and evolution. Ethologists often study one type of behaviour (for example, aggression) in a number of unrelated animals.

Evolution of Emotion

Perspectives on emotions from evolution theory were initiated in the late 19th century with Charles Darwin's book *The Expression of Emotions in Man and Animals*. Darwin's original thesis was that emotions evolved via natural selection and therefore have cross-culturally universal counterparts. Furthermore, animals undergo emotions comparable to our own. Evidence of universality in the human case has been provided by Paul Ekman's seminal research on facial expression. Other research in this area focuses on physical displays of emotion including body language of animals and humans. The increased potential in neuroimaging has also allowed investigation into evolutionarily ancient parts of the brain. Important neurological advances were made from these perspectives in the 1990s by, for example, Joseph E. LeDoux and António Damásio.

American evolutionary biologist Robert Trivers argues that moral emotions are based on the principle of reciprocal altruism. The notion of group selection is of particular relevance. This theory posits the different emotions have different reciprocal effects. Sympathy prompts a person to offer the first favor, particularly to someone in need for whom the help would go the furthest. Anger protects a person against cheaters who accept a favor without reciprocating, by making him want to punish the ingrate or sever the relationship.

Gratitude impels a beneficiary to reward those who helped him in the past. Finally, guilt prompts a cheater who is in danger of being found out, by making them want to repair the relationship by redressing the misdeed. As well, guilty feelings encourage a cheater who has been caught to advertise or promise that he will behave better in the future.

Sociology

We try to regulate our emotions to fit in with the norms of the situation, based on many—sometimes conflicting—demands upon us which originate from various entities studied by sociology on a micro level—such as social roles and 'feeling rules' the everyday social interactions and situations are shaped by—and, on a macro level, by social institutions, discourses, ideologies etc. For example, (post-)modern marriage is, on one hand, based on the emotion of love and on the other hand the very emotion is to be worked on and regulated by it. The sociology of emotions also focuses on general attitude changes in a population. Emotional appeals are commonly found in advertising, health campaigns and political messages. Recent examples include no-smoking health campaigns and political campaign advertising emphasizing the fear of terrorism.

Psychotherapy

Depending on the particular school's general emphasis either on cognitive components of emotion, physical energy discharging, or on symbolic movement and facial expression components of emotion, different schools of psychotherapy approach human emotions differently. While, for example, the school of Re-evaluation Counseling proposes that distressing emotions are to be relieved by "discharging" them—hence crying, laughing, sweating, shaking, and trembling; other more cognitively oriented schools approach them via their cognitive components, such as rational emotive behaviour therapy. Yet others approach emotions via symbolic movement and facial expression components (like in contemporary Gestalt therapy.)

In Artificial Languages

EARL

The HUMAINE Emotion Annotation and Representation Language (EARL) classifies the following 48 emotions.

- Negative and forceful
  - Anger
  - Annoyance
  - Contempt

  * Disgust
  * Irritation
- Negative and not in control
  * Anxiety
  * Embarrassment
  * Fear
  * Helplessness
  * Powerlessness
  * Worry
- Negative thoughts
  * Doubt
  * Envy
  * Frustration
  * Guilt
  * Shame
- Negative and passive
  * Boredom
  * Despair
  * Disappointment
  * Hurt
  * Sadness
- Agitation
  * Stress
  * Shock
  * Tension
- Positive and lively
  * Amusement
  * Delight
  * Elation
  * Excitement
  * Happiness
  * Joy
  * Pleasure

- Caring
  - Affection
  - Empathy
  - Friendliness
  - Love
- Positive thoughts
  - Courage
  - Hope
  - Pride
  - Satisfaction
  - Trust
- Quiet positive
  - Calm
  - Content
  - Relaxed
  - Relieved
  - Serene
- Reactive
  - Interest
  - Politeness
  - Surprised

Emotions and Culture

Emotions are universal phenomena; however, they are affected by culture. While some emotions are universal and are experienced in similar ways as a reaction to similar events across all cultures, other emotions show considerable cultural differences in their antecedent events, the way they are experienced, the reactions they provoke and the way they are perceived by the surrounding society.

Bases of Cultural Differences

Self Construal

The way a person perceives her/himself in relation to the surrounding human environment affects one's emotional world.

Collectivistic cultures emphasize the fundamental relatedness of individuals to each other, for example by valuing attending to others, fitting in, and harmonious interdependence with them.

Thus the self in collectivistic cultures is interdependent, and the individual is focused predominantly on his or her relationship with ingroup members or with the ingroup as a whole. In individualistic cultures, on the other hand, individuals hold an independent view of the self and seek to maintain their independence from others by attending to the self and by discovering and expressing their unique inner attributes.

Subjective vs. Objective Emotions

The view of the self as independent in individualistic cultures leads to the perception of emotions as a unique personal experience. The emotional reality is therefore taken as subjective: different people are expected to have different emotional worlds, and to react in different ways to the same experiences. On the contrary, in collectivistic cultures, emotions are experienced out of relationships. They reflect the outer, rather than the inner world and are therefore taken as objective: it is assumed that all people experience the same emotion in a given social situation.

Self and Emotions

The construal of the self affect the personal emotional experienced. The need to enhance the self and its independence in individualistic cultures leads to prevalence of emotions that stress the uniqueness and separation of the individual. In collectivistic cultures emotion relate more to the relationships with others and to the fitness of the individual to its social environment.

Hence, the same situation might lead to different emotions in collectivistic and in individualistic cultures. In a research held by Mesquita (2001) it was found that achievements related to higher education in Turkey (a collectivistic culture) led to pride as a result of the honor brought to the family, while in Holland (an individualistic culture) similar achievements led to self satisfaction and content.

Cultural Norms for Emotions

Social norms exist for various aspects of emotions.

- General emotional norms: what emotions are considered to be good or bad? Which should be more prevalent?
- Feeling rules: how should one feel when encountering certain event (does being criticized lead to anger or embarrassment?)
- Display rules: how should one act when experiencing certain emotion (does anger manifest as aggression or withdrawal?)

While individualistic cultures are loose regarding to the display rules (one can express one's feelings as preferred at the moment), norms for positive feeling rules in individualistic cultures are very tight. According to those norms, one should be happy and strive for happiness, and if one is not happy, that means one has failed to achieve life's goals. In collectivistic cultures such as China, the feeling rules are rather loose: there are no strict expectations about how one should generally feel. However, the display rules are much tighter: there are certain expectations about the way one should show one's feelings in a given context. For example, Confucian cultures consider expression of emotions (both positive and negative) as a possible threat to the social order. Hence, the norms are of not-showing personal emotions. One may feel as one pleases, as long as one doesn't express it.

Cultural effects on Emotional Aspects

Culture and Life Satisfaction

Culture affects the subjective well-being. Well-being includes both general life satisfaction, and the relative balance of positive affect verses negative affect in daily life. Culture directs the attention to different sources of information for making the life satisfaction judgments, thus affecting subjective well-being appraisal.

Individualistic cultures direct attention to inner states and feelings (such as positive or negative affects), while in collectivistic cultures the attention is directed to outer sources (i.e. adhering to social norms or fulfilling one's duties). Indeed,

Suh et al. (1998) found that the correlation between life satisfaction and the prevalence of positive affect is higher in individualistic cultures, whereas in collectivistic cultures affect and adhering to norms are equally important for life satisfaction.

Shame and Culture in the Work Context

Shame is an automatic involuntary response to a personal failure attributed to the self. The failure is relative to other's expectations, thus shame is a social emotion that involves self-consciousness. A study examined the effects of shame on salespersons in Holland (an individualistic culture) and the Philippines (a collectivistic culture). They found that bad experiences with clients led to similar shame emotions in both cultures. However, the responses to this shame were opposite: shame caused Dutch salespersons to withdraw and to perform poorer on their job, apparently because they directed most of their mental resources inwards, to defend the self. Filipino salespersons felt shame all the same; however, the shame caused them to put more efforts in building relationship and thus to perform better on the job. Moreover, Filipino salespersons demonstrated more Organizational Citizenship Behaviours (OCB) after experiencing shame. The reason for this is that in collectivistic cultures shame signals that social harmony has been hampered and that the individual should act to rebuild it.

Problems in Cross Cultural Research of Emotions

Several problems exist when trying to compare emotions between different cultures.

Translation

- Words describing emotions might not be equivalent across cultures. For example, happiness has a buoyant meaning in English. However for the Kipsigis, happiness occurs "when nothing is bothering you" thus has quiet calm meaning.
- Some feelings are idiosyncratic, and do not have equivalent terms in other languages: *Emotions across cultures and methods*. Journal of Cross-Cultural Psychology.

* Abhiman is an Indian term best described as a feeling of prideful loving anger.
* Sukhi is an Indian term similar to peace and happiness.
* Fureai: Fureai is a Japanese term used when feeling a sense of connectedness to someone else.
* Rettokan is a Japanese term that means to feel inferior
* Schadenfreude is a German term defined by German philosopher Theodor Adorno as "the largely unanticipated delight in the suffering of another which is cognized as trivial and/or appropriate".

Clustering

Across cultures, people report that they ideally want to feel more positive than negative. Personality and Social Psychology Bulletin. All cultures classify emotions as either pleasant or unpleasant, and desirable or undesirable, and most emotions are classified in the same way across all cultures. For example, sadness is classified as an unpleasant undesirable feeling everywhere, and happiness is always a pleasant desirable feeling. The classification of certain other emotions is not identical in all cultures, depending if the emotion is seen as either beneficial or detrimental to a person's goals and well-being and to the society norms. Examples for such differences include:

- Pride is sometimes seen as a positive emotion in western cultures (such as the USA), in India it is considered to be a negative emotion.
- Love is a purely positive emotion in western cultures, however in China it is seen as closer to sadness and negative loss emotions.

In the beginning babies are programmed to seek out the things that they want by crying. As they mature, though, children's emotional capabilities expand, allowing them to develop a variety of skills that they will need in their adult lives. Emotional development encompasses the feelings that we have about ourselves and others, as well as our capabilities to function well in the world from a social standpoint.

Babies and Their Emotions

While babies seem to be born with some of their emotional qualities in place, much of how they develop initially can be credited to the lessons that they are taught by their primary caregivers.

Warm, attentive care, especially during the first year of life, helps babies to gain a sense that the world is a safe and welcoming place. That sense of security can be a good base for the development of other healthy emotional responses. Babies form attachments to the people closest to them when they are quite young, showing increased anxiety and restlessness when with unfamiliar people. These first and ost important relationships serve as a child's earliest lessons in forming close, emotional bonds.

Toddlers-the Beginning of Independence

As children move from infancy into the toddler era, they gain a sense of self, separate from their parents and siblings. Since this is a whole new world for them, frustrations can run high (for mum and dad, too!) and they may be prone to temper tantrums or other behaviours that their parents find objectionable. As with any new skill, learning to control negative emotional responses takes time, so parents should try to be patient with their temperamental toddlers. Children need to learn that there are better and more effective ways to get what they want than to throw tantrums, and parents can help them by exercising firm kindness.

While they may be a bit emotionally high-strung, toddlers are also likely to show the first signs of compassion, expressing worry when a playmate or family member seems sad or upset. These expressions of positive emotion should be complimented by parents and caregivers who are striving to encourage healthy emotional development.

Kindness and Self-Control

By the time that they are school-aged, children begin to take pride in their ability to exert self-control, and enjoy the feedback that they receive from being responsible and cooperative. This presents parents and educators with the opportunity to foster desirable emotional responses by pointing out situations in which children behaved in mature, compassionate ways.

School aged children are also faced with their own unique challenges, of course, so parents must do all that they can to help kids to navigate unfamiliar situations. Sibling rivalry is common, which can be exasperating for parents who harbour hopes that their children will get along famously. Allowing the children to work things out for themselves is wise (unless the situation gets truly out of control) because each time that the kids resolve an issue, they take steps toward emotional maturity.

Almost Adults

The teen years can be turbulent (a true understatement!), with additional stresses put on adolescents that they may not have encountered in the past. Social and school responsibilities, coupled with a natural desire to make their own decisions without the input of their parents, can be cause for distress as well as opportunities for growth.

Depending on the teen's emotional development up to that point, adolescents may find themselves dealing with feelings of depression, anxiety, or helplessness, in which case, parents must do all that they can to ease their child's stress level. Encouraging activities that promote self-esteem and a sense of community will serve teens well, since they are only steps away from taking full responsibility for their lives.

Expert Opinions

Lawrence Kohlberg, an American psychologist, felt that people continued to grow and develop emotionally and socially, throughout their entire lives. He determined that we work through six stages (in three levels, with two stages each) of moral development in order to reach our highest potential. His theory seems especially plausible as he acknowledged that not all people will attain the highest levels of morality and emotional maturity. The goal then, for parents, is to encourage their children's emotional development whilst paying close attention to the examples they are setting for their impressionable youngsters.

Personal, Social and Emotional Development

Requirements

Children must be provided with experiences and support which will help them to develop a positive sense of themselves and of others; respect for others; social skills; and a positive disposition to learn. Providers must ensure support for children's emotional well-being to help them to know themselves and what they can do.

Aspects of Personal, Social and Emotional Development

Personal, Social and Emotional Development is made up of the following aspects:

Dispositions and Attitudes – is about how children become interested, excited and motivated about their learning.

Self-confidence and Self-esteem – is about children having a sense of their own value and understanding the need for sensitivity to significant events in their own and other people's lives.

Making Relationships– is about the importance of children forming good relationships with others and working alongside others companionably.

Behaviour and Self-control – is about how children develop a growing understanding of what is right and wrong and why, together with learning about the impact of their words and actions on themselves and others.

Self-care – is about how children gain a sense of self-respect and concern for their own personal hygiene and care and how they develop independence.

Sense of Community – is about how children understand and respect their own needs, views, cultures and beliefs and those of other people.

What Personal, Social and Emotional Development means for children

- For children, being special to someone and well cared-for is vital for their physical, social and emotional health and well-being.

- Being acknowledged and affirmed by important people in their lives leads to children gaining confidence and inner strength through secure attachments with these people.
- Exploration within close relationships leads to the growth of self-assurance, promoting a sense of belonging which allows children to explore the world from a secure base.
- Children need adults to set a good example and to give them opportunities for interaction with others so that they can develop positive ideas about themselves and others.
- Children who are encouraged to feel free to express their ideas and their feelings, such as joy, sadness, frustration and fear, can develop strategies to cope with new, challenging or stressful situations.

6

Moral Development and Juvenile Delinquency

A moral (from Latin *morâlis*) is a message conveyed or a lesson to be learned from a story or event. The moral may be left to the hearer, reader or viewer to determine for themselves, or may be explicitly encapsulated in a maxim. As an example of the latter, at the end of Aesop's fable of the Tortoise and the Hare, in which the plodding and determined tortoise wins a race against the much-faster yet extremely arrogant hare, the stated moral is "slow and steady wins the race". However, other morals can often be taken from the story itself; for instance, that "arrogance or overconfidence in one's abilities may lead to failure or the loss of an event, race, or contest". The use of stock characters is a means of conveying the moral of the story by eliminating complexity of personality and so spelling out the issues arising in the interplay between the characters, enables the writer to generate a clear message. With more rounded characters, such as those typically found in Shakespeare's plays, the moral may be more nuanced but no less present, and the writer may point it up in other ways.

Throughout the history of recorded literature, the majority of fictional writing has served not only to entertain but also to instruct, inform or improve their audiences or readership. In classical drama, for example, the role of the chorus was to comment on the proceedings and draw out a message for the audience to take away with them; while the novels of Charles Dickens are a vehicle for morals regarding the social and economic system of Victorian Britain.

Morals have typically been more obvious in children's literature, sometimes even being introduced with the phrase: "The moral of the story is ...". Such explicit techniques have grown increasingly out of fashion in modern storytelling, and are now usually only included for ironic purposes.

Some examples are: "Better to be safe than sorry", "The evil deserves no aid", "Be friends with whom you don't like", "Don't judge people by the way they look", "Sticks and stones will break my bones, but words will never hurt me", "Slow and steady wins the race", and "Your overconfidence is your weakness".

Moral is also understood as an individual understanding or translation of mannerisms at which they abide.

Kohlberg's Stages of Moral Development

Kohlberg's stages of moral development constitute an adaptation of a psychological theory originally conceived of by the Swiss psychologist Jean Piaget. Lawrence Kohlberg began work on this topic while a psychology postgraduate student at the University of Chicago, and expanded and developed this theory throughout the course of his life.

The theory holds that moral reasoning, the basis for ethical behaviour, has six identifiable developmental stages, each more adequate at responding to moral dilemmas than its predecessor. Kohlberg followed the development of moral judgment far beyond the ages studied earlier by Piaget, who also claimed that logic and morality develop through constructive stages. Expanding on Piaget's work, Kohlberg determined that the process of moral development was principally concerned with justice, and that it continued throughout the individual's lifetime, a notion that spawned dialogue on the philosophical implications of such research.

Kohlberg relied for his studies on stories such as the Heinz dilemma, and was interested in how individuals would justify their actions if placed in similar moral dilemmas. He then analysed the form of moral reasoning displayed, rather than its conclusion, and classified it as belonging to one of six distinct stages. There have been critiques of the theory from several perspectives. Arguments include that it emphasizes justice to the exclusion of other moral values, such as caring; that there is such an overlap between stages that they should more properly be regarded as separate domains; or that evaluations of the reasons for moral choices are mostly *post hoc* rationalizations (by both decision makers and psychologists studying them) of essentially intuitive decisions. Nevertheless, an entirely new field within psychology was created as a result of Kohlberg's theory, and according to Haggbloom et al.'s study of the most eminent psychologists of the 20th century, Kohlberg was the 16th most frequently cited psychologist in introductory psychology textbooks throughout the century, as well as the 30th most eminent overall. Kohlberg's scale is about how people justify behaviours and his stages are not a method of ranking how moral someone behaves: there should however be a correlation between how someone scores on the scale and how they behave and the general hypothesis is that moral behaviour is more responsible, consistent and predictable from people at higher levels.

Stages

Kohlberg's six stages can be more generally grouped into three levels of two stages each: pre-conventional, conventional and post-conventional. Following Piaget's constructivist requirements for a stage model, as described in his theory of cognitive development, it is extremely rare to regress backward in stages—to lose the use of higher stage abilities. Stages cannot be skipped; each provides a new and necessary perspective, more comprehensive and differentiated than its predecessors but integrated with them.

Level 1 (Pre-Conventional)

1. Obedience and punishment orientation

(*How can I avoid punishment?*)

2. Self-interest orientation

(*What's in it for me?*)

Level 2 (Conventional)

3. Interpersonal accord and conformity

(*Social norms*)

(*The good boy/good girl attitude*)

4. Authority and social-order maintaining orientation

(*Law and order morality*)

Level 3 (Post-Conventional)

5. Social contract orientation

6. Universal ethical principles

(*Principled conscience*).

Pre-Conventional

The pre-conventional level of moral reasoning is especially common in children, although adults can also exhibit this level of reasoning. Reasoners at this level judge the morality of an action by its direct consequences. The pre-conventional level consists of the first and second stages of moral development, and is solely concerned with the self in an egocentric manner. A child with preconventional morality has not yet adopted or internalized society's conventions regarding what is right or wrong, but instead focuses largely on external consequences that certain actions may bring.

In Stage one (obedience and punishment driven), individuals focus on the direct consequences of their actions on themselves. For example, an action is perceived as morally wrong because the perpetrator is punished. "The last time I did that I got spanked so I will not do it again." The worse the punishment for the act is, the more "bad" the act is perceived to be. This can give rise to an inference that even innocent victims are guilty in proportion to their suffering. It is "egocentric", lacking recognition that others' points of view are different from one's own. There is "deference to superior power or prestige".

Stage two (self-interest driven) espouses the "what's in it for me" position, in which right behaviour is defined by whatever is in the individual's best interest. Stage two reasoning shows a limited interest in the needs of others, but only to a point where it might further the individual's own interests. As a result, concern for others is not based on loyalty or intrinsic respect, but rather a "you scratch my back, and I'll scratch yours" mentality. The lack of a societal perspective in the pre-conventional level is quite different from the social contract (stage five), as all actions have the purpose of serving the individual's own needs or interests. For the stage two theorist, the world's perspective is often seen as morally relative.

Conventional

The conventional level of moral reasoning is typical of adolescents and adults. Those who reason in a conventional way judge the morality of actions by comparing them to society's views and expectations. The conventional level consists of the third and fourth stages of moral development. Conventional morality is characterized by an acceptance of society's conventions concerning right and wrong. At this level an individual obeys rules and follows society's norms even when there are no consequences for obedience or disobedience. Adherence to rules and conventions is somewhat rigid, however, and a rule's appropriateness or fairness is seldom questioned.

In Stage three (interpersonal accord and conformity driven), the self enters society by filling social roles. Individuals are receptive to approval or disapproval from others as it reflects society's accordance with the perceived role. They try to be a "good boy" or "good girl" to live up to these expectations, having learned that there is inherent value in doing so. Stage three reasoning may judge the morality of an action by evaluating its consequences in terms of a person's relationships, which now begin to include things like respect, gratitude and the "golden rule". "I want to be liked and thought well of; apparently, not being naughty makes people like me." Desire to maintain rules and authority exists only to further support these social roles. The intentions of actions play a more significant role in reasoning at this stage; "they mean well ...".

In Stage four (authority and social order obedience driven), it is important to obey laws, dictums and social conventions because of their importance in maintaining a functioning society. Moral reasoning in stage four is thus beyond the need for individual approval exhibited in stage three; society must learn to transcend individual needs. A central ideal or ideals often prescribe what is right and wrong, such as in the case of fundamentalism. If one person violates a law, perhaps everyone would—thus there is an obligation and a duty to uphold laws and rules. When someone does violate a law, it is morally wrong; culpability is thus a significant factor in this stage as it separates the bad domains from the good ones. Most active members of society remain at stage four, where morality is still predominantly dictated by an outside force.

Post-Conventional

The post-conventional level, also known as the principled level, consists of stages five and six of moral development. There is a growing realization that individuals are separate entities from society, and that the individual's own perspective may take precedence over society's view; they may disobey rules inconsistent with their own principles. These people live by their own abstract principles about right and wrong—principles that typically include such basic human rights as life, liberty, and justice. Because of this level's "nature of self before others", the behaviour of post-conventional individuals, especially those at stage six, can be confused with that of those at the pre-conventional level.

People who exhibit postconventional morality view rules as useful but changeable mechanisms—ideally rules can maintain the general social order and protect human rights. Rules are not absolute dictates that must be obeyed without question. Contemporary theorists often speculate that many people may never reach this level of abstract moral reasoning.

In Stage five (social contract driven), the world is viewed as holding different opinions, rights and values. Such perspectives should be mutually respected as unique to each person or community. Laws are regarded as social contracts rather than rigid edicts. Those that do not promote the general welfare should be changed when necessary to meet "the greatest good for the greatest number of people". This is achieved through majority decision, and inevitable compromise. Democratic government is ostensibly based on stage five reasoning.

In Stage six (universal ethical principles driven), moral reasoning is based on abstract reasoning using universal ethical principles. Laws are valid only insofar as they are grounded in justice, and a commitment to justice carries with it an obligation to disobey unjust laws. Rights are unnecessary, as social contracts are not essential for deontic moral action. Decisions are not reached hypothetically in a conditional way but rather categorically in an absolute way, as in the philosophy of Immanuel Kant. This involves an individual imagining what they would do in another's shoes, if they believed what that other person imagines to be true. The resulting consensus is the action taken. In this way action is never a means but always an end in itself; the individual acts because it is right, and not because it is instrumental, expected, legal, or previously agreed upon. Although Kohlberg insisted that stage six exists, he found it difficult to identify individuals who consistently operated at that level.

Further Stages

In Kohlberg's empirical studies of individuals throughout their life Kohlberg observed that some had apparently undergone moral stage regression. This could be resolved either by allowing for moral regression or by extending the theory. Kohlberg chose the latter, postulating the existence of sub-stages in which the emerging stage has not yet been fully integrated into the personality. In particular Kohlberg noted a stage 4½ or 4+, a transition from stage four to stage five, that shared characteristics of both. In this stage the individual is disaffected with the arbitrary nature of law and order reasoning; culpability is frequently turned from being defined by society to viewing society itself as culpable. This stage is often mistaken for the moral relativism of stage two, as the individual views those interests of society that conflict with their own as being relatively and morally wrong. Kohlberg noted that this was often observed in students entering college.

Kohlberg suggested that there may be a seventh stage—Transcendental Morality, or Morality of Cosmic Orientation—which linked religion with moral reasoning. Kohlberg's difficulties in obtaining empirical evidence for even a sixth stage, however, led him to emphasize the speculative nature of his seventh stage.

Theoretical Assumptions (Philosophy)

The picture of human nature Kohlberg begins with is that humans are inherently communicative and capable of reason. They also possess a desire to understand others and the world around them. The stages of Kohlberg's model relate to the qualitative moral *reasonings* adopted by individuals, and so do not translate directly into praise or blame of any individual's actions or character. Arguing that his theory measures moral reasoning and not particular moral conclusions, Kohlberg insists that the *form and structure* of moral arguments is independent of the *content* of those arguments, a position he calls "formalism".

Kohlberg's theory centres on the notion that justice is the essential characteristic of moral reasoning. Justice itself relies heavily upon the notion of sound reasoning based on principles. Despite being a justice-centered theory of morality, Kohlberg considered it to be compatible with plausible formulations of deontology and eudaimonia.

Kohlberg's theory understands values as a critical component of the right. Whatever the right is, for Kohlberg, it must be universally valid across societies (a position known as "moral universalism"): there can be no relativism. Moreover, morals are not natural features of the world; they are prescriptive. Nevertheless, moral judgments can be evaluated in logical terms of truth and falsity.

According to Kohlberg: someone progressing to a higher stage of moral reasoning cannot skip stages. For example, an individual cannot jump from being concerned mostly with peer judgments (stage three) to being a proponent of social contracts (stage five). On encountering a moral dilemma and finding their current level of moral reasoning unsatisfactory, however, an individual will look to the next level. Realizing the limitations of the current stage of thinking is the driving force behind moral development, as each progressive stage is more adequate than the last. The process is therefore considered to be constructive, as it is initiated by the conscious construction of the individual, and is not in any meaningful sense a component of the individual's innate dispositions, or a result of past inductions.

Formal Elements

Progress through Kohlberg's stages happens as a result of the individual's increasing competence, both psychologically and in balancing conflicting social-value claims. The process of resolving conflicting claims to reach an equilibrium is called "justice operation". Kohlberg identifies two of these justice operations: "equality," which involves an impartial regard for persons, and "reciprocity," which means a regard for the role of personal merit. For Kohlberg, the most adequate result of both operations is "reversibility," in which a moral or dutiful act within a particular situation is evaluated in terms of whether or not the act would be satisfactory even if particular persons were to switch roles within that situation (also known colloquially as "moral musical chairs").

Knowledge and learning contribute to moral development. Specifically important are the individual's "view of persons" and their "social perspective level", each of which becomes more complex and mature with each advancing stage. The "view of persons" can be understood as the individual's grasp of the psychology of other persons; it may be pictured as a spectrum, with stage one having no view of other persons at all, and stage six being entirely sociocentric. Similarly, the social perspective level involves the understanding of the social universe, differing from the view of persons in that it involves an appreciation of social norms.

Examples of Applied Moral Dilemmas

Kohlberg established the *Moral Judgement Interview* in his original 1958 dissertation. During the roughly 45-minute tape recorded semi-structured interview, the interviewer uses moral dilemmas to determine which stage of moral reasoning a person uses. The dilemmas are fictional short stories that describe situations in which a person has to make a moral decision. The participant is asked a systemic series of open-ended questions, like what they think the right course of action is, as well as justifications as to why certain actions are right or wrong. The form and structure of these replies are scored and not the content; over a set of multiple moral dilemmas an overall score is derived.

Heinz Dilemma

A dilemma that Kohlberg used in his original research was the druggist's dilemma: *Heinz Steals the Drug In Europe.*

A woman was near death from a special kind of cancer. There was one drug that the doctors thought might save her.

It was a form of radium that a druggist in the same town had recently discovered. The drug was expensive to make, but the druggist was charging ten times what the drug cost him to produce. He paid $200 for the radium and charged $2,000 for a small dose of the drug. The sick woman's husband, Heinz, went to everyone he knew to borrow the money, but he could only get together about $ 1,000, which is half of what it cost. He told the druggist that his wife was dying and asked him to sell it cheaper or let him pay later. But the druggist said, "No, I discovered the drug and I'm going to make money from it." So Heinz got desperate and broke into the man's store to steal the drug for his wife. Should Heinz have broken into the laboratory to steal the drug for his wife? Why or why not?

From a theoretical point of view, it is not important what the participant thinks that Heinz should *do*. Kohlberg's theory holds that the justification the participant offers is what is significant, the *form* of their response. Below are some of many examples of possible arguments that belong to the six stages:

Stage one (*obedience*): Heinz should not steal the medicine because he would consequently be put in prison, which would mean he is a bad person. Or: Heinz should steal the medicine because it is only worth $200, not how much the druggist wanted for it. Heinz had even offered to pay for it and was not stealing anything else.

Stage two (*self-interest*): Heinz should steal the medicine because he will be much happier if he saves his wife, even if he will have to serve a prison sentence. Or: Heinz should not steal the medicine because prison is an awful place, and he would probably experience anguish over a jail cell more than his wife's death.

Stage three (*conformity*): Heinz should steal the medicine because his wife expects it; he wants to be a good husband. Or: Heinz should not steal the drug because stealing is bad and he is not a criminal; he tried to do everything he could without breaking the law, you cannot blame him.

Stage four (*law-and-order*): Heinz should not steal the medicine because the law prohibits stealing, making it illegal. Or: Heinz should steal the drug for his wife but also take the prescribed punishment for the crime as well as paying the druggist what he is owed. Criminals cannot just run around without regard for the law; actions have consequences.

Stage five (*human rights*): Heinz should steal the medicine because everyone has a right to choose life, regardless of the law. Or: Heinz should not steal the medicine because the scientist has a right to fair compensation. Even if his wife is sick, it does not make his actions right.

Stage six (*universal human ethics*): Heinz should steal the medicine, because saving a human life is a more fundamental value than the property rights of another person. Or: Heinz should not steal the medicine, because others may need the medicine just as badly, and their lives are equally significant.

Criticisms

One criticism of Kohlberg's theory is that it emphasizes justice to the exclusion of other values, and so may not adequately address the arguments of those who value other moral aspects of actions. Carol Gilligan has argued that Kohlberg's theory is overly androcentric. Kohlberg's theory was initially developed based on empirical research using only male participants; Gilligan argued that it did not adequately describe the concerns of women. Although research has generally found no significant pattern of differences in moral development between sexes, Gilligan's theory of moral development does not focus on the value of justice. She developed an alternative theory of moral reasoning based on the ethics of caring. Critics such as Christina Hoff Sommers, however, argued that Gilligan's research is ill-founded, and that no evidence exists to support her conclusion.

Kohlberg's stages are not culturally neutral, as demonstrated by its application to a number of different cultures. Although they progress through the stages in the same order, individuals in different cultures seem to do so at different rates. Kohlberg has responded by saying that although different cultures do indeed inculcate different beliefs, his stages correspond to underlying modes of reasoning, rather than to those beliefs.

Other psychologists have questioned the assumption that moral action is primarily a result of formal reasoning. Social intuitionists such as Jonathan Haidt, for example, argue that individuals often make moral judgments without weighing concerns such as fairness, law, human rights, or abstract ethical values. Thus the arguments analysed by Kohlberg and other rationalist psychologists could be considered *post hoc* rationalizations of intuitive decisions; moral reasoning may be less relevant to moral action than Kohlberg's theory suggests.

Developmental theories, according to Siegel (2004) are either "latent trait" theories, which hold that criminal behaviour is controlled by some master trait present at birth or soon after which remains stable and unchanging throughout a lifetime; or "life course" theories, which view criminality as a dynamic process, influenced by individual characteristics as well as social experiences. Moral development theories tend to be embraced by those with an interest in ethics; latent trait theories by those with an interest in the root psychological causes of crime; and life course theories tend to be attract researchers interested in asking why and when do offenders *stop* offending (i.e., the study of *desistance*).

It should be noted that despite the inroads of some fairly good ideas in criminology, *moral development theories* are most often regarded as "eclectic" theories in the field. Eclectic means "everything causes delinquency or crime." They're subject to what is also called the "evil causes evil fallacy." Blaming delinquency on being an adolescent is the same as saying "moods" or "states of mind" cause crime, and, of course, there are many things to blame delinquency on. Theoretical efforts are likewise diverse, shooting out in multiple directions. Neo-cognitive theory (Kelley 1994), for example, draws heavily upon the quite mysterious process of alienation that typically occurs in adolescence, and then, to take another example, there are important down-to-earth biological processes to note, such as the concept of "pubertal development" advanced by Felson & Haynie (2002), who incidently found that puberty (and an associated property crime to violent crime to drug crime pattern) was as reliable a predictor of delinquency as school performance and peer association. There is tremendous variability to be explained from this approach, and it is quite likely that this theoretical project will remain unfinished for some time in criminology.

Adolescence as a Stage of Development

It's been called the "transition" stage with no accomplishment nor completion. Its existence has been called an "historical accident." Experts can't even agree on when it begins (most simply use the age of puberty) and when it ends (some say an "extended" adolescence is possible up to age 25 or 30; other say there's an "early" 12-14 stage, a "middle" 15-17 stage, and a "late" 18-19 stage). There's more mythology than science when it comes to notions of "typical" or "normal" adolescence, and explaining the breakdown that occurs.

Daedalus, an inventor, and his son, Icarus (so the ancient Greek myth goes) were both imprisoned in a tower on the island of Crete. To escape, Daedalus built a set of wings out of feathers and wax, but only his son, Icarus was small enough to fit thru the tower window. Daedalus warned Icarus not to fly too high because Apollo, God of the Sun, would become jealous of someone entering his domain and melt the wax. But Icarus, exhilarated by being able to soar above the Earth, flies too high, and his wings melt, plunging him into the Hellspont. Ever since, "adolescents" have been seen as: (a) disobedient toward parents; (b) wanting to "fly" too high; and, in some interpretations, (c) condemned to hell.

Hippocrates, the father of medicine, recommended two kinds of treatments for unruly children. For females, they should be made pregnant. For males, they should be flogged. Philo, a friend of Socrates, advocated infanticide if beatings didn't work. History actually records a long record of using sex, corporal punishment, and infanticide against unruly children. The common law doctrine of *in loco parentis* has deep roots in almost all civilizations. Historically, adolescence can be considered a by-product of the Industrial Revolution. Prior to child labor laws, there had been no need to define any special period of life for those too young to work but too old to not be given at least some adult responsibilities. Over the years, the age at which society permits children to assume adult roles has gradually been raised. This "stretch" of time, then, has come to be associated with the "stress" of adolescence.

By the late 19th Century, numerous experts were popularizing the idea of adolescence being a "critical" stage of life. Baden-Powell (founder of the Boy Scouts) pioneered the technique of "not too much" but "not too little" discipline as a cure for the problems of adolescence. Dr. Spock, later in the 1950s, would advocate complete and total leniency. Counterculture experts such as Keniston and Roscak in the 1960s also advocated toleration as well as popularized the idea of being "stuck in adolescence." Freudian and Neo-Freudian ideas abounded, but it was Stanley Hall's ideas about the *Six Themes of Adolescence* that became the most popular hallmarks of "normal," as follows:

The Six Themes of Adolescence

1. Self-definition — a concern for finding one's "real" self, a concern for habit formation, and little unstructured time to deal with these concerns, hence, a constant state of urgency.
2. Estrangement and Omnipotentiality — estrangement takes the form of feeling like a marginal member of society, with unrealistic mobility aspirations and intense job anxieties. Omnipotentiality is the feeling of absolute freedom, a reveling in all the pure possibilities that the future may hold. For many, the "car" becomes a symbol for this.
3. Refusal of Socialization — a critical if not rebellious stance at continued efforts to instruct, educate, or train for society's purposes. There's a feeling of always being under observation by a critical audience of all adult socializing agents.
4. Celebration of Youth Culture — a rebellious sense of solidarity based on the perceived sharing of fads, fashions, and styles by others in the same age group or generation; intense age-consciousness.
5. Stasis as Death — stasis means "standing still" or being in a rut, and this is avoided and despised at all costs. There's an irrational devotion to change, to putting oneself through changes merely for the sake of change. It takes two forms: a need to move (geographic restlessness); and a need to be moved (experimentation with states of consciousness).

6. Physical Obsession — there's an obsessiveness or inadmissible sense of shame over uncontrollable physical changes, like sex fantasies, body weight and contours, dietary habits, the outgrowing of clothing, outbreaks of acne, etc.

Indicators of Normal and Abnormal Adolescence

Indicators of being on a "normal" course of moral development:

1. Obsessive concern for bodily appearance
2. Fear of abandonment expressed as assertion of independence
3. Desire to be different in terms of "fads"
4. Sexual desire and manipulativeness
5. Wanting to be like other races or cultures
6. Persistent wisecracking as long as it's witty
7. Obsessive desire for success and recognition
8. Lack of self-identity or distinct self-concept
9. Emotional extremes expressed as sensitivity to criticism.

Indicators of being on an "abnormal" course of moral development:

1. Driven by whim or caprice rather than purpose or gain
2. Unmoved by overtures of help & harms helpers
3. Shows no loyalty to other adolescents
4. Words are inconsistent with feelings, language is strange, humour missing
5. Claims to have always been the first to do something
6. Pathological lying for no good reason
7. Superficially charming but unable to maintain intimate relations.

Indicators of being an "at-risk" youth (Middle Schools):

1. Frequent absenteeism, tardiness, or suspension
2. Academic performance below grade level or repeating a grade

3. Oppositional stance towards authority
4. Drug/alcohol involvement
5. Police/probation involvement
6. Being a "latch-key" child
7. Coming from a single parent family or foster home.

Indicators of "delinquent pathways" (Justice Dept.):

1. Authority Conflict Pathway: Early signs of stubbornness, outright defiance by age 11, running away, avoiding authorities, truancy, staying out late
2. Covert Pathway: Early signs of minor mischievousness, frequent lying, shoplifting by age 10, property damage, firestarting, vandalism
3. Overt Pathway: Early acts of aggression or bullying, annoying everyone around them by age 12, having no friends and numerous enemies, interested only in escalating problems.

Notes on Piaget's Moral Development Theory

1. Sensorimotor Stage 0-2
2. PreOperational Stage 2-7
3. Concrete Stage 7-14
4. Formal Stage 14-adult.

In short, delinquents are seen as "stuck" in the Concrete stage, only seeing things as black or white, right or wrong. In short, they have a dualistic morality. They're only concerned with classifying things, and no other reasoning about them.

Notes on Erikson's Moral Development Theory

1. Trust/Mistrust Stage 0-1
2. Autonomy/Doubt Stage 2-3
3. Initiative/Guilt Stage 3-6
4. Industry/Inferiority Stage 7-12
5. Identity/Identity Diffusion Stage 12-18
6. Intimacy/Isolation Stage "Twenty-something"
7. Generativity/Stagnation Stage 20s-50s
8. Integrity/Despair Stage 60s—

In short, delinquents are seen as "stuck" in the Identity Stage, in a semi-permanent state of identity crisis. Male delinquents experience identity without intimacy, and female delinquents experience intimacy without identity. Self-worth and fidelity are virtues that have not yet developed.

Notes on Kohlberg's Moral Development Theory

1. Punishment Concern stage-obedience to power and avoiding punishment
2. Individualistic Concern stage-meeting one's own needs, me first
3. Interpersonal Concern stage-having good motives, some concern for others
4. Conscience Concern stage-serving welfare of the group or society
5. Social Contract Concern stage-agreed-upon individual rights in society
6. Universal Ethics Concern stage-principles of justice for all humankind.

In short, delinquents are seen as "stuck" in a state of moral immaturity. It doesn't depend on age, and any of the first three stages may be where they're stuck. Most hardcore delinquents would be at the Punishment stage, where they only believe something is right or wrong because it hurts if you do what society thinks is wrong. Others are in the Individualistic stage, where they decide what is right or wrong by reference to an egoistic sense of whether they can be blamed or not for doing wrong. A few may be in the Interpersonal stage, where they determine right or wrong by a sense of group honor. Kohlberg actually did some research with adult criminals, finding that they are more likely to be in stages 1 and 2 (deterred from crime by fear of sanctions).

Notes on Gilligan's Moral Development Theory

The differences between males and females are seen as the difference between an ethics of justice and an ethics of caring. Boys *game* (for winners and losers) while girls *play* (for enjoyment of the game). The theory is a feminist critique of justice, as traditional justice conceptions are seen as not allowing room for an ethics of caring. Similar ideas can be found in what is called restorative justice or peacemaking criminology. Although these viewpoints in criminology have separate traditions, there is enough of a connection to mention them here.

Developmental Theories

The "latent trait" view holds that there is some personal attribute or characteristic present in all people which controls their inclination or propensity to commit crime. The most sophisticated model of this idea can be found in Rowe, Osgood & Nicewander (1990), but there have been a number of efforts since then to identify which trait is the "master" trait.

Suspected traits include defective intelligence, impulsive personality, genetic abnormalities, physical-chemical functioning of the brain, and/or environmental influences on brain function. Wilson & Herrstein (1985), for example, attempted to develop a human nature theory of crime which argued that personal traits outweigh the importance of social variables. In a latter work, similar authors (Gottfredson & Hirschi 1990) argued that "low self-control" was the "master" trait, the root cause of which was inadequate child-rearing. Gottfredson & Hirschi's ideas in this regard are often treated as a control theory of crime.

A fairly new "latent trait" approach has been that of Mark Colvin who argues that chronic criminals emerge from a developmental process characterized by recurring, erratic episodes of coercion. There are two types of coercion: interpersonal (which is direct, involving the use or threat of force from parents, peers, and significant others); and impersonal (which involves pressures beyond individual control). Colvin's *differential coercion theory* integrates several existing criminological perspectives, but in brief, attempts to locate the root cause of chronic offending in the fact that such offenders grew up in homes where parents used erratic control and applied it in an erratic and inconsistent fashion.

Also fairly new is Tittle's *control balance theory* (Tittle 1995), which expands on the notion of personal control as a predisposing element of criminality. Control, as a concept, can refer to either the amount of control one is subject to by others, or it can refer to the amount of control one can exercise over others. Those who have an excess of the first kind of control tend to engage in exploitation, plunder, and decadence. Those who have a deficit of the second kind of control tend to engage in predation, defiance, and submission. All six behaviours are ways to restore a balance.

The "life course" view can probably be traced back at least to the Gluecks (Glueck & Glueck 1950), but most modern criminologists trace it to Sampson & Laub's (1993) book, *Crime in the Making*. Two concepts are important from this point of view. One is the concept of "*trajectory*" which is the pathway of development over the life course marked by a sequence of transactions. Every trajectory has an entry point, success point, and the element of timing. Normal development is characterized by avoiding any event that may be called an "off-age" event. Two is the concept of "*transition*" which refers to the life events themselves which are embedded in the trajectories. Transitions can consist of tipping points or turning points, but generally refer to radical turnaround points in life. Most life course theorists presume that the seeds of a criminal career are planted early in life, point to "age of onset" as being the best predictor of later, more serious criminality, and research things like getting married or joining the military as turning points. However, people may begin their trajectory into crime at different times in their life. For example, the forensic psychologist, Terrie Moffit argues that there are two (2) main trajectories, as explained below.

The Moffit Developmental Theory of Crime

University of Wisconsin psychology professor Terrie Moffitt's developmental theory (Moffitt 1993) begins with empirical research indicating that signs of persistent antisocial behaviour can be detected early in life, as early as the preschool years, and extends to the idea that adolescent deviant behaviour is greatly influenced by the behaviour of peer groups even after parental variables are taken into account. The theory states that two groups of antisocial youth can be distinguished based on their ages of onset and trajectories of conduct problems. These two groups differ enough to require separate causal explanations. It might be helpful to illustrate some of the distinctions between these two groups in the following table:

The Dual Trajectories in the Origins of Conduct Disorder (CD)	
"Early Starters" Life-course-persistent (LCP) offenders DSM-IV conduct disorder: childhood-onset type Minor aggression (bullying, fighting), lying, hurting animals, biting and hitting by age 4	"Late Starters" Adolescent limited (AL) offenders DSM-IV conduct disorder: adolescent-onset type Serious aggression (mugging, forced sex, use of weapon), stealing, running away, truancy, breaking & entering
Neurological problems: attention deficit or hyperactivity 5-10% of the male juvenile offender population (2% females)	Little to no problems with peer rejection; have learned how to get along with others Majority of juvenile offender population; ceases or stops offending around age 18

During the teenage years, the two types are indistinguishable, and no existing paper-and-pencil test for antisocial tendencies or psychopathy will be able to discriminate the two types. That's because many of the "late starters" will "begin" with rather serious delinquency, and many of the "early starters" will be just "escalating" into serious delinquent behaviour at about the same time. Because many of the "late starters" may only be engaging in symbolic adolescent rebellion (perhaps because something is forbidden), have usually maintained empathy and avoided peer rejection, and are smart enough to see the rewards in more socially approved behaviour, they usually "dropout" or desist from any pathway toward crime. Not so with the "early starters" (*the most frequently studied group*) who may only be precociously escalating into serious offenses as a way of expanding the versatility of their antisocial ways across all kinds of conditions and situations. In fact, a trajectory toward versatility might be apparent with early starters at a very young age. The research indicates that increasingly higher levels of early conduct problems are associated with increasingly higher levels of late conduct problems, and Tremblay's (2003) research also shows that the best predictors of early starters are: having a target (sibling); parental separation before birth; and low income.

Although the number of early starters in the population of interest may only amount to 5-10% of the total, such children and adolescents usually account for more than 50% of referrals to authorities and mental health services. Their behaviour is disruptive not only to authorities, but to their peers, and for this reason, they experience significant amounts of peer rejection. Not only does this limit their chances for "getting ahead" on the basis of normal, lasting relationships, but their *poor interpersonal or social skills* are combined with three other prominent features, as follows, and discussed in separate paragraphs below:

- *hyperactive-impulsive-attention problems*
- *conduct problems*
- *below-average intelligence or low-IQ.*

The first feature — attention deficit/hyperactivity disorder (ADHD) — refers to a complex set of behaviours characterized by three central features: (1) excessive motor activity (cannot sit still, fidgets, runs about, is talkative and noisy); (2) impulsivity (acts before thinking, shifts quickly from one activity to another, interrupts others, does not consider consequences of behaviour); and (3) inattention (does not seem to listen, is easily distracted, loses things necessary for essential tasks). ADHS should not be confused with ODD (oppositional defiant disorder) which has the following cluster of symptoms: (1) arguing with adults; (2) refusing adults' requests; (3) deliberately trying to annoy others; (4) blaming others for mistakes; and (5) being spiteful or vindictive. ADHS afflicts as many as 20% of American school-age children, boys more than girls (by a ratio of 9:1), and blacks more than other ethnic groups, for debatable reasons ranging from speculations about genetic predisposition to the possibility of exposure to hazardous toxins in black communities. Many people afflicted with ADHD never "outgrow" it, and theories about the continuity of learning disabilities into adulthood are also controversial. The most common treatment is methylphenidate, also known as Ritalin, but it has mixed effects, and a successful treatment regimen for ADHD has yet to be found.

Conduct problems refer to the variety of symptoms found in the diagnostic category of Conduct Disorder (CD), and among delinquent youth, these are usually "co-occurring psychopathologies" that exist between one or more of these symptoms and ADHD symptoms.

In fact, Bartol & Bartol (2004) report on research indicating that as many as 50% of disruptive children exhibit having the symptoms of CD half the time and the symptoms of ADHD the other half of the time. According to the APA, the central feature of CD is a repetitive and persistent pattern of behaviour that violates the rights of others, and early-onset CD generally begins before age 10.

Symptoms of CD include stealing, fire setting, running away, truancy, destroying property, fighting, telling lies on a frequent basis, and being cruel to animals and people. It is the consensus of scholars that conduct disorder (CD) is roughly the juvenile equivalent of adult antisocial personality disorder. Conduct disorder typically gets worse as the child gets older, and it is often misdiagnosed as a learning disability (because there are frequent problems with school assignments) whereas someone with a "true" learning disability may not be conduct-disordered. CD afflicts about 16% of the male population and about 9% of the female population.

Below-average intelligence or low IQ refers to a lower cognitive ability and slow language development that, at times, is called by other names, such as "neuropsychological dysfunction" or impairment of "executive functioning." Low IQ is strongly associated with an early age of onset for Conduct Disorder (CD) and has a relationship to delinquency which holds even when socioeconomic status (SES) is controlled for. An 8 to 10 point difference is usually found on any standard intelligence test comparing delinquents with nondelinquents. There are some interesting findings regarding ethnic differences in how low-IQ is related to delinquency, as low-IQ whites tend to follow a "susceptibility" pathway to the typical personality disorders, and low-IQ minorities (blacks, Latinos, and Asians) tend to follow a "school failure" (being held back) pathway to lower "emotional intelligence" which results in decreased empathy and violent misreading of emotional cues from others.

7

Intellectual Development

Intelligence is an umbrella term describing a property of the mind including related abilities, such as the capacities for abstract thought, understanding, communication, reasoning, learning, learning from past experiences, planning, and problem solving.

Theories of intelligence are two-fold: (i) the "single intelligence" based upon the unilinear construct of "general intelligence," and (ii) the construct of multiple intelligences. Influenced by his cousin Charles Darwin, Francis Galton was the first scientist to propose a theory of general intelligence; that intelligence is a true, biologically-based mental faculty that can be studied by measuring a person's reaction times to cognitive tasks. Galton's research in measuring the head sizes of British scientists and laymen led to the conclusion that head-size is unrelated to a person's intelligence.

Alfred Binet, and the French school of intelligence, believed intelligence was a median average of dissimilar abilities, not a unitary entity with specific, identifiable properties.

Definitions

Scientists have proposed two major definitions of intelligence:

1. from *Mainstream Science on Intelligence* (1994), an editorial statement by fifty-two researchers:

   A very general mental capability that, among other things, involves the ability to reason, plan, solve problems, think abstractly, comprehend complex ideas, learn quickly and learn from experience. It is not merely book learning, a narrow academic skill, or test-taking smarts. Rather, it reflects a broader and deeper capability for comprehending our surroundings—"catching on," "making sense" of things, or "figuring out" what to do.

2. from *Intelligence: Knowns and Unknowns* (1995), a report published by the Board of Scientific Affairs of the American Psychological Association:

   Individuals differ from one another in their ability to understand complex ideas, to adapt effectively to the environment, to learn from experience, to engage in various forms of reasoning, to overcome obstacles by taking thought. Although these individual differences can be substantial, they are never entirely consistent: a given person's intellectual performance will vary on different occasions, in different domains, as judged by different criteria. Concepts of "intelligence" are attempts to clarify and organize this complex set of phenomena. Although considerable clarity has been achieved in some areas, no such conceptualization has yet answered all the important questions, and none commands universal assent. Indeed, when two dozen prominent theorists were recently asked to define intelligence, they gave two dozen, somewhat different, definitions.

Besides the foregoing organizational definitions, these psychology and learning researchers also have defined intelligence as:

Researcher	*Quotation*
Alfred Binet	Judgment, otherwise called "good sense," "practical sense," "initiative," the faculty of adapting one's self to circumstances... auto-critique.
David Wechsler	The aggregate or global capacity of the individual to act purposefully, to think rationally, and to deal effectively with his environment.
Cyril Burt	Innate general cognitive ability

Howard Gardner	To my mind, a human intellectual competence must entail a set of skills of problem solving — enabling the individual to resolve genuine problems or difficulties that he or she encounters and, when appropriate, to create an effective product — and must also entail the potential for finding or creating problems — and thereby laying the groundwork for the acquisition of new knowledge.
Linda Gottfredson	The ability to deal with cognitive complexity.
Sternberg & Salter	Goal-directed adaptive behaviour.
Reuven Feuerstein	The theory of Structural Cognitive Modifiability describes intelligence as "the unique propensity of human beings to change or modify the structure of their cognitive functioning to adapt to the changing demands of a life situation."

Practical application — Furthermore, in clinical and therapeutic practice, such theoretic and academic definitions of intelligence might not apply to patients with borderline intellectual and adaptive functioning, whose treatments require comprehensive analysis of every diagnostic, testing, educational placement, and psychosocial factor. The eighth (2005) and ninth (2009) editions of the *Kaplan & Sadock's Comprehensive Textbook of Psychiatry*, by Frank John Ninivaggi, MD, address these matters.

Human Intelligence

Theories of Human Intelligence

A popular theory of intelligence is based on psychometric testing, i.e. intelligence quotient (IQ) tests; however, some researchers' dissatisfaction with traditional IQ tests prompted their developing alternative theories of intelligence suggesting that intelligence results from independent capabilities that uniquely contribute to human intellectual performance.

Psychometric Approach

Despite the variety of concepts of intelligence, the approach to understanding intelligence with the most supporters and published research over the longest period of time is based on psychometric testing. Such intelligence quotient (IQ) tests include the Stanford-Binet, Raven's Progressive Matrices, the Wechsler Adult Intelligence Scale and the Kaufman Assessment Battery for Children.

Charles Spearman is generally credited with defining general intelligence, which he reported in his 1904 *American Journal of Psychology* article titled "'General Intelligence,' Objectively Determined and Measured." Based on the results of a series of studies collected in Hampshire, England, Spearman concluded that there was a common function (or group of functions) across intellectual activities including what he called intelligence (i.e., school rank, which Spearman thought of as "present efficiency" in school courses; the difference between school rank and age, which was conceptualized as "native capacity;" teacher ratings; and peer ratings provided by the two oldest students, which was termed "common sense") and sensory discriminations (i.e., discrimination of pitch, brightness, and weight). This common function became known as "g" or general intelligence.

To objectively determine and measure general intelligence, Spearman invented the first technique of factor analysis (the method of Tetrad Differences) as a mathematical proof of the Two-Factor Theory. The factor analytic results indicated that every variable measured a common function to varying degrees, which led Spearman to develop the somewhat misleadingly named Two-Factor Theory of Intelligence. The Two-Factor Theory of Intelligence holds that every test can be divided into a "g" factor and an "s" factor. The g-factor measures the "general" factor or common function among ability tests. The s-factor measures the "specific" factor unique to a particular ability test. Spearman's g factor account for positive correlations among any cognitive ability tests. However, the necessary condition for g-factor to exist is routinely violated in correlation matrices of cognitive tests, according to the work by Peter Schönemann and others..

L.L. Thurstone extended and generalized Spearman's method of factor analysis into what is called the Centroid method and which became the basis for modern factor analysis. Thurstone demonstrated that Spearman's one common factor method (Spearman's method yielded only a single factor) was a special case of his multiple factor analysis. Thurstone's research led him to propose a model of intelligence that included seven orthogonal (unrelated) factors (i.e., verbal comprehension, word fluency, number facility, spatial visualization, associative memory, perceptual speed and reasoning) referred to as the Primary Mental Abilities.

In a critical review of the adult testing literature, Raymond B. Cattell found that a considerable percentage of intelligence tests that purported to measure adult intellectual functioning had all of the trappings of using college students in their development. To account for differences between children/ adolescents and adults, which past theory did not address, Cattell proposed two types of cognitive abilities in a revision of Spearman's concept of general intelligence. Fluid intelligence (Gf) was hypothesized as the ability to discriminate and perceive relations (e.g., analogical and syllogistic reasoning), and crystallized intelligence (Gc) was hypothesized as the ability to discriminate relations that had been established originally through Gf, but no longer required the identification of the relation (commonly assessed using information or vocabulary tests). In addition, fluid intelligence was hypothesized to increase until adolescence and then to slowly decline, and crystallized intelligence increases gradually and stays relatively stable across most of adulthood until it declines in late adulthood.

With his student John L. Horn, Cattell indicated that Gf and Gc were only two among several factors manifest in intelligence tests scores under the umbrella of what became known as Gf/Gc Theory. General visualization (Gv; visual acuity, depth perception), general fluency (F, facility in recalling words), general speediness (Gs; performance on speeded, simple tasks) were among several cognitive ability factors added to Gf/Gc Theory.

J.P. Guilford sought to more fully explore the scope of the adult intellect by providing the concept of intelligence with a strong, comprehensive theoretical backing. The Structure-of-Intellect model (SI model) was designed as a cross classification system with intersections in the model providing the basis for abilities similar to Mendeleev's periodic table in chemistry. The three-dimensional cube—shaped model includes five content categories (the way in which information is presented on a test; visual, auditory, symbolic, semantic, and behavioral), six operation categories (what is done on a test; evaluation, convergent production, divergent production, memory retention, memory recording, and cognition), and six product categories (the form in which information is processed on a test; units, classes, relations, systems, transformations, and implications). The intersection of three categories provides a frame of reference for generating one or more new hypothetical factors of intelligence.

John B. Carroll re-analysed 461 datasets in the single most comprehensive study of cognitive abilities. This analysis led him to propose the Three Stratum Theory, which is a hierarchical model of intellectual functioning. The strata represent three different levels of generality over the domain of cognitive abilities. At the bottom is the first stratum, which is represented by narrow abilities that are highly specialized (e.g., induction, spelling ability). The second stratum is represented by broad abilities that include moderate specializations in various domains. Carroll identified eight second-stratum factors: fluid intelligence, crystallized intelligence, general memory and learning, broad visual perception, broad auditory perception, broad retrieval ability, broad cognitive speediness, and processing speed (reaction time decision speed). Carroll has noted the similarity of his second stratum abilities and the Gf/Gc factors, although the Three-Stratum Theory does not incorporate the developmental trajectories associated with Gf/Gc Theory. Carroll accepted Spearman's concept of general intelligence, for the most part, as a representation of the uppermost third stratum.

More recently, an amalgamation of the Gf-Gc theory of Cattell and Horn with Carroll's Three-Stratum theory has led to the Cattell-Horn-Carroll (CHC) Theory of cognitive abilities. CHC researchers have produced numerous studies that have influenced diagnostic issues and test development.

Intelligence tests are widely used in educational, business, and military settings due to their efficacy in predicting behaviour. *g* is highly correlated with many important social outcomes—individuals with low IQs are more likely to be divorced, have a child out of marriage, be incarcerated, and need long-term welfare support, while individuals with high IQs are associated with more years of education, higher status jobs and higher income. Intelligence is significantly correlated with successful trainin, and performance outcomes, and *g* is the single best predictor of successful job performance.

Controversies

IQ tests were originally designed to identify mentally "defective" children. The inventors of the IQ did not necessarily believe they were measuring fixed intelligence. Despite this, critics argue that intelligence tests have been used to support nativistic theories which view intelligence as a qualitative object with a relatively fixed quantity.

Critics of the psychometrics point out that intelligence is often more complex and broader in conception than what is measured by IQ tests. Furthermore, skeptics argue that even though tests of mental abilities are correlated, people still have unique strengths and weaknesses in specific areas. Consequently they argue that psychometric theorists over-emphasize *g*, despite the fact that *g* was defined so as to encompass all inter-correlated capabilities and skills.

Researchers in the field of human intelligence have encountered a considerable amount of public concern and criticism—much more than scientists in other areas normally receive. A number of critics have challenged the relevance of psychometric intelligence in the context of everyday life. There have also been controversies over genetic factors in intelligence, particularly questions regarding the relationship between race and intelligence and sex and intelligence. Another controversy in the field is how to interpret the increases in test scores that have occurred over time, the so-called Flynn effect.

Stephen Jay Gould was one of the most vocal critics of intelligence testing. In his book *The Mismeasure of Man* Gould argued that intelligence could not be quantified to a single numerical entity. He also challenged the hereditarian viewpoint on intelligence. Many of Gould's criticisms were aimed at Arthur Jensen, who responded that his work had been misrepresented. Gould also investigated the methods of 19th-century craniometry. Jensen stated that drawing conclusions from early intelligence research is like condemning the auto industry by criticizing the performance of the Model T.

Multiple Intelligences

Howard Gardner's theory of multiple intelligences is based on studies not only of normal children and adults but also by studies of gifted individuals (including so-called "savants"), of persons who have suffered brain damage, of experts and virtuosos, and of individuals from diverse cultures. This led Gardner to break intelligence down into at least eight different components: logical, linguistic, spatial, musical, kinesthetic, interpersonal, intrapersonal in 1983 and naturalist intelligences added in 1999. He argues that psychometric tests address only linguistic and logical plus some aspects of spatial intelligence. A major criticism of Gardner's theory is that it has never been tested, or subjected to peer review, by Gardner or anyone else, and indeed that it is unfalsifiable.

Triarchic Theory of Intelligence

Robert Sternberg proposed the triarchic theory of intelligence to provide a more comprehensive description of intellectual competence than traditional differential or cognitive theories of human ability. The triarchic theory describes three fundamental aspects of intelligence. Analytic intelligence comprises the mental processes through which intelligence is expressed. Creative intelligence is necessary when an individual is confronted with a challenge that is nearly, but not entirely, novel or when an individual is engaged in automatizing the performance of a task. Practical intelligence is bound in a sociocultural milieu and involves adaptation to, selection of, and shaping of the environment to maximize fit in the context. The triarchic theory does not argue against the validity of a general intelligence factor; instead, the theory posits that general intelligence is part of analytic intelligence, and only by considering all three aspects of intelligence can the full range of intellectual functioning be fully understood.

More recently, the triarchic theory has been updated and renamed the Theory of Successful Intelligence by Sternberg. Intelligence is defined as an individual's assessment of success in life by the individual's own (idiographic) standards and within the individual's sociocultural context. Success is achieved by using combinations of analytical, creative, and practical intelligence. The three aspects of intelligence are referred to as processing skills. The processing skills are applied to the pursuit of success through what were the three elements of practical intelligence: adapting to, shaping of, and selecting of one's environments. The mechanisms that employ the processing skills to achieve success include utilizing one's strengths and compensating or correcting for one's weaknesses.

Sternberg's theories and research on intelligence remain contentious within the scientific community.

Developmental Approach

Jean Piaget was the founder of the developmental approach to the study of intelligence. According to his theory of cognitive development, intelligence is the basic mechanism of ensuring equilibrium in the relations between the person and the environment. This is achieved through the actions of the developing person on the world. At any moment in development, the environment is assimilated in the schemes of action that are already available and these schemes are transformed or accommodated to the peculiarities of the objects of the environment, if they are not completely appropriate. Thus, the development of intelligence is a continuous process of assimilations and accommodations that lead to increasing expansion of the field of application of schemes, increasing coordination between them, increasing interiorization, and increasing abstraction. Piaget described four main periods or stages in the development towards completely equilibrated thought and problem solving. In the sensorimotor stage (0–2 years), thought is based on perceptions and external actions and their coordination. In the preoperational stage, sensorimotor schemes are internalized and thought occurs mentally rather than externally, through the manipulation of representations and symbols that stand for sensorimotor schemes and objects.

At the beginning, however, mental schemes are not coordinated. As a result, systematic logical reasoning is not possible (that, for example, A = C, if A = B and B = C). When mental schemes are coordinated, thinking enters the concrete operational stage. In this period, thinking is logical, but limited to the concrete aspects of the world. That is, children can grasp several important aspects of the world, such as the conservation of number, matter, length, weight, volume, etc. despite external transformation. Gradually, concrete operational schemes are coordinated with each other and cognitive development enters the final formal operational stage. In this period reality is subsumed to possibilities and reasoning becomes formal. As a result, abstract scientific concepts such as the concept of inertia, energy, algebra, and proportionality can be grasped and scientific experiments can be designed. All in all, for Piaget intelligence is not the same at different ages. It changes qualitatively, thereby allowing access to different levels of organization of the world. Research shows that Piagetian intelligence is correlated but it is not identical with psychometric intelligence and IQ.

The neo-Piagetian theories of cognitive development advanced by Case, Demetriou, Halford, and Pascual-Leone, attempted to integrate Piaget's theory with cognitive and differential theories of cognitive organization and development. Their aim was to better account for the cognitive factors of development and for intra-individual and inter-individual differences in cognitive development. They suggested that development along Piaget's stages is due to increasing processing efficiency which is defined in terms of speed of processing and working memory capacity. Moreover, Demetriou's theory ascribes an important role to hypercognitive processes of self-recording, self-monitoring, and self-regulation and it recognizes the operation of several relatively autonomous domains of thought.

Overall, this approach suggests that there indeed is a general intelligence factor. This factor is geared on general processing efficiency functions that enable humans to represent and process information, that processing involves general inferential processes that are gradually constructed, and self-awareness and reflection are instrumental in this construction. The general understanding and problem solving ability associated with this factor changes qualitatively with age and this change is related to the succession of Piagetian stages. At the same time, individual differences in the state of the general efficiency factors may cause differences in the rate of intellectual development of different individuals and these differences may be reflected in psychometric measures of cognitive ability, such as the IQ tests. Moreover differences between individuals may come from differences in their predispositions or facility related to different domains of knowledge and problem solving.

Emotional Intelligence

Daniel Goleman and several other researchers have developed the concept of emotional intelligence and claim it is at least as "important" as traditionally proposed components of intelligence. These theories grew from observations of human development and of brain injury victims who demonstrate an acute loss of a particular cognitive function—e.g. the ability to think numerically, or the ability to understand written language—without showing any loss in other cognitive areas.

Many researchers believe that emotional intelligence is a composite of general intelligence and agreeableness, one of the five dimensions of personality in the five-factor model of personality. In this model, an emotionally intelligent person would score higher than average in both dimensions, and vice versa. Moreover, an emotionally intelligent person cannot score high on only one of the two traits. For example, an individual with low general mental ability and high agreeableness would be impaired in his ability to produce emotionally intelligent behaviour despite his intentions, while an individual with high general mental ability and low agreeableness would be perfectly capable of being emotionally intelligent, but not inclined to do so.

PASS Theory

PASS theory has been offered as an alternative to general intelligence, and is based on a description of neuropsychological processes. These authors suggested that a unidimensional model with just intelligence fails to assist researchers and clinicians who study learning disabilities, disorders of attention, mental retardation, and interventions designed for special populations who face those challenges. The PASS model covers four kinds of competencies that are associated with areas of the brain.

1. The planning processes involve decision making, problem solving, and performing activities and requires goal setting and self-monitoring.
2. The attention/arousal component involves selectively attending to a particular stimulus, ignoring distractions, and maintaining vigilance.
3. Simultaneous processing involves the integration of stimuli into a group and requires the observation of relationships.
4. Successive processing involves the integration of stimuli into serial order.

The planning and attention/arousal components comes from structures located in the frontal lobe, and the simultaneous and successive processes come from structures located in the posterior region of the cortex.

Empirical Evidence

IQ proponents have claimed that IQ's predictive validity has been demonstrated, for example in predicting non-academic outcomes such as job performance (see IQ), and that the various multiple intelligence theories have little or no such support. Meanwhile, it has been claimed that the relevance and existence of multiple intelligences have not been borne out when tested. A set of ability tests that do not correlate together would support the claim that multiple intelligences are independent of each other.

Evolution of Intelligence

Our hominid and human ancestors evolved large and complex brains exhibiting an ever-increasing intelligence through a long and mostly unknown evolutionary process. This process was either driven by the direct adaptive benefits of intelligence, or, alternatively, driven by its indirect benefits within the context of sexual selection as a reliable signal of genetic resistance against pathogens.

Factors Affecting Intelligence

Intelligence is an ill-defined, difficult to quantify concept. Accordingly, the IQ tests used to measure intelligence provide only approximations of the posited "real" intelligence. In addition, a number of theoretically unrelated properties are known to correlate with IQ such as race, gender and height but since correlation does not imply causation the true relationship between these factors is uncertain. Factors affecting IQ may be divided into biological and environmental.

Intelligence Quotient

An intelligence quotient, or IQ, is a score derived from one of several different standardized tests designed to assess intelligence. The term "IQ," from the German *Intelligenz-Quotient,* was devised by the German psychologist William Stern in 1912 as a proposed method of scoring children's intelligence tests such as those developed by Alfred Binet and Théodore Simon in the early 20th Century. Lewis Terman accepted that form of scoring, expressing a score as a quotient of "mental age" and "chronological age," for his revision of the Binet-Simon test, the first version of the Stanford-Binet Intelligence Scales.

Although the term "IQ" is still in common use, the scoring of modern IQ tests such as the Wechsler Adult Intelligence Scale is now based on standard scoring of the subject's rank order on the test item content with the median score set to 100, and a standard deviation of 15, although not all tests adhere to that assignment of 15 IQ points to each standard deviation.

IQ scores have been shown to be associated with such factors as morbidity and mortality, parental social status, and, to a substantial degree, parental IQ. While the heritability of IQ has been investigated for nearly a century, controversy remains regarding the significance of heritability estimates, and the mechanisms of inheritance are still a matter of some debate. IQ scores are used in many contexts: as predictors of educational achievement or special needs, by social scientists who study the distribution of IQ scores in populations and the relationships between IQ score and other variables, and as predictors of job performance and income.

The average IQ scores for many populations have been rising at an average rate of three points per decade since the early 20th century, a phenomenon called the Flynn effect. It is disputed whether these changes in scores reflect real changes in intellectual abilities, or merely methodological problems with past or present testing.

History

Psychometrics

Englishman Francis Galton, influenced by Darwinism, founded eugenics (and later psychometrics) to measure differences between upper and lower classes. Galton argued that due to heredity, white aristocrats were intellectually superior to other humans; nurture, meanwhile, played a lesser role in intellectual capacity.

Clinical Diagnostics

French psychologist Alfred Binet gave more weight to nurture, arguing that intelligence could be improved. Binet and fellow French psychologist Théodore Simon later developed the Binet-Simon test for measuring intellectual development or mental age to diagnose French children in need of special assistance classes. Binet-Simon tasks were diverse in order to neutralize individual differences in types of intelligence and provide a general measure.

Intelligence Testing

English psychologist Charles Spearman, however, did not believe there were different types of intelligence. He devised a correlational formula to define a common intellective factor (which he called "general intelligence"), a factor that Binet argued did not exist.

Intelligence Quotient (IQ)

In 1910 the eugenics movement in the USA seized on the Binet-Simon test as means to give them credibility in diagnosing mental retardation after American psychologist Henry H. Goddard published a translation of it that same year. American psychologist Lewis Terman revised the Binet-Simon scale, implementing German psychologist William Stern's intelligence quotient (I.Q.) ratio of mental age to chronological age and used the resulting Stanford-Binet scale as a measure of general intelligence.

World War I: Large Scale Testing

A team of psychologists led by eugenicist Robert Yerkes assisted the US army to rapidly assess and assign huge numbers of personnel. They developed two group-administered intelligence tests for this purpose: an alpha test for literate personnel; and a beta for the illiterate. They successfully tested 1,726,000 recruits. However, there was too little time for validity testing and not enough staff to administer tests correctly. Many officers distrusted the psychologists, accusing them of conducting research for their own purposes using culturally biased tests. Orders were issued that low test scores should not bar men from officer training and that a disability board should consider all discharges. The outcome was that 0.5% of recruits were discharged as mentally inferior, whilst Yerkes would have preferred to have discharged 3% whose results showed a mental age of under 10.

In contrast, another team of psychologists led by Walter Dill Scott defined intelligence as a diverse complex of capacities, as Binet had. They stressed an individual differences approach emphasizing environmental adjustments of mental qualities as functions. Soon they developed a rating scale to classify and place enlisted men according to how they used their intelligence, not their base levels of intelligence. The army was enthusiastic about Scott's classification of personnel. By the time the war ended they had already been incorporated into the military and had classified 3½ million men and assigned 973,858 to technical units.

Post War to 1929

The army abolished Yerkes' team after the war but employed two psychologists to continue intelligence testing research. However, a great deal of positive post war publicity on army psychological testing helped to make psychology a respected field. Subsequently there was an increase in jobs and funding in psychology. Group intelligence tests were developed for and became widely used in both primary and secondary schools, universities and industry. But controversy followed when one of Yerkes' team, Goddard, admitted that they had been guilty of bad logic in finding that 45% of army recruits had a mental age of 12 or less. In addition, there was no agreement on what the intelligence tests measured, and the publication of racial differences in scores led to much criticism that environmental influences on score had not been considered.

Wechsler's Innovation in Scoring

The modern IQ scale is a mathematical transformation of a raw score on an IQ test, based on the rank of that score in a normalization sample. This procedure was pioneered by David Wechsler. Modern scores are sometimes referred to as "deviation IQs," while older method age-specific scores are referred to as "ratio IQs." IQ scales of either kind are ordinal scales and thus IQ points are not units of measurement.

The two scoring methodologies yield similar results near the population median, but the older ratio IQs yielded far higher scores for high-scoring (gifted) children. Current IQ tests do not yield such high scores, as recent validation studies have shown that concerns about ceiling effects in identifying gifted children are exaggerated. In any event error of estimation is greatest for scores above the population median and likely to overestimate the true score (in the sense of formal testing theory) of a test-taker who obtains a score above the median.

Since the publication of the Wechsler Adult Intelligence Scale (WAIS), almost all intelligence scales have adopted the deviation method of scoring. The use of this scoring method makes the term "intelligence quotient" an inaccurate description, mathematically speaking, but the term "IQ" still enjoys colloquial usage, and is used to label the standard scoring of most cognitive ability tests currently in use.

Reliability

IQ scores can differ for the same individual even on the most sophisticated current IQ scales. (IQ score table data and pupil pseudonyms adapted from description of KABC-II norming study cited in Kaufman 2009.)

Psychometricians generally regard IQ tests as highly reliable (in the technical sense of testing theory) and clinical psychologists generally regard them as having sufficient validity for many clinical purposes. A test-taker's score on any one IQ test is surrounded by an error band that shows, to a specified degree of confidence, what the test-taker's true score (in that same technical sense) is likely to be. Test-takers can have varying scores on differing occasions of taking IQ tests and can vary in scores on different IQ tests taken at the same age.

Pupil	*KABC-II*	*WISC-III*	*WJ-III*
Asher	90	95	111
Brianna	125	110	105
Colin	100	93	101
Danica	116	127	118
Elpha	93	105	93
Fritz	106	105	105
Georgi	95	100	90
Hector	112	113	103
Imelda	104	96	97
Jose	101	99	86
Keoku	81	78	75
Le*	116	124	102

Trends in IQ

Since the twentieth century, IQ scores have increased at an average rate of around three IQ points per decade in most parts of the world. This phenomenon has been named the *Flynn effect* (a.k.a. the "Lynn-Flynn effect") named after Richard Lynn and James R. Flynn. Attempted explanations have included improved nutrition, a trend towards smaller families, better education, greater environmental complexity, and heterosis. Some researchers believe that modern education has become more geared toward IQ tests, thus rendering higher scores, but not necessarily higher intelligence. As a result, tests are routinely renormalized to obtain mean scores of 100, for example WISC-R (1974), WISC-III (1991) and WISC-IV (2003). This adjustment specifically addresses the variation over time, allowing scores to be compared longitudinally.

Some researchers argue that the Flynn effect may have ended in some developed nations, starting in the 1980s in the United Kingdom, and in the mid-1990s in Denmark and in Norway.

Environmental and Genetic Influences and Malleability

Environmental Influences

Environmental factors play a role in determining IQ. Proper childhood nutrition appears critical for cognitive development; malnutrition can lower IQ. For example, iodine deficiency causes a fall, in average, of 12 IQ points. It is expected that average IQ in third world countries will increase dramatically if the deficiencies of iodine and other micronutrients are eradicated.

A recent study found that the FADS2 gene, along with breastfeeding, adds about seven IQ points to those with the "C" version of the gene. Those with the "G" version of the FADS2 gene see no advantage.

Musical training in childhood may also increase IQ. Recent studies have shown that training in using one's working memory may increase IQ.

Family Environment

Some studies in the developed world have shown that inherited personality traits cause non-related children raised in the same family ("adoptive siblings") to be as different as children raised in different families. There are some family effects on the IQ of children, accounting for up to a quarter of the variance; however, by adulthood, this correlation approaches zero. For IQ, adoption studies show that, after adolescence, adoptive siblings are no more similar in IQ than strangers (IQ correlation near zero), while full siblings show an IQ correlation of 0.6. Twin studies reinforce this pattern: monozygotic (identical) twins raised separately are highly similar in IQ (0.86), more so than dizygotic (fraternal) twins raised together (0.6) and much more than adoptive siblings. However these results make no correction for the social and emotional effects frequently associated with adoption.

Possible Bias in Older Studies

Stoolmiller (1999) found that the range restriction of family environments that goes with adoption, that adopting families tend to be more similar on, for example, socio-economic status than the general population, suggests a possible underestimation of the role of the shared family environment in previous studies. Corrections for range correction applied to adoption studies indicate that socio-economic status could account for as much as 50% of the variance in IQ. However, the effect of restriction of range on IQ for adoption studies was examined by Matt McGue and colleagues, who wrote that "restriction in range in parent disinhibitory psychopathology and family socio-economic status had no effect on adoptive-sibling correlations [in] IQ".

Eric Turkheimer and colleagues (2003) studied the heritability of IQ in impoverished US families. Results demonstrated that in small children the proportions of IQ variance attributable to genes and environment vary nonlinearly with socio-economic status. The models suggest that in impoverished families, 60% of the variance in early childhood IQ is accounted for by the shared family environment, and the contribution of genes is close to zero; in affluent families, the result is almost exactly the reverse. They suggest that the role of shared environmental factors may have been underestimated in older studies which often only studied affluent middle class families.

Maternal (Fetal) Environment

A meta-analysis, by Devlin and colleagues in *Nature* (1997), of 212 previous studies evaluated an alternative model for environmental influence and found that it fits the data better than the 'family-environments' model commonly used. The shared maternal (fetal) environment effects, often assumed to be negligible, account for 20% of covariance between twins and 5% between siblings, and the effects of genes are correspondingly reduced, with two measures of heritability being less than 50%.

Bouchard and McGue reviewed the literature in 2003, arguing that Devlin's conclusions about the magnitude of heritability is not substantially different from previous reports and that their conclusions regarding prenatal effects stands in contradiction to many previous reports. They write that:

Chipuer et al. and Loehlin conclude that the postnatal rather than the prenatal environment is most important. The Devlin et al. conclusion that the prenatal environment contributes to twin IQ similarity is especially remarkable given the existence of an extensive empirical literature on prenatal effects. Price (1950), in a comprehensive review published over 50 years ago, argued that almost all MZ twin prenatal effects produced differences rather than similarities. As of 1950 the literature on the topic was so large that the entire bibliography was not published. It was finally published in 1978 with an additional 260 references. At that time Price reiterated his earlier conclusion. Research subsequent to the 1978 review largely reinforces Price's hypothesis.

Dickens and Flynn Model

Dickens and Flynn postulate that the arguments regarding the disappearance of the shared family environment should apply equally well to groups separated in time. This is contradicted by the Flynn effect. Changes here have happened too quickly to be explained by genetic heritable adaptation. This paradox can be explained by observing that the measure "heritability" includes both a direct effect of the genotype on IQ and also indirect effects where the genotype changes the environment, in turn affecting IQ. That is, those with a higher IQ tend to seek out stimulating environments that further increase IQ. The direct effect can initially have been very small but feedback loops can create large differences in IQ. In their model an environmental stimulus can have a very large effect on IQ, even in adults, but this effect also decays over time unless the stimulus continues (the model could be adapted to include possible factors, like nutrition in early childhood, that may cause permanent effects). The Flynn effect can be explained by a generally more stimulating environment for all people. The authors suggest that programs aiming to increase IQ would be most likely to produce long-term IQ gains if they taught children how to replicate outside the program the kinds of cognitively demanding experiences that produce IQ gains while they are in the program and motivate them to persist in that replication long after they have left the program.

Genetic Influences

Various studies find the heritability of IQ between 0.4 and 0.8 in the United States; that is, depending on the study, a little less than half to substantially more than half of the variation in IQ among the children studied was estimated to be due to genetic variation. Heritability measures the proportion of variation that can be attributed to genes within any measured population (however defined), and not the extent that genes contribute to intelligence. It should also be noted that the idea that genetic and environmental influences on intelligence are independent is not necessarily accepted, or as Jeremy Freese says "The lucidity of Lewontin's arguments has historically proven no match for the allure of overly simple characterizations of outcomes as being x% due to genes and (1 – x)% not due to genes". That means that genes affect environment and environment affects genes. A heritability in the range of 0.4 to 0.8 implies that IQ is "substantially" heritable, that is, some substantial part of the variation within a population is caused at least in part by genes.

The effect of restriction of range on IQ was examined by Matt McGue and colleagues, who wrote that "restriction in range in parent disinhibitory psychopathology and family SES had no effect on adoptive-sibling correlations... IQ." On the other hand, a 2003 study by Eric Turkheimer, Andreana Haley, Mary Waldron, Brian D'Onofrio, Irving I. Gottesman demonstrated that the proportions of IQ variance attributable to genes and environment vary with socioeconomic status. They found that in impoverished families, 60% of the variance in IQ "in a sample of 7-year-old twins" is accounted for by the shared environment, and the contribution of genes was close to zero.

It is reasonable to expect that genetic influences on traits like IQ should become less important as one gains experiences with age. However, the opposite occurs. Heritability measures in infancy are as low as 20%, around 40% in middle childhood, and as high as 80% in adulthood. The *American Psychological Association's* 1995 task force on "Intelligence: Knowns and Unknowns" concluded that within the white population the heritability of IQ is "around.75." The *Minnesota Study of Twins Reared Apart*, a multiyear study of 100 sets of reared-apart twins which was started in 1979, concluded that about 70% of the variance in IQ was found to be associated with genetic variation. Some of the correlation of IQs of twins may be a result of the effect of the maternal environment before birth, shedding some light on why IQ correlation between twins reared apart is so robust. There are a number of points to consider when interpreting heritability:

- A high heritability does not mean that the environment has no effect on the development of a trait, or that learning is not involved. Vocabulary size, for example, is very substantially heritable (and highly correlated with general intelligence) although every word in an individual's vocabulary is learned. In a society in which plenty of words are available in everyone's environment, especially for individuals who are motivated to seek them out, the number of words that individuals actually learn depends to a considerable extent on their genetic predispositions.
- A common error is to assume that because something is heritable it is necessarily unchangeable. As previously noted, heritable traits can depend on learning, and they may be subject to other environmental effects as well. The value of heritability can change if the distribution of environments (or of genes) in the population is substantially altered. For example, an impoverished or suppressive environment could fail to support the development of a trait, and hence restrict individual variation. Differences in variation of heritability are found between developed and developing nations. This could affect estimates of heritability. Another example is Phenylketonuria which previously caused mental retardation for everyone who had this genetic disorder. Today, this can be prevented by following a modified diet.
- On the other hand, there can be effective environmental changes that do not change heritability at all. If the environment relevant to a given trait improves in a way that affects all members of the population equally, the mean value of the trait will rise without any change in its heritability (because the differences among individuals in the population will stay the same). This has evidently happened for height: the heritability of stature is high, but average heights continue to increase.

- Even in developed nations, high heritability of a trait within a given group has no necessary implications for the source of a difference between groups.

IQ and the Brain

In 2004, Richard ꓲlaier, professor of psychology in the Department of Pediatrics and colleagues at University of California, Irvine and the University of New Mexico used MRI to obtain structural images of the brain in 47 normal adults who also took standard IQ tests. The study demonstrated that general human intelligence appears to be based on the volume and location of gray matter tissue in the brain, and also demonstrated that, of the brain's gray matter, only about 6 percent appeared to be related to IQ.

Many different sources of information have converged on the view that the frontal lobes are critical for fluid intelligence. Patients with damage to the frontal lobe are impaired on fluid intelligence tests (Duncan et al. 1995). The volume of frontal grey (Thompson et al. 2001) and white matter (Schoenemann et al. 2005) have also been associated with general intelligence. In addition, recent neuroimaging studies have limited this association to the lateral prefrontal cortex. Duncan and colleagues (2000) showed using Positron Emission Tomography that problem-solving tasks that correlated more highly with IQ also activate the lateral prefrontal cortex. More recently, Gray and colleagues (2003) used functional magnetic resonance imaging (fMRI) to show that those individuals that were more adept at resisting distraction on a demanding working memory task had both a higher IQ and increased prefrontal activity. For an extensive review of this topic.

A study involving 307 children (aged from six to nineteen) measuring the size of brain structures using magnetic resonance imaging (MRI) and measuring verbal and non-verbal abilities has been conducted (Shaw et al. 2006). This study indicated that higher intelligence is not directly related to cortical thickness, but rather the change in cortical thickness over time. More intelligent children would develop a thicker cortex initially, and then their cortex would go through a more rigorous thinning process. Garlick (2010) has argued that this reduction in cortical thickness reflects a pruning process of the neural connections, and this pruning process results in a better ability to identify abstractions in the environment.

There is "a highly significant association" between the CHRM2 gene and intelligence according to a 2006 Dutch family study. The study concluded that there was an association between the CHRM2 gene on chromosome 7 and Performance IQ, as measured by the Wechsler Adult Intelligence Scale-Revised. The Dutch family study used a sample of 667 individuals from 304 families. A similar association was found independently in the *Minnesota Twin and Family Study* (Comings et al. 2003) and by the Department of Psychiatry at the Washington University.

Significant injuries isolated to one side of the brain, especially those occurring at a young age, may not significantly affect IQ.

Studies reach conflicting conclusions regarding the controversial idea that brain size correlates positively with IQ. Jensen and Reed claim no direct correlation exists in nonpathological subjects. A more recent meta-analysis suggests otherwise.

Malleability (Mutability or Changeability)

Although IQ is believed by many to be immutable, recent research suggests that certain mental activities can change the brain's ability to process information, leading to the conclusion that intelligence can be altered or changed over time. The brain is now properly understood to be neuroplastic and hence far more amenable to change than once was thought. Studies into the neuroscience of animals indicate that challenging activities can produce changes in gene expression patterns of the brain. (Training Degus to Use Rakes and Iriki's earlier research with macaque monkeys indicating brain changes.)

A study on young adults published in April 2008 by a team from the Universities of Michigan and Bern supports the possibility of the transfer of fluid intelligence from specifically designed working memory training. Further research will be needed to determine nature, extent and duration of the proposed transfer. Among other questions, it remains to be seen whether the results extend to other kinds of fluid intelligence tests than the matrix test used in the study, and if so, whether, after training, fluid intelligence measures retain their correlation with educational and occupational achievement or if the value of fluid intelligence for predicting performance on other tasks changes. It is also unclear whether the training is durable of extended periods of time.

The peak capacity for both fluid intelligence and crystallized intelligence is 26 years. This is followed by a slow decline

Validity and Social Significance

While IQ is sometimes treated as an end unto itself, scholarly work on IQ focuses to a large extent on IQ's validity, that is, the degree to which IQ correlates with outcomes such as job performance, social pathologies, or academic achievement. Different IQ tests differ in their validity for various outcomes. Traditionally, correlation for IQ and outcomes is viewed as a means to also predict performance; however readers should distinguish between prediction in the hard sciences and the social sciences.

Health

People with a higher IQ have generally lower adult morbidity and mortality. Post-Traumatic Stress Disorder, and schizophrenia are less prevalent in higher IQ bands. People in the midsts of a major depressive episode have been shown to have a lower IQ than when without symptoms and lower cognitive ability than people without depression of equivalent verbal intelligence.

A study of 11,282 individuals in Scotland who took intelligence tests at ages 7, 9 and 11 in the 1950s and 1960s, found an "inverse linear association" between childhood IQ scores and hospital admissions for injuries in adulthood. The association between childhood IQ and the risk of later injury remained even after accounting for factors such as the child's socioeconomic background. Research in Scotland has also shown that a 15-point lower IQ meant people had a fifth less chance of living to 76, while those with a 30-point disadvantage were 37% less likely than those with a higher IQ to live that long. A decrease in IQ has also been shown as an early predictor of late-onset Alzheimer's Disease and other forms of dementia. In a 2004 study, Cervilla and colleagues showed that tests of cognitive ability provide useful predictive information up to a decade before the onset of dementia. However, when diagnosing individuals with a higher level of cognitive ability, in this study those with IQs of 120 or more, patients should not be diagnosed from the standard norm but from an adjusted high-IQ norm that measured changes against the individual's higher ability level. In 2000, Whalley and colleagues published a paper in the journal *Neurology,* which examined links between childhood mental ability and late-onset dementia. The study showed that mental ability scores were significantly lower in children who eventually developed late-onset dementia when compared with other children tested.

Several factors can lead to significant cognitive impairment, particularly if they occur during pregnancy and childhood when the brain is growing and the blood-brain barrier is less effective. Such impairment may sometimes be permanent, or may sometimes be partially or wholly compensated for by later growth. Several harmful factors may also combine, possibly causing greater impairment.

Developed nations have implemented several health policies regarding nutrients and toxins known to influence cognitive function. These include laws requiring fortification of certain food products and laws establishing safe levels of pollutants (e.g. lead, mercury, and organochlorides). Comprehensive policy recommendations targeting reduction of cognitive impairment in children have been proposed.

In terms of the effect of one's intelligence on health, in one British study, high childhood IQ was shown to correlate with one's chance of becoming a vegetarian in adulthood. In another British study, high childhood IQ was shown to inversely correlate with the chances of smoking.

Other Tests

One study found a correlation of.82 between *g* (general intelligence factor) and SAT scores; another has found correlation of.81 between *g* and GCSE scores.

Correlations between IQ scores (general cognitive ability) and achievement test scores are reported to be.81 by Deary and colleagues, with the percentage of variance accounted for by general cognitive ability ranging "from 58.6% in Mathematics and 48% in English to 18.1% in Art and Design".

School Performance

The American Psychological Association's report *Intelligence: Knowns and Unknowns* states that wherever it has been studied, children with high scores on tests of intelligence tend to learn more of what is taught in school than their lower-scoring peers. The correlation between IQ scores and grades is about.50. However, this means that they explain only 25% of the variance. Achieving good grades depends on many factors other than IQ, such as "persistence, interest in school, and willingness to study".

Job Performance

According to Frank Schmidt and John Hunter, "for hiring employees without previous experience in the job the most valid predictor of future performance is general mental ability." The validity of IQ as a predictor of job performance is above zero for all work studied to date, but varies with the type of job and across different studies, ranging from 0.2 to 0.6. While IQ is more strongly correlated with reasoning and less so with motor function IQ-test scores predict performance ratings in all occupations. That said, for highly qualified activities (research, management) low IQ scores are more likely to be a barrier to adequate performance, whereas for minimally-skilled activities, athletic strength (manual strength, speed, stamina, and coordination) are more likely to influence performance. It is largely mediated through the quicker acquisition of job-relevant knowledge that IQ predicts job performance.

In establishing a causal direction to the link between IQ and work performance, longitudinal studies by Watkins and others suggest that IQ exerts a causal influence on future academic achievement, whereas academic achievement does not substantially influence future IQ scores. Treena Eileen Rohde and Lee Anne Thompson write that general cognitive ability but not specific ability scores predict academic achievement, with the exception that processing speed and spatial ability predict performance on the SAT math beyond the effect of general cognitive ability. The American Psychological Association's report *Intelligence: Knowns and Unknowns* states that other individual characteristics such as interpersonal skills, aspects of personality etc. are probably of equal or greater importance, but at this point we do not have equally reliable instruments to measure them. More recently, others argue that since most professional tasks are now standardized or automated, and ranked IQ is a stable measurement over time with high correlation with many positive personal traits from the general population, it is the best tool to help determine hiring and job placement at any stage in a career, independently of experience, personality bias or any formal training one may acquire.

Income

Some researchers claim that "in economic terms it appears that the IQ score measures something with decreasing marginal value. It is important to have enough of it, but having lots and lots does not buy you that much."

Other studies show that ability and performance for jobs are linearly related, such that at all IQ levels, an increase in IQ translates into a concomitant increase in performance. Charles Murray, coauthor of *The Bell Curve,* found that IQ has a substantial effect on income independently of family background.

Taking the above two principles together, very high IQ produces very high job performance, but no greater income than slightly high IQ. Studies also show that high IQ is related to higher net worth.

The American Psychological Association's report *Intelligence: Knowns and Unknowns* states that IQ scores account for about one-fourth of the social status variance and one-sixth of the income variance. Statistical controls for parental SES eliminate about a quarter of this predictive power. Psychometric intelligence appears as only one of a great many factors that influence social outcomes.

Some studies claim that IQ only accounts for a sixth of the variation in income because many studies are based on young adults (many of whom have not yet completed their education).

On pg 568 of *The g Factor*, Arthur Jensen claims that although the correlation between IQ and income averages a moderate 0.4 (one sixth or 16% of the variance), the relationship increases with age, and peaks at middle age when people have reached their maximum career potential. In the book, *A Question of Intelligence*, Daniel Seligman cites an IQ income correlation of 0.5 (25% of the variance).

A 2002 study further examined the impact of non-IQ factors on income and concluded that an individual's location, inherited wealth, race, and schooling are more important as factors in determining income than IQ.

Other Correlations with IQ

In addition, IQ and its correlation to health, violent crime, gross state product, and government effectiveness are the subject of a 2006 paper in the publication *Intelligence*. The paper breaks down IQ averages by U.S. states using the federal government's National Assessment of Educational Progress math and reading test scores as a source.

There is a correlation of-0.19 between IQ scores and number of juvenile offences in a large Danish sample; with social class controlled, the correlation dropped to-0.17. Similarly, the correlations for most "negative outcome" variables are typically smaller than 0.20, which means that test scores are associated with less than 4% of their total variance. It is important to realize that the causal links between psychometric ability and social outcomes may be indirect. Children with poor scholastic performance may feel alienated. Consequently, they may be more likely to engage in delinquent behaviour, compared to other children who do well.

IQ is also negatively correlated with certain diseases.

Tambs *et al.* found that occupational status, educational attainment, and IQ are individually heritable; and further found that "genetic variance influencing educational attainment... contributed approximately one-fourth of the genetic variance for occupational status and nearly half the genetic variance for IQ." In a sample of U.S. siblings, Rowe *et al.* report that the inequality in education and income was predominantly due to genes, with shared environmental factors playing a subordinate role. In 2008, intelligence researcher Helmuth Nyborg examined whether IQ relates to denomination and income, using representative data from the National Longitudinal Study of Youth. His results demonstrated that on average, Atheists scored 1.95 IQ points higher than Agnostics, 3.82 points higher than Liberal persuasions, and 5.89 IQ points higher than Dogmatic persuasions.

Group Differences

Among the most controversial issues related to the study of intelligence is the observation that intelligence measures such as IQ scores vary between ethnic and racial groups and sexes. While there is little scholarly debate about the *existence* of some of these differences, their *causes* remain highly controversial both within academia and in the public sphere.

Sex

Men and women have statistically significant differences in average scores on tests of particular abilities. Studies also illustrate consistently greater variance in the performance of men compared to that of women.

IQ tests are weighted on these sex differences so there is no bias on average in favor of one sex, however the consistent difference in variance is not removed. Because the tests are defined so there is no average difference it is difficult to put any meaning on a statement that one sex has a higher intelligence than the other. However some people have made claims like this even using unbiased IQ tests. For instance, there are claims that men tend to outperform women on average by three to four IQ points based on tests of medical students where the greater variance of men's IQ can be expected to contribute to the result, or where a 'correction' is made for different maturation ages.

Race

The 1996 Task Force investigation on Intelligence sponsored by the American Psychological Association concluded that there are significant variations in I.Q. across races. The problem of determining the causes underlying this variation relates to the question of the contributions of "nature and nurture" to I.Q.

Psychologists such as Alan S. Kaufman and Nathan Brody and statisticians such as Bernie Devlin point out there are insufficient data to conclude that this is because of genetic influences. One of the most notable authors arguing for a strong genetic influence on this score difference is Arthur Jensen. In contrast, Richard Nisbett, the long-time director of the Culture and Cognition program at the University of Michigan, argues that environmental influences are not sufficiently taken into account in Jensen's writings.

Public Policy

In the United States, certain public policies and laws regarding military service, education, public benefits, capital punishment, and employment incorporate an individual's IQ into their decisions. However, in the case of Griggs v. Duke Power Co. in 1971, for the purpose of minimizing employment practices that disparately impacted racial minorities, the U.S. Supreme Court banned the use of IQ tests in employment, except in very rare cases. Internationally, certain public policies, such as improving nutrition and prohibiting neurotoxins, have as one of their goals raising, or preventing a decline in, intelligence.

Criticism and Views

Binet

Alfred Binet, a French psychologist, did not believe that IQ test scales qualified to measure intelligence. He neither invented the term "intelligence quotient" nor supported its numerical expression. He stated:

The scale, properly speaking, does not permit the measure of intelligence, because intellectual qualities are not superposable, and therefore cannot be measured as linear surfaces are measured. —Binet, *1905*

Binet had designed the Binet-Simon intelligence scale in order to identify students who needed special help in coping with the school curriculum. He argued that with proper remedial education programs, most students regardless of background could catch up and perform quite well in school. He did not believe that intelligence was a measurable fixed entity.

Binet cautioned: Some recent thinkers seem to have given their moral support to these deplorable verdicts by affirming that an individual's intelligence is a fixed quantity, a quantity that cannot be increased. We must protest and react against this brutal pessimism; we must try to demonstrate that it is founded on nothing.

The Mismeasure of Man

Some scientists dispute psychometrics entirely. In *The Mismeasure of Man*, Harvard professor and paleontologist Stephen Jay Gould argued that intelligence tests were based on faulty assumptions and showed their history of being used as the basis for scientific racism. He criticized, ...the abstraction of intelligence as a single entity, its location within the brain, its quantification as one number for each individual, and the use of these numbers to rank people in a single series of worthiness, invariably to find that oppressed and disadvantaged groups—races, classes, or sexes—are innately inferior and deserve their status.

He spends much of the book criticizing the concept of IQ, including a historical discussion of how the IQ tests were created and a technical discussion of why *g* is simply a mathematical artifact. Later editions of the book included criticism of *The Bell Curve.*

Bernard Davis wrote that while the nonscientific reviews of The Mismeasure of Man were almost uniformly laudatory, the reviews in the scientific journals were almost all highly critical.

Peter H. Schönemann

Psychologist Peter Schönemann has been a persistent critic of IQ, calling it "the IQ myth". He argued that Spearman's g is a flawed theory and the high heritability estimates of IQ are based on false assumptions.

Relation between IQ and Intelligence

According to Dr. C. George Boeree of Shippensburg University, intelligence is a person's capacity to (1) acquire knowledge (i.e. learn and understand), (2) apply knowledge (solve problems), and (3) engage in abstract reasoning. It is the power of one's intellect, and as such is clearly a very important aspect of one's overall well-being. Psychologists have attempted to measure it for well over a century.

IQ is associated with intelligence, but may fail to act as an accurate measure of "intelligence" in its broadest sense. This is partly because IQ tests only examine particular areas embodied by the broadest notion of "intelligence", failing to account for certain areas which are also associated with "intelligence" such as creativity or emotional intelligence.

Several other ways of measuring intelligence have been proposed. Daniel Schacter, Daniel Gilbert, and others have moved beyond general intelligence and IQ as the sole means to describe intelligence.

Test Bias

The American Psychological Association's report *Intelligence: Knowns and Unknowns* states that IQ tests as predictors of social achievement are not biased against people of African descent since they predict future performance, such as school achievement, similarly to the way they predict future performance for people of European descent.

However, IQ tests may well be biased when used in other situations. A 2005 study stated that "differential validity in prediction suggests that the WAIS-R test may contain cultural influences that reduce the validity of the WAIS-R as a measure of cognitive ability for Mexican American students," indicating a weaker positive correlation relative to sampled white students. Other recent studies have questioned the culture-fairness of IQ tests when used in South Africa. Standard intelligence tests, such as the Stanford-Binet, are often inappropriate for children with autism; the alternative of using developmental or adaptive skills measures are relatively poor measures of intelligence in autistic children, and may have resulted in incorrect claims that a majority of children with autism are mentally retarded.

Outdated Methodology

A 2006 review article says that contemporary mainstream test analysis does not reflect substantial recent developments in the field and "bears an uncanny resemblance to the psychometric state of the art as it existed in the 1950s."

The View of the American Psychological Association

In response to the controversy surrounding *The Bell Curve*, the American Psychological Association's Board of Scientific Affairs established a task force in 1995 to write a consensus statement on the state of intelligence research which could be used by all sides as a basis for discussion. The full text of the report is available through several websites.

In this paper the representatives of the association regret that IQ-related works are frequently written with a view to their political consequences: "research findings were often assessed not so much on their merits or their scientific standing as on their supposed political implications".

The task force concluded that IQ scores do have high predictive validity for individual differences in school achievement. They confirm the predictive validity of IQ for adult occupational status, even when variables such as education and family background have been statistically controlled. They found that individual differences in intelligence are substantially influenced by genetics and that both genes and environment, in complex interplay, are essential to the development of intellectual competence.

They state there is little evidence to show that childhood diet influences intelligence except in cases of severe malnutrition. The task force agrees that large differences do exist between the average IQ scores of blacks and whites, and that these differences cannot be attributed to biases in test construction.

The task force suggests that explanations based on social status and cultural differences are possible, and that environmental factors have raised mean test scores in many populations. Regarding genetic causes, they noted that there is not much direct evidence on this point, but what little there is fails to support the genetic hypothesis.

The APA journal that published the statement, *American Psychologist,* subsequently published eleven critical responses in January 1997, several of them arguing that the report failed to examine adequately the evidence for partly-genetic explanations.

High IQ Societies

There are social organizations, some international, which limit membership to people who have scores as high as or higher than the 98th percentile on some IQ test or equivalent. Mensa International is perhaps the most well known of these. There are other groups requiring a score above the 98th percentile.

Popular Culture Usage

Many websites and magazines use the term IQ to refer to technical or popular knowledge in a variety of subjects not related to intelligence, including sex, poker, and American football, among a wide variety of other topics. These tests are generally not standardized and do not fit within the normal definition of intelligence. Intelligence tests such as the Wechsler Adult Intelligence Scale, Wechsler Intelligence Scale for Children, Stanford-Binet, Woodcock-Johnson III Tests of Cognitive Abilities, or the Kaufman Assessment Battery for Children-II, to name some of the best constructed, are not merely placing a test taker's score within the norm, as presumably are the thousands of alleged "IQ Tests" found on the internet, but they are also testing factors (e.g., fluid and crystallized intelligence, working memory, and the like) that were previously found to represent pure measures of intelligence using factor analysis. This claim may not be made for the hundreds of online tests marketing themselves as IQ Tests, a distinction that may be unfortunately lost upon the public taking them.

"Heritability refers to the genetic contribution to variance within a population and in a specific environment... ; if the environment changes, the heritability measure changes." Heritability of a trait in a particular population does not set any limit on how malleable the trait is under changes of environment, because "even highly heritable traits can be strongly manipulated by the environment, so heritability has little if anything to do with controllability." The debate about IQ heritability touches on the nature versus nurture divide, and there has been significant controversy in the academic community about it ever since research began in the

19th century. Most of the heritable variance in IQ correlates strongly with variance in the general intelligence factor (or *g*). Destructive mutation of individual genes associated with development can severely affect intelligence, with Phenylketonuria as an example. An abnormal number of chromosomes carrying genes that ordinarily would result in normal or above average IQ, as in Down syndrome, is an example of normally harmless genes resulting in mental retardation if their pattern of expression is unusual.

Background

Heritability is defined as the proportion of variance in a trait which is attributable to genotype within a defined population in a specific environment. Heritability takes a value ranging from 0 to 1; a heritability of 1 indicates that all variation in the trait in question is genetic in origin and a heritability of 0 indicates that *none* of the variation is genetic. The heritability of many traits can be considered primarily genetic under similar environmental backgrounds. For example, Visscher *et al.* (2006) found that adult height has a heritability estimated at 0.80, when a similar environmental background is present, to control for environment the study only looked at the contribution of heritability to variation within families. The paper stated that "one can never be sure that the estimates are correct, because nature and nurture can be confounded without one knowing it. The authors got around this problem by comparing the similarity between relatives as a function of the exact proportion of genes that they have in common, looking only within families." Other traits have low heritabilities, which indicate a large relative environmental influence. For example, a twin study on the heritability of depression in men calculated it as 0.29, while it was 0.42 for women in the same study.

Heritability for a trait is calculated by measuring how strongly traits covary in people of a given genetic and environmental similarity. The most common method is to consider identical twins reared apart, with any similarities which exists between such twin pairs attributed to genotype. In terms of correlation statistics, this means that theoretically the correlation of tests scores between monozygotic twins would be 1.00 if genetics alone accounted for variation in IQ scores;

likewise, siblings and dizygotic twins share on average half of their alleles and the correlation of their scores would be 0.50 if IQ were affected by genes alone. Practically, however, the upper bound of these correlations are given by the reliability of the test, which tends to be 0.90 to 0.95 for typical IQ tests Thus, the actual heritability of IQ will tend to be slightly higher than attained by estimates derived from studies of monozygotic twins, though this effect is small.

In the case of the inheritance of IQ or a certain degree of giftedness, the relatives of probands with a high IQ exhibit a comparably high IQ with a much higher probability than the general population. In 1982, Bouchard and McGue reviewed such correlations reported in 111 original studies in the United States. The mean correlation of IQ scores between monozygotic twins was 0.86, between siblings, 0.47, between half-siblings, 0.31, and between cousins, 0.15. From such data the heritability of IQ was estimated at anywhere between 0.40 and 0.80 in the United States. The reason for this wide margin appeared to be that the heritability of IQ rises through childhood and adolescence, peaking at 0.68 and 0.78 in adults, leaving the overwhelming majority of IQ differences between individuals to be explained genetically.

The finding of rising heritability with age is counter-intuitive; it is reasonable to expect that genetic influences on traits like IQ should become less important as one gains experiences with age. However, that the opposite occurs is well documented. According to work by Robert Plomin, heritability estimates calculated on infant samples are as low as 20%, rising to around 40% in middle childhood, and ultimately as high as 80% in adult samples in the United States. This suggests that the underlying genes actually express themselves by affecting a person's predisposition to build, learn, and develop mental abilities throughout the lifespan.

Estimates and Caveats to Them

In 2006, *The New York Times Magazine* listed about three quarters as a figure held by the majority of studies, while a 2004 meta-analysis of reports in *Current Directions in Psychological Science* gave an overall estimate of around.85 for 18-year-olds and older. As well, a 1996 statement by the

American Psychological Association gave about.45 for children and about.75 during and after adolescence.

The 2006 edition of *Assessing adolescent and adult intelligence* by Alan S. Kaufman and Elizabeth O. Lichtenberger reports correlations of 0.86 for identical twins raised together compared to 0.76 for those raised apart and 0.47 for siblings.

There are a number of points to consider when interpreting heritability:

- A high heritability does not mean that the environment has no effect on the development of a trait, or that learning is not involved. Vocabulary size, for example, is very substantially heritable (and highly correlated with general intelligence) although every word in an individual's vocabulary is learned. In a society in which plenty of words are available in everyone's environment, especially for individuals who are motivated to seek them out, the number of words that individuals actually learn depends to a considerable extent on their genetic predispositions.
- A common error is to assume that because something is heritable it is necessarily unchangeable. This is wrong. Heritability does not imply immutability. As previously noted, heritable traits can depend on learning, and they may be subject to other environmental effects as well. The value of heritability can change if the distribution of environments (or genes) in the population is substantially altered. For example, an impoverished or suppressive environment could fail to support the development of a trait, and hence restrict individual variation. This could affect estimates of heritability. Another example is Phenylketonuria which previously caused mental retardation for everyone who had this genetic disorder. Today, this can be prevented by following a modified diet.
- On the other hand, there can be effective environmental changes that do not change heritability at all. If the environment relevant to a given trait improves in a way that affects all members of the population equally, the mean value of the trait will rise without any change

in its heritability (because the differences among individuals in the population will stay the same). This has evidently happened for height: the heritability of stature is high, but average heights continue to increase.

- Even in developed nations, high heritability of a trait within a given group has no necessary implications for the source of a difference between groups.
- Heritability increases with education and with social class, such that the children of highly educated parents are more likely to inherit traits. Most of the studies done about heritability have used middle class families-not because of any intentional choice made by researchers but because, on average, lower income people are less likely to volunteer to be studied in the first place.
- Even among close groups such as families, different individuals—such as siblings—will still experience different environments, which matter in determining intelligence scores.

Test Score Differences

Intelligence tests measure many important abilities, such as verbal and quantitative reasoning, and can predict socially-relevant outcomes such as academic performance and occupational outcomes. However, intelligence test scores do not reflect all of the intricacies of the everyday meaning of intelligence, so researchers take care to distinguish between IQ test results and intelligence.

Some studies of intelligence tests use statistical methods to extract so-called latent variables from the IQ test scores. One such variable is the general intelligence factor, or *g*, which accounts for most of the differences in IQ test scores between individuals. There are other latent variables in addition to *g*, and IQ tests vary in their ability to measure these latent variables, if they measure them at all. IQ tests scores, while often summarized as a single overall number, are actually multidimensional in nature. Transforming IQ test scores into latent variables is an attempt to find one or dimensions on which to compare IQ test scores.

IQ scores can vary substantially for the same person, even on tests taken at the same age. (IQ score table data and pupil pseudonyms adapted from description of KABC-II norming study cited in Kaufman 2009.)

Pupil	*KABC-II*	*WISC-III*	*WJ-III*
Asher	90	95	111
Brianna	125	110	105
Colin	100	93	101
Danica	116	127	118
Elpha	93	105	93
Fritz	106	105	105
Georgi	95	100	90
Hector	112	113	103
Imelda	104	96	97
Jose	101	99	86
Keoku	81	78	75
Le*	116	124	102

Latent variables are also sometimes called factors or constructs. The construct validity of an IQ test score is a key criteria for judging whether the IQ test score differences are meaningful. Tests which do not measure difference in latent variables for some group are said to have measurement bias. The construct validity of most commonly used IQ tests has been fairly well established within multiple racial-ethnic groups in developing countries such as the United States. That is, test score difference within each racial-ethnic group are valid indicators of differences in latent variables such as *g*. A related question is whether test-score differences between groups are valid. There is a consensus that test score differences between Black and White people in the United States have predictive validity (also called predictive invariance), meaning that test scores predict the same socially-relevant outcomes regardless of the race of the person being tested.

To further address this question, three studies using sophisticated statistical techniques have shown that Black-White differences in IQ test scores are not a result of measurement bias (a criterion called measurement invariance). These studies imply that Black-White IQ differences reflect very general differences in some underlying latent variables, but they are unable to differentiate precisely which latent variables differ under a variety of models. These studies were performed in response to previous investigations which suggested that Black-White IQ differences are primarily differences in *g* in particular.

United States

There are observed differences in average test score achievement between racial-ethnic groups, which vary depending on the populations studied and the type of tests used. Self-defined black and white United States citizens have been the subjects of the greatest number of studies. Black-white average IQ differences appear to increase with age, reaching an average of nearly 17 points by age 24, which is slightly more than one standard deviation. According to James Flynn and others, the overall average black-white gap has reduced by one-third over the course of the 20th century. For example, the black men inducted into the U.S. armed forces during World War II averaged about 1.5 standard deviations below their white counterparts. This improvement is also reflected in black-white differences on school achievement tests, which have shrunk from about 1.2 to about 0.8 standard deviations. However, these improvements may have stalled for people born after the early 1970s.

The average black-white IQ difference also varies depending on test content. For example, two subsections of the WISC IQ test, known as forward and reverse digit-span, ask children to repeat a long series of numbers either forwards or backwards. The black-white difference on forward digit span is relatively small, while the difference on reverse digit span is relatively large. Across a battery of tests, the size of the black-white gap is correlated with the extent to which the tests measure the psychometric factor *g*, which also accounts for most of the variation in interindividual differences in IQ test performance. Gaps are seen in other tests of cognitive ability or aptitude, including university admission exams such as the SAT and GRE as well as employment tests for corporate settings and the military. The IQ distributions of other racial and ethnic groups in the United States are less well studied. Hispanic and

Native American populations, including Arctic Natives, tend to score worse on average than white populations but better on average than black populations. East Asian populations may score higher on average than white populations in the United States as they do elsewhere. A 1960 study of 1,236 American teenagers calculated six IQ measures for Jews relative to white gentiles. The results found that the relative IQ of American Jews varied from a low of 91.3 (visual reasoning) to a high of 109.7 (mathematics). A recent review by Lynn (2004) used a 10 word vocabulary test to estimate the IQ of American Jews. The population of 150 Jews scored half a standard deviation above the 5,300 white gentiles in verbal IQ.

For each of these populations, there is some evidence that the mixture of ability factors that distinguish individuals are differentially distributed between groups. For example, East Asian populations tend to outscore white populations in performance IQ, whereas the test score differences skew towards higher verbal IQ for Ashkenazi Jew-white differences. However, the mixture of abilities within groups appears to be nearly identical across many ethnic groups. The stability of these differences is also less well studied than black-white differences.

Worldwide

According to Richard Lynn, J. Philippe Rushton, and others, IQ test score differences are observed cross-culturally and around the world. Lynn has published three books summarizing IQ test scores from around the world. The inaccuracy of the cross cultural IQ scores is well documented, but many scholars use the results as an estimate of worldwide IQ scores. Lynn's meta-analysis lists East Asians (105), Europeans (99), Inuit (91), Southeast Asians and Amerindians (87 each), Pacific Islanders (85), South Asians/North Africans (84), Non-Bushmen sub-Saharan Africans (67), Australian Aborigines (62) and Bushmen (54).. However, critics point out that different researchers using different data get different results. For example, James Flynn found out that Lynn's comparisons between nations were skewed and that the IQ values should be recalculated.

International achievement test scores, including TIMSS and PISA, have also been used to estimate average IQ worldwide with similar results where data is available. The very low IQ scores reported for sub-Saharan African populations are especially controversial. For example, Wicherts argues that the average IQ of sub-Saharan Africans is poorly measured and is more likely 78. According to anthropologist Mark Cohen, the frequently reported African mean IQ of 70 is "preposterous". Using Western standards, this would mean that African countries evidencing such a low IQ would be largely dysfunctional. Given that individuals in these countries lead "vibrant artistic, symbolic and spiritual lives", this is, according to Cohen, clearly not the case. Thus, he concludes, the IQ test results from Africa do not reflect actual intelligence levels.

Differences in education, prolonged malnutrition, exposure to toxin, exposure to stress, and exposure to disease are all generally expected to contribute to the lower scores observed in developing countries. However, direct experimental evidence to confirm the role of individual factors is difficult to acquire in most cases because each of these factors tends to also be associated with one another and with unfavorable socioeconomic conditions. In the case of some toxins, such as lead, a negative effect on IQ scores has been established. Two other factors that have as well established negative association with IQ are severely premature birth and severe low birth weight.

Developing Nations

Almost all studies on heritability have been in the developed world, mostly in the United States. In developing nations there are many environmental factors affecting IQ which are much less important in developed nations. Examples include nutrition, diseases, environmental toxins, and health care. For example, iodine deficiency causes a fall, in average, of 12 IQ points in China..

Issues in the Calculations

Family Environment

In the developed world, nearly all personality traits show that, contrary to some expectations, environmental effects actually cause non-related children raised in the same family ("adoptive siblings") to be as different as children raised in different families (Harris, 1998; Plomin & Daniels, 1987). There are some family effects on the IQ of children, accounting for up to a quarter of the variance. However, by adulthood, this correlation disappears, such that adoptive siblings are not more similar in IQ than strangers, while adult full siblings show an IQ correlation of 0.6. Twin studies reinforce this pattern: monozygotic (identical) twins raised separately are highly similar in IQ (0.86), more so than dizygotic (fraternal) twins raised together (0.6) and much more than adoptive siblings (~0.0). The American Psychological Association's report *Intelligence: Knowns and Unknowns* (1995) states that there is no doubt that normal child development requires a certain minimum level of responsible care. Severely deprived, neglectful, or abusive environments must have negative effects on a great many aspects of development, including intellectual aspects. Beyond that minimum, however, the role of family experience is in serious dispute.

There is no doubt that such variables as resources of the home and parents' use of language are correlated with children's IQ scores, but such correlations may be mediated by genetic as well as (or instead of) environmental factors. But how much of that variance in IQ results from differences between families, as contrasted with the varying experiences of different children in the same family? Recent twin and adoption studies suggest that while the effect of the family environment is substantial in early childhood, it becomes quite small by late adolescence. These findings suggest that differences in the life styles of families whatever their importance may be for many aspects of children's lives make little long-term difference for the skills measured by intelligence tests. It also stated

"We should note, however, that low-income and non-white families are poorly represented in existing adoption studies as well as in most twin samples. Thus it is not yet clear whether these studies apply to the population as a whole. It remains possible that, across the full range of income and ethnicity, between-family differences have more lasting consequences for psychometric intelligence."

A study of French children adopted between the ages of four and six shows the continuing interplay of nature and nurture. The children came from poor backgrounds with IQs that initially averaged 77, putting them near retardation. Nine years later after adoption, they retook the IQ tests, and all of them did better. The amount they improved was directly related to the adopting family's socioeconomic status. "Children adopted by farmers and laborers had average IQ scores of 85.5; those placed with middle-class families had average scores of 92. The average IQ scores of youngsters placed in well-to-do homes climbed more than 20 points, to 98."

Biased Older Studies?

Stoolmiller (1999) found that the range restriction of family environments that goes with adoption, that adopting families tend to be more similar on for example SES than the general population, means that role of the shared family environment have been underestimated in previous studies. Corrections for range correction applied to adoption studies indicate that SE could account for as much as 50% of the variance in IQ. However, the effect of restriction of range on IQ for adoption studies was examined by Matt McGue and colleagues, who write that "restriction in range in parent disinhibitory psychopathology and family SES had no effect on adoptive-sibling correlations [in] IQ". Eric Turkheimer and colleagues (2003), not using an adoption study, included impoverished US families. Results demonstrated that the proportions of IQ variance attributable to genes and environment vary nonlinearly with SES. The models suggest that in impoverished families, 60% of the variance in IQ is accounted for by the shared family environment, and the contribution of genes is close to zero; in affluent families, the result is almost exactly the reverse. They suggest that the role of shared environmental factors may have been underestimated in older studies which often only studied affluent middle class families. When comparing late 1970s to pre-1963 recorded data, researches DeFries and Plomin found that IQ correlation between parent and child living together fell significantly, from 0.50 to 0.35.

Maternal (Fetal) Environment

A meta-analysis, by Devlin and colleagues in *Nature* (1997), of 212 previous studies evaluated an alternative model for environmental influence and found that it fits the data better than the 'family-environments' model commonly used. The shared maternal (foetal) environment effects, often assumed to be negligible, account for 20% of covariance between twins and 5% between siblings, and the effects of genes are correspondingly reduced, with two measures of heritability being less than 50%. They argue that the shared maternal environment may explain the striking correlation between the IQs of twins, especially those of adult twins that were reared apart.

Bouchard and McGue reviewed the literature in 2003, arguing that Devlin's conclusions about the magnitude of heritability is not substantially different than previous reports and that their conclusions regarding prenatal effects stands in contradiction to many previous reports. They write that:

Chipuer et al. and Loehlin conclude that the postnatal rather than the prenatal environment is most important. The Devlin et al. (1997a) conclusion that the prenatal environment contributes to twin IQ similarity is especially remarkable given the existence of an extensive empirical literature on prenatal effects. Price (1950), in a comprehensive review published over 50 years ago, argued that almost all MZ twin prenatal effects produced differences rather than similarities. As of 1950 the literature on the topic was so large that the entire bibliography was not published. It was finally published in 1978 with an additional 260 references. At that time Price reiterated his earlier conclusion (Price, 1978). Research subsequent to the 1978 review largely reinforces Price's hypothesis.

The Dickens and Flynn Model

Dickens and Flynn (2001) argue that the arguments regarding the disappearance of the shared family environment should apply equally well to groups separated in time. This is contradicted by the Flynn effect. Changes here have happened too quickly to be explained by genetics. This paradox can be explained by observing that the measure "heritability" includes both a direct effect of the genotype on IQ and also indirect effects where the genotype changes the environment, in turn effecting IQ. That is, those with a higher IQ tend to seek out stimulating environments that further increase IQ. The direct effect can initially have been very small but feedback loops can create large differences in IQ. In their model an environmental stimulus can have a very large effect on IQ, even in adults, but this effect also decays over time unless the stimulus continues (the model could be adapted to include possible factors, like nutrition in early childhood, that may cause permanent effects). The Flynn effect can be explained by a generally more stimulating environment for all people. The authors suggest that programs aiming to increase IQ would be most likely to produce long-term IQ gains if they taught children how to replicate outside the program the kinds of cognitively demanding experiences that produce IQ gains while they are in the program and motivate them to persist in that replication long after they have left the program.

Regression Towards the Mean

The heritability of IQ measures the extent to which the IQ of a child is measurably influenced by the IQ of its parents. As IQ is a quantifiable phenotype, one can estimate the expected IQ of child using the equation, where

- is the expected IQ of the child,
- is the mean IQ of the population to which the parents belong,
- h^2 is the heritability of IQ,
- m and f are the IQs of the mother and father, respectively.

The equation asserts that, on average, the IQ of a child tends to the mean IQ of the population. For instance, if the heritability of IQ is 50% and the mean IQ of a population is 100, then a couple with an average IQ of 120 will, on average, have a child with an IQ of 110. Similarly, a couple with an average IQ of 80 will, on average, have a child with an IQ of 90. It is noted that the above equation relates only statistical averages and is not deterministic. Furthermore, the equation is a general equation based in the inheritance of genetically-based characteristics (in this case, phenotypes), and so it is implicitly assumed that environmental factors are, for the sake of correctly assessing the genetic contribution to IQ, the same across the population.

Operating under the assumption that child and parent are raised in the exact same environment (unlikely, but usually closer to the truth than in the completely dissimilar environment that the previous equation assumes), h^2 can be replaced by h, which is simply the correlation between parent and offspring IQ. In this case, regression towards the mean is no longer partially caused by environmental differences and therefore only by random genetic variation.

Finally, it is important to note that the expected IQ of the offspring is normally distributed around the mean calculated using the above equation, so in many cases regression towards the mean does not actually occur; as the values are normally distributed, there is a chance that offspring IQ will be more deviant from the mean than that of the parental average.

Historical Research

As early as 1869, Francis Galton replaced mere speculations by statistical data through his book, *Hereditary Genius*:

Highly Gifted Men and the Percentage of their Highly Gifted Male Relatives (classified by occupation and achievement)

	Galton	Terman	Brimhall	Weiss	
	%	%	%	%	*n*
Probands	100	84+	100	97+	1972: *1329* 1994: *357*
Fathers	26	41	29	40	*346*
Brothers	47	–	49	49	*220*
Sons	60	64*	–	55	*77*
Grandfathers	14	–	9	9	*681*
Uncles	16	–	13	14	*615*
Nephews	23	–	–	22	*76*
Grandsons	14	–	–	–	–
Greatgrandfathers	0	–	–	4	*1290*
Uncles of the parents	5	–	–	5	*1996*
Cousins	16	–	9#	18	*570*
Greatgrandsons	7	–	–	–	–
Cousins of parents	–	–	–	11	*2250*

"+": classified by occupation; 100%, if classified by test

"*": classified only by IQ; classification by occupation gives about 55%;

n = 820.

"#": some cousins were still too young and did not have full opportunity to become distinguished

"–": no data

Sources

- Francis Galton: Hereditary Genius. London 1869. "100 famous Famous men (n = 43) of science and the percentage of their famous male relatives."
- M. H. Oden: The fulfillment of promise: 40-year follow-up of the Terman gifted group. *Genetical Psychology Monographs 77 (1968) 3-93. "The mean IQ (transformed to 100;15) of the sample of probands was 146 (n = 724); the cut-off score IQ 137."*
- Dean R. Brimhall: Family resemblances among American men of science. *The American Naturalist* 56 (1922) 504-547; 57 (1923) 74-88, 137-152, and 326-344. "In 1915 questionnaires were filled in by 956 distinguished American men of science and their relatives."
- Volkmar Weiss: Mathematical giftedness and family relationship. European Journal for High Ability 5 (1994) 58-67.[2] *"Highly gifted males (mean IQ 135 +/-9) and their relatives in professions and occupational positions, typically associated with an IQ above 123."*

Despite the differences in methods and societies, there is a notable parallelism in the published statistics. The ITO-method by Li and Sacks (1954) allows from this set of data the estimation of the underlying number of genes and their allele frequencies.

The Inheritance of Cognitive Deficits

There are many genetic variants known to cause lower IQ. The number of such mutations already known is in the hundreds. For example, an allele of the gene GDI1 is associated with an IQ below 70. Copy number variation has also been associated with idiopathic learning disability.

There are number of known cases where the homozygotes have severe cognitive deficits and the heterozygotes show a small decrease of IQ. In such cases further alleles are investigated to estimate their influence on IQ. For example, one minor allele of the gene ALDH5A1 is associated with an IQ difference of around 1.5 points.

Interindividual (between individuals) differences in learning ability are also known in mice, dogs and other animals, and the achievements of pure strains can be improved by selective breeding. In such a way also behaviour genetics is contributing to our knowledge of the inheritance of mental traits. There is an open question to which degree differences of animal behaviour have any meaning for differences in human intelligence.

The Search for Specific Genes

Unfortunately, most of the research done about the heritability of intelligence have focused on children and young adults. Thus, the role of genetic factors to intelligence, which most likely increases over time, is mostly unknown. Many studies attempting to find loci in the genome relating to IQ have had little success. For example, a study by Robert Plomin using groups of around 100 people investigated 1,842 DNA markers in a high-IQ group and in an average-IQ control group. The study used a five-step replication process to eliminate false positives, and no gene met this rigid criterion for replicability

The failure to find a specific gene associated with IQ indicates that cognitive abilities are very complex and are likely to involve several genes (polygenic). Some estimate that as much as 40% of all genes may contribute to IQ. The more genes that contribute to a trait the more the trait will be continuous instead of discrete. A 2008 study of 500,000 single nucleotide polymorphisms (SNPs) from 7,089 children did not substantially improve on earlier studies. The study did not find any SNPs that accounted for more than 0.5% of the variance in general intelligence.

A 2007 study did find that a gene called FADS2 along with breastfeeding adds about 7 IQ points to those with the "C" version of the gene. Those with the "G" version see no advantage.

There is "a highly significant association" between the CHRM2 gene and intelligence according to a 2006 Dutch family study. The study concluded that there was an association between the CHRM2 gene on chromosome 7 and Performance IQ, as measured by the Wechsler Adult Intelligence Scale-Revised. The Dutch family study used a sample of 667 individuals from 304 families. A similar association was found independently in the *Minnesota Twin and Family Study* (Comings et al. 2003) and by the Department of Psychiatry at the Washington University. Microcephalin and ASPM are two genes that are associated with brain development. Mutations in these genes are associated with microcephaly, and hence they were initially associated with general intelligence. However recent studies have found no association with general cognitive abilities.

STX1A correlates significantly with intelligence in Williams syndrome patients.

Between-group Heritability

Although IQ differences between individuals are shown to have a large genetic component, it does not automatically follow that mean group-level disparities (between-group differences) in IQ can be assumed to have a genetic basis. An analogy, attributed to Richard Lewontin, illustrates this point:

Suppose two handfuls are taken from a sack containing a genetically diverse variety of corn, and each grown under carefully controlled and standardized conditions, except that one batch is lacking in certain nutrients that are supplied to the other. After several weeks, the plants are measured. There is variability of growth within each batch, due to the genetic variability of the corn. Given that the growing conditions are closely controlled, nearly all the variation in the height of the plants within a batch will be due to differences in their genes. Thus, within populations, heritabilities will be very high. Nevertheless, the difference between the two groups is due entirely to an environmental factor-differential nutrition. Lewontin didn't go so far as to have the one set of pots painted white and the other set black, but you get the idea. The point of the example, in any case, is that the causes of between-group differences may in principle be quite different from the causes of within-group variation.

However, differences in IQ between reportedly discrete genetic groups has been observed, and some researchers, such as Arthur Jensen, maintain that environmental differences are too small to account for these differences. They propose that therefore genetic differences must provide the primary explanation. This view is challenged by Peter Schönemann who claims that Arthur Jensen and others routinely confuse the first principal component (PC1) with *g* as Charles Spearman defined it. Schönemann argues that the high IQ heritability estimates reported in the literature derive from restrictive formal models whose underlying assumptions are rarely tested and usually violated by the data. Jensen's view is also rebutted by James Flynn in his book *What Is Intelligence.*

The issue of observed between-group IQ differences is controversial *vis-a-vis* considerations on both the nature of race and the meaning and measurement of intelligence. Important related questions include whether intelligence can be accurately described by a single number, and whether the nature of intelligence is the same across cultures.

Other biological factors correlating with IQ include ratio of brain weight to body weight and the volume and location of gray matter tissue in the brain.

Because intelligence appears to be at least partly dependent on brain structure and the genes shaping brain development, it has been proposed that genetic engineering could be used to enhance the intelligence of animals, a process sometimes called biological uplift in science fiction. Experiments on mice have demonstrated superior ability in learning and memory in various behavioral tasks.

Environmental

Evidence suggests that family environmental factors may have an effect upon childhood IQ, accounting for up to a quarter of the variance. Other variance in IQ results from environmental influences not shared by siblings who grow up in the same home. Another important influence on IQ that was often neglected in earlier human genetic studies is the "maternal effect" of the prenatal environment of the mother's womb. In the context of follow-up research on the nature versus nurture debate, it is still unclear whether the "nature" component is more important than the "nurture" component in explaining IQ variance in the general population.

There are indications that in middle age intelligence is influenced by life style choices (e.g. long working hours).

Cultural factors also play a role in intelligence. For example, on a sorting task to measure intelligence, Westerners tend to take a taxonomic approach while the Kpelle people take a more functional approach. For example, instead of grouping food and tools into separate categories, a Kpelle participant stated "the knife goes with the orange because it cuts it."

Ethical issues

Conscious efforts to influence intelligence raise ethical issues. Transhumanist theorists study the possibilities and consequences of developing and using techniques to enhance human abilities and aptitudes, and individuals ameliorating what they regard as undesirable and unnecessary aspects of the human condition; eugenics is a social philosophy which advocates the improvement of human hereditary traits through various forms of intervention. Eugenics has variously been regarded as meritorious or deplorable in different periods of history, falling greatly into disrepute after the defeat of Nazi Germany in World War II. Policies promoted on supposed eugenic grounds usually favor the ethnic group in political authority, without regard to evidence of genetic superiority. For example, Jewish people were disfavored by the Nazis even though Jews in Germany had conspicuous achievements in the arts and sciences.

Neuroethics considers the ethical, legal and social implications of neuroscience, and deals with issues such as the difference between treating a human neurological disease and enhancing the human brain, and how wealth impacts access to neurotechnology. Neuroethical issues interact with the ethics of human genetic engineering.

8

Development of Interests and Attitudes

Interest is a feeling or emotion that causes attention to focus on an object or an event or a process. In contemporary psychology of interest, the term is used as a general concept that may encompass other more specific psychological terms, such as curiosity and to a much lesser degree surprise. The emotion of interest does have its own facial expression, of which the most prominent component is having dilated pupils.

Attitude

An attitude is a hypothetical construct that represents an individual's degree of like or dislike for an item. Attitudes are generally positive or negative views of a person, place, thing, or event—this is often referred to as the attitude object. People can also be conflicted or ambivalent toward an object, meaning that they simultaneously possess both positive and negative attitudes toward the item in question.

Attitudes are judgments. They develop on the ABC model (affect, behaviour, and cognition). The *affective* response is an emotional response that expresses an individual's degree of preference for an entity. The *behavioral* intention is a verbal indication or typical behavioral tendency of an individual. The *cognitive* response is a cognitive evaluation of the entity that constitutes an individual's beliefs about the object. Most attitudes are the result of either direct experience or observational learning from the environment.

Attitude Formation

Unlike personality, attitudes are expected to change as a function of experience. Tesser (1993) has argued that hereditary variables may affect attitudes-but believes that they may do so indirectly. For example, consistency theories, which imply that we must be consistent in our beliefs and values. The most famous example of such a theory is Dissonance-reduction theory, associated with Leon Festinger, although there are others, such as the balance theory.

Attitude Change

Attitudes can be changed through persuasion and we should understand attitude change as a response to communication. Experimental research into the factors that can affect the persuasiveness of a message include:

1. Target Characteristics: These are characteristics that refer to the person who receives and processes a message. One such trait is intelligence-it seems that more intelligent people are less easily persuaded by one-sided messages. Another variable that has been studied in this category is self-esteem. Although it is sometimes thought that those higher in self-esteem are less easily persuaded, there is some evidence that the relationship between self-esteem and persuasibility is actually curvilinear, with people of moderate self-esteem being more easily persuaded than both those of high and low self-esteem levels (Rhodes & Woods, 1992). The mind frame and mood of the target also plays a role in this process.
2. Source Characteristics: The major source characteristics are expertise, trustworthiness and interpersonal attraction or attractiveness. The credibility of a perceived message has been found to be a key variable here; if one reads a report about health and believes it came from a professional medical journal, one may be more easily persuaded than if one believes it is from a popular newspaper. Some psychologists have debated whether this is a long-lasting effect and Hovland and Weiss (1951) found the effect of telling people that a

message came from a credible source disappeared after several weeks (the so-called "sleeper effect"). Whether there is a sleeper effect is controversial. Perceived wisdom is that if people are informed of the source of a message before hearing it, there is less likelihood of a sleeper effect than if they are told a message and then told its source.

3. Message Characteristics: The nature of the message plays a role in persuasion. Sometimes presenting both sides of a story is useful to help change attitudes.

Cognitive Routes: A message can appeal to an individual's cognitive evaluation to help change an attitude. In the *central route* to persuasion the individual is presented with the data and motivated to evaluate the data and arrive at an attitude changing conclusion. In the *peripheral route* to attitude change, the individual is encouraged to not look at the content but at the source. This is commonly seen in modern advertisements that feature celebrities. In some cases, physician, doctors or experts are used. In other cases film stars are used for their attractiveness.

Emotion and Attitude Change

Emotion is a common component in persuasion, social influence, and attitude change. Much of attitude research emphasized the importance of affective or emotion components. Emotion works hand-in-hand with the cognitive process, or the way we think, about an issue or situation. Emotional appeals are commonly found in advertising, health campaigns and political messages. Recent examples include no-smoking health campaigns and political campaign advertising emphasizing the fear of terrorism. Attitudes and attitude objects are functions of cognitive, affective and conative components. Attitudes are part of the brain's associative networks, the spider-like structures residing in long term memory that consist of affective and cognitive nodes.

By activating an affective or emotion node, attitude change may be possible, though affective and cognitive components tend to be intertwined. In primarily affective networks, it is more difficult to produce cognitive counterarguments in the resistance to persuasion and attitude change.

Affective forecasting, otherwise known as intuition or the prediction of emotion, also impacts attitude change. Research suggests that predicting emotions is an important component of decision making, in addition to the cognitive processes. How we feel about an outcome may override purely cognitive rationales.

In terms of research methodology, the challenge for researchers is measuring emotion and subsequent impacts on attitude. Since we cannot see into the brain, various models and measurement tools have been constructed to obtain emotion and attitude information. Measures may include the use of physiological cues like facial expressions, vocal changes, and other body rate measures. For instance, fear is associated with raised eyebrows, increased heart rate and increase body tension (Dillard, 1994). Other methods include concept or network mapping, and using primes or word cues.

Components of Emotion Appeals

Any discrete emotion can be used in a persuasive appeal; this may include jealousy, disgust, indignation, fear, and anger. Fear is one of the most studied emotional appeals in communication and social influence research.

Important consequences of fear appeals and other emotion appeals include the possibility of reactance which may lead to either message rejections or source rejection and the absence of attitude change. As the EPPM suggests, there is an optimal emotion level in motivating attitude change. If there is not enough motivation, an attitude will not change; if the emotional appeal is overdone, the motivation can be paralyzed thereby preventing attitude change.

Emotions perceived as negative or containing threat are often studied more than perceived positive emotions like humour. Though the inner-workings of humour are not agreed upon, humour appeals may work by creating incongruities in the mind. Recent research has looked at the impact of humour on the processing of political messages. While evidence is inconclusive, there appears to be potential for targeted attitude change is receivers with low political message involvement. Important factors that influence the impact of emotion appeals include self efficacy, attitude accessibility, issue involvement, and message/source features. Self efficacy is a perception of one's own human agency; in other words, it is the perception of our own ability to deal with a situation. It is an important variable in emotion appeal messages because it dictates a person's ability to deal with both the emotion and the situation. For example, if a person is not self-efficacious about their ability to impact the global environment, they are not likely to change their attitude or behaviour about global warming.

Dillard (1994) suggests that message features such as source non-verbal communication, message content, and receiver differences can impact the emotion impact of fear appeals. The characteristics of a message are important because one message can elicit different levels of emotion for different people. Thus, in terms of emotion appeals messages, one size does not fit all.

Attitude accessibility refers to the activation of an attitude from memory in other words, how readily available is an attitude about an object, issue, or situation. Issue involvement is the relevancc and salience of an issue or situation to an individual. Issue involvement has been correlated with both attitude access and attitude strength. Past studies conclude accessible attitudes are more resistant to change.

Implicit and Explicit Attitudes

There is also considerable research on implicit attitudes, which are generally unacknowledged or outside of awareness, but have effects that are measurable through sophisticated methods using people's response times to stimuli. Implicit and explicit attitudes seem to affect people's behaviour, though in different ways. They tend not to be strongly associated with each other, although in some cases they are. The relationship between them is poorly understood.

Jung's Definition

Attitude is one of Jung's 57 definitions in Chapter XI of *Psychological Types*. Jung's definition of attitude is a "readiness of the psyche to act or react in a certain way". Attitudes very often come in pairs, one conscious and the other unconscious. Within this broad definition Jung defines several attitudes.

The main (but not only) attitude dualities that Jung defines are the following.

- Consciousness and the unconscious. The "presence of two attitudes is extremely frequent, one conscious and the other unconscious. This means that consciousness has a constellation of contents different from that of the unconscious, a duality particularly evident in neurosis".
- Extraversion and introversion. This pair is so elementary to Jung's theory of types that he labeled them the "attitude-types".
- Rational and irrational attitudes. "I conceive reason as an attitude".
- The rational attitude subdivides into the thinking and feeling psychological functions, each with its attitude.
- The irrational attitude subdivides into the sensing and intuition psychological functions, each with its attitude. "There is thus a typical thinking, feeling, sensation, and intuitive attitude".
- Individual and social attitudes. Many of the latter are "isms".

In addition, Jung discusses the abstract attitude. "When I take an abstract attitude...". Abstraction is contrasted with concretism. "CONCRETISM. By this I mean a peculiarity of thinking and feeling which is the antithesis of abstraction".

MBTI Definition

The MBTI write-ups limit the use of "attitude" to the extraversion-introversion (EI) and judging-perceiving (JP) indexes. The JP index is sometimes referred to as an orientation to the outer world and sometimes JP is classified as an "attitude." In Jungian terminology the term *attitude* is restricted to EI. In MBTI terminology *attitude* can include EI and also JP.

The above MBTI Manual statement, is restricted to EI," is directly contradicted by Jung's statement above that there is "a typical thinking, feeling, sensation, and intuitive attitude" and by his other uses of the term "attitude". Regardless of whether the MBTI simplification (or oversimplification) of Jung can be attributed to Myers, *Gifts Differing* refers only to the

"EI preference", consistently avoiding the label "attitude". Regarding the JP index, in *Gifts Differing* Myers does use the terms "the *perceptive* attitude and the *judging* attitude" (Myers, 1980:8). The JP index corresponds to the irrational and rational attitudes Jung describes, except that the MBTI focuses on the preferred orientation in the outer world in order to identify the function hierarchy. To be consistent with Jung, it can be noted that a rational extraverted preference is accompanied by an irrational introverted preference.

Formation and Expression of Attitudes

Antecedents to beliefs – those conditions that "set the stage" for beliefs to develop (e.g., community, past experiences, family and friends, individual characteristics).

Beliefs – what people perceive to be true. They may or may not be correct.

Attitude – a learned predisposition to respond in a consistently favorable or unfavorable manner with respect to a given object. "Attitudes are the enduring positive or negative feeling about some person, object, or issue."

Intentions – those behavioral plans individuals make with respect to the presence of another person. *It has been said that the road to a not so desirable location is paved with good intentions.*

Behaviours – any observable and measurable act, response, or movement by an individual. The impact of attitudes is reflected in people's behaviours.

All of the components listed above are interrelated in a dynamic process of attitude development and expression. Each is influenced by another, therefore, when one component is changed, frequently the other components are altered.

Development of Negative Attitudes

When interacting with one another, individuals with and without disabilities can experience stress. It has been noted that when people without disabilities interact with people with disabilities they experience:

- greater emotional distress

- exhibited higher physiological arousal
- showed less motor activity
- displayed less variability in their verbal behaviour
- expressed opinions that were less representative of their previously reported beliefs
- terminated interactions sooner

The perception of a person with a disability as being "different" may result in that person experiencing personal stress. This stress can cause interactions to become strained followed by emotions such as fear, anxiety and actions such as avoidance and segregation.

Perception of Being Different

Stigma – an undesired differentness which separates the person from others in a society. It is not just a difference, but a characteristic that deeply discredits a person's moral character.

An individual may be devalued as a total person because their disabling condition is so negatively valued. Living with stigmatized characteristics transforms ordinary social tasks such as shopping and meeting strangers into socially demanding ones. When people with disabilities become aware of their stigmatized label, their self-perceptions are affected.

Generalized Attitudes

Stereotype – a standardized mental picture held in common by members of a group and represents an oversimplified opinion, attitude, or judgment.

People with disabilities and professionals both agree that one of the biggest problems facing people with disabilities are stereotypes. Stereotypes of people result in a very narrow view of them.

Prejudice – the development of a judgment in disregard of a person's rights, resulting in that individual being injured or damaged in some way

"Prejudice" – *"pre"*, meaning beforehand, and root word, *"judic,"* meaning to judge.

Prejudicial outlooks toward individuals are created by stereotypes.

Generalized Actions

Discrimination – making a distinction categorically rather than individually about another person, then acting towards that person differently than another person.

Discrimination involves people making judgments about people based on the affiliation with a group, instead of who they are as an individual.

Segregation – the separation or isolation of a group or individual in a restricted area because of discrimination. The end result would be receiving treatment that is different from others.

The practice of segregation may occur when people are stigmatized and perceived as deviant because of their disabilities. It is suggested that when people with disabilities are segregated from their peers who don't have disabilities, they may only model those behaviours exhibited by other people with similar disabilities. They do not get a chance to learn a full range of behaviours.

Labels and Expectations

There are three possible reactions by people with disabilities that can occur as a result of negative attitudes and expectations:

Self-fulfilling prophecy

- Labeling of a person may result in the person's behaviour being consistent with the label.
- Self-fulfilling prophecy may make it difficult for people with disabilities to develop a positive self-concept.
- The tendency of individuals with disabilities to accept negative stereotyping about themselves is often referred to as *internalized oppression.*

Spread Phenomenon

- Associations of additional disabilities to a person on the basis of the actual disabling condition (e.g., speaking loudly to a person who is blind).
- The spread phenomenon further "handicaps" a person with a disability.

Psychosexual Development

The concept of psychosexual development, as envisioned by Sigmund Freud at the end of the 19th and the beginning of the 20th century, is a central element in his sexual drive theory, which posits that, from birth, humans have instinctual sexual appetites (libido), which unfold in a series of stages. Each stage is characterized by the erogenous zone that is the source of the libidinal drive during that stage. These stages are, in order: oral, anal, phallic, latency, and genital. Freud believed that if, during any stage, the child experienced anxiety in relation to that drive, that themes related to this stage would persist into adulthood as neurosis.

Background

Freud observed that, at somewhat predictable points during early development, children's behaviour often orients around certain body parts (the mouth during breast-feeding, the anus during Toilet-training, and later the genitals). Believing, due to his previous work with hysterical patients, that adult neurosis often has root in childhood sexuality, Freud proposed that these behaviours were childhood expressions of sexual fantasy and desire. He suggested that humans are born "polymorphously perverse", meaning that infants can derive sexual pleasure from any part of the body., and that it is only through socialization that libidinal drives are focused into adult heterosexuality.

Due to the fairly predictable time-line that the childhood behaviours in question follow, Freud developed a model for what he considered to be the normal sexual development of the child, which he called "libido development". According to this theory, each child passes through five psychosexual stages. During each stage, the libido has a different erogenous zone as the source of its drives. The libido refers to various kinds of sensual pleasures and gratifications.

However, in the pursuit of satisfying these sexual urges, the child may experience failure or reprimands from its parents or society and may thus come to associate anxiety with this erogenous zone. To avoid this anxiety, the child becomes preoccupied with themes related to this zone, a phenomenon

Freud termed fixation. Freud believed the fixation persists into adulthood and underlies the personality structure and psychopathology, including neurosis, hysteria and personality disorders. Freud called this psychosexual infantilism.

Freud's Model of Psychosexual Development

Oral Phase

The first stage of psychosexual development is the oral stage, which lasts from the beginning of one's life up to 2 years. During this stage, the focus of gratification is on the mouth and pleasure is the result of nursing, but also of exploration of the surroundings (as infants tend to put new objects in their mouths). In this stage the Id is dominant since neither the ego nor the super ego is yet fully formed. Thus the baby does not have a sense of self and all actions are based on the pleasure principle.

The ego, however, is under formation during this first stage. There are two factors that contribute to the formation of the ego. Firstly, body image is developed, which implies that the infant recognizes that the body is distinct from the outer world. For instance, one starts understanding that one feels pain only when force is applied on one's own body. By the identification of the body boundaries, one starts developing the sense of ego. Ego formation is attributed to a second factor: experiences that involve delay of gratification and that lead to the understanding that specific behaviours can satisfy some needs. The infant gradually realises that gratification is not immediate, and that he or she must produce certain behaviours to initiate actions that lead to gratification. An example of such behaviour is crying, which seems to be purposeless during the first 2 months of the baby's life, but later seems to be used productively and is connected to certain needs.

The key experience in this stage is weaning, during which the child loses much of the intimate contact with the mother and leads to the first feeling of loss ever experienced by the baby. Weaning also adds to the baby's awareness of self, since he or she learns that not everything is under his or her control, but also that gratification is not always immediate.

In this stage, the gratification of needs lead to the formation of independence (since the baby forms a clear idea about the limits of the self and has formed his or her ego), and trust (since the baby learned that specific behaviours lead to gratification). On the other hand, a fixation can lead to passivity, gullibility, immaturity and unrealistic optimism, and also to the formation of a generally manipulative personality due to improper formation of the ego. This can be the result of either too much or too little gratification. In the case of too much gratification, the child does not learn that not everything is under his or her control and that gratification is not always immediate (which are the results of weaning), forming an immature personality. On the other hand, the child's needs may be insufficiently met, and thus the child becomes passive since he or she has learned that whether producing behaviour or not, no gratification comes. In some societies it is common for a child to be nursed by his or her mother for several years, whereas in others the stage is much shorter. Sucking and eating, however, compose the earliest memories for infants in every society. This stage holds special importance because some tribal societies commonly found in the Southwest Pacific and Africa, consider the stomach to be the seat of emotions.

Anal Phase

In the anal stage of the psychosexual development the focus of drive energy (erogenous zone) moves from the upper digestive tract to the lower end and the anus. This stage lasts from about the 15th month to the third year of age. In this stage, the formation of ego continues.

According to the theory, the major experience during this stage is toilet training. This occurs around the age of two (there may be fluctuations among different societies as to the age in which toilet training occurs), and results to conflict between the id, which asks for immediate gratification of its drives that involves elimination and activities related to it (such as handling feces) and the demands of their parents. The resolution of this conflict can be gradual and non-traumatic, or intense and stormy, depending on how the parents handle the situation. The ideal resolution comes if the child tries to adjust and the parents are moderate, so that the child learns the importance of cleanliness and order gradually, which leads to a self-controlled adult. If the parents put too much emphasis on toilet training while the child decides to accommodate, this may lead to the development of compulsive personality, extensively concerned about order and neatness. On the other hand, if the child decides to heed the demands of the id and the parents give in, the child may develop a messy and self-indulgent personality. If the parents react, the child must comply, but it develops a weakened sense of self, since the parents were the ones who controlled the situation, not the ego.

Phallic Phase

The phallic stage extends from about three to five years of age, and the erogenous zone associated with it as the area of the genitals. Even though the gratification is focused on the genitals, this is not in the form of adult sexuality, since the children are physically immature. However, stimulation of genitals is welcomed as pleasurable and boys, like adult males, may have erections during their sleep. Children become increasingly aware of their body and are curious about the bodies of other children, but also their parents. Freud observed that children of this age can very often be observed taking off their clothes and playing "doctor" with each other, or asking their mothers whether she has a penis. These observations persuaded Freud that the gratification is focused on and around the genitals during this period.

The major conflict of this stage is called Oedipal conflict, the name deriving from Oedipus, who killed his father and unintentionally slept with his mother. Freud used the term Oedipal for both sexes, but other analysts proposed the female variant to be referred to as "Electra complex". In the beginning, for both sexes the primary care giver (at least in most societies) and main source of gratification is the mother. As the child develops, however, it starts forming a sexual identity and the dynamics for boys and girls alter. For both sexes, the parents become the focus of drive energy.

For the boy, the mother becomes more desired, while the father is the focus of jealousy and rivalry, since he is the one who sleeps with the mother, but still he is one of the main caregivers. The id wants to unite with the mother and kill the father (like Oedipus did), but the ego, based on the reality principle, knows that the father is stronger. The child also feels affectionate towards the father, one of the caregivers, and his feelings are ambivalent. The fear that the father will object to the boy's feelings is expressed by the id as fear that the father will castrate him. The castration fear is not rational, and occurs in a subconscious irrational level.

Freud argued that young girls followed more or less the same psychosexual development as boys. Whereas the boy would develop a castration anxiety, the girl would go on to develop penis envy, envy felt by females toward the males because the males possess a penis. The envy is rooted in the fact that without a penis, the female cannot sexually possess the mother as driven to by the Id. As a result of this realization, she is driven to desire sexual union with the father. After this stage, the woman has an extra stage in her development when the clitoris should wholly or in part hand over its sensitivity and its importance to the vagina. The young girl must also at some point give up her first object-choice, the mother, in order to take the father as her new proper object-choice. Her eventual move into heterosexual femininity, which culminates in giving birth, grows out of her earlier infantile desires, with her own child taking place of the penis in accordance with an ancient symbolic equivalence. Generally, Freud considered the Oedipal conflict experienced by girls more intense than that experienced by boys, potentially resulting in a more submissive and less confident personality.

In both cases the conflict between the id drives and the ego is resolved through two basic defence mechanisms of the ego. One of them is repression, which involves the blocking of memories, impulses and ideas from the conscious mind, but does not lead to resolution of the conflict. The second is identification, which involves incorporation of characteristics of the same-sex parent into the child's own ego. The boy by adopting this mechanism seeks for the reduction of castration fears, since his similarity with the father is thought to protect the boy from him. The identification of girls with the mother is easier, since the girl realizes that neither she, nor her mother have a penis. Freud's theory regarding the psychosexual dynamic present in female children in this point of their psychosexual development is termed, though not by Freud himself, the Electra complex. Freud's theory of feminine sexuality, particularly penis envy, has been sharply criticized in both gender theory and feminist theory.

If the conflict is not resolved, a fixation in this stage may lead to adult women striving for superiority over men, if she had overwhelming feelings of devastation due to lack of penis, being seductive and flirtatious, or very submissive and with low self-esteem. On the other hand, men can exhibit excessive ambition and vanity. Overall, the Oedipal conflict is very important for the super-ego development, since by identifying with one of the parents, morality becomes internalized, and compliance with rules is not any more the result of punishment fear. A poor identification with the same sex parent may lead to recklessness or even immorality.

Latency Phase

The latency stage is typified by a solidifying of the habits that the child developed in the earlier stages. Whether the Oedipal conflict is successfully resolved or not, the drives of the Id are not accessible to the Ego during this stage of development, since they have been repressed during the phallic stage. Hence the drives are seen as dormant and hidden (latent), and the gratification the child receives is not as immediate as it was during the three previous stages. Now pleasure is mostly related to secondary process thinking. Drive energy is redirected to new activities, mainly related to schooling, hobbies and friends. Problems however might occur during this stage, and this is attributed to inadequate repression of the Oedipal conflict, or to the inability of the Ego to redirect the drive energy to activities accepted by the social environment.

Genital Phases

The fifth and last stage of psycho-sexual development, the genital stage, lasts from puberty onward (i.e. starting at 12 years of age). It is said to continue until development stops, which is supposedly at 18 years of age when adulthood starts. This stage represents a major portion of life and the basic task for the individual is detachment from parents. It is also the time when the individual tries to come to terms with unresolved residues of early childhood. In this stage, the focus is again on the genitals, like in the phallic stage, but this time the energy is expressed in terms of adult sexuality. Another crucial difference between these two stages is that, while phallic gratification is linked with satisfaction of primary drives, the ego in the genital stage is well-developed. It uses secondary, process thinking, which allows for symbolic gratification. This symbolic gratification may include the formation of love relationships, development of families, or acceptance of responsibilities associated with adulthood.

Criticism of Freud's theory of psychosexual development. A common scientific criticism regarding Freudian theory of human psychosexual development is that Freud was personally overly fixated on human sexuality himself, which may have served to subjectively bias his work in favor of defining human development solely upon normative human sexual development. It is possible that said fixation regarding human sexuality could have negatively influenced Freud in manners that may have led to him ignoring other significant variables that contribute to human's psychosexual development, such as hormonal and pheromonal activity. The stage that has caused the most controversy is the phallic stage. Freud supported his assertions on the Oedipal complex with a series of clinical observations. In 1909, he published a case study of a boy called "little Hans," who had a phobia of horses. Freud connected Hans' fear for horses to his fear for his father. Hans' fear and anxiety were thought to be the result of various factors, including the birth of his sister, the desire of his id to replace his father as his mother's companion and conflicts over masturbation. Hans admitted his want to have children with his mother, which was considered an adequate proof for patient's sexual attraction for the opposite-sex parent. Little Hans, however, was unable to connect the fear for the horses with his father, and, as Freud admitted, "Hans had to be told many things that he could not say himself" and that "he had to be presented with thoughts which he had so far shown no signs of possessing," so that one may suggest that Freud manipulated the patient's mind.

Scientifically minded researchers have criticized Freud's statement, in his 1914 paper, "*On Narcissism*," that "It is impossible to suppose that a unity comparable to the ego can exist in the individual from the very start". Ample evidence documents a functioning ego in infants, even in neonates, contrary to Freud's speculation. The neonate shows surprising ability to track moving targets, to differentiate a familiar from an unfamiliar stimulus, and to react meaningfully with the care giver. Further, children show signs of superego behaviour earlier than Freud's suggestion that it does not arise until after the Oedipal complex has been resolved.

Cultural considerations have largely influenced the assumptions within the psychodynamic perspective. Freud stated that the Oedipal Complex is universal and essential for development. Bronis³aw Malinowski, an anthropologist who studied the behaviour of villagers in the Trobriand Islands, challenged common western views such as Freud's Oedipus complex and their claim to universality. In the Trobriand society the boys are disciplined by their mothers' brothers instead of their biological fathers (avuncular society). As he recounts in his work, *Sex and Repression in Savage Society* (1927), Malinowski found that boys had dreams in which the target of fears was not their father, but their uncle. Based on this observation, Malinowski argued that power, not sexual jealousy, is the base for the oedipal tension. As a result, Segall et al. hypothesized that Freud's theory was based on a misinterpretation of a confounding variable.

A survey of scientific research showed that while personality traits corresponding to Freud's oral, anal, phallic, and genital phases can be observed, they cannot be observed as stages in the development of children, nor can it be confirmed that such traits in adults result from childhood experiences.

Feminist Critique

Despite their popularity among psychoanalytical psychologists, Freud's psychosexual theories are commonly criticized as being sexist. Freud's theories were often informed by his own introspection and self-analysis, and thus were infused with an inherently male perspective, resulting in a great deal of criticism from feminists as well as from gender theory practitioners. He had difficulty incorporating female desire into his theories and attempted to provide a theoretical explanation for feminine psychosexual development only rather late in his career. Freud personally confessed a lack of understanding of female sexuality and did not hold out hope that psychology would ever explain the phenomenon.

For example, Freud stated that young females develop "penis envy" toward the males during their psychosexual development. In response, Karen Horney, a German Freudian psychoanalyst, argued that young females develop "power envy" instead of "penis envy" toward the male. She also suggested the concept of "womb envy" in males, which is defined as jealousy of ability to bear children. However, more modern formulations consider this as an envy of the perceived right of women to be nurturing.

9

The Developing Individual and his Educational Environment

Education in the largest sense is any act or experience that has a formative effect on the mind, character or physical ability of an individual. In its technical sense, education is the process by which society deliberately transmits its accumulated knowledge, skills and values from one generation to another.

Etymologically, the word education is derived from *educare* (Latin) "bring up", which is related to *educere* "bring out", "bring forth what is within", "bring out potential" and *ducere*, "to lead".

Teachers in educational institutions direct the education of students and might draw on many subjects, including reading, writing, mathematics, science and history. This process is sometimes called schooling when referring to the education of teaching only a certain subject, usually as professors at institutions of higher learning. There is also education in fields for those who want specific vocational skills, such as those required to be a pilot. In addition there is an array of education possible at the informal level, such as in museums and libraries, with the Internet and in life experience. Many non-traditional education options are now available and continue to evolve.

Education is a concept, referring to the process in which students can learn something:

- Instruction refers to the facilitating of learning toward identified objectives, delivered either by an instructor or other forms.

- Teaching refers to the actions of a real live instructor designed to impart learning to the student.
- Learning refers to learning with a view toward preparing learners with specific knowledge, skills, or abilities that can be applied immediately upon completion.

Preschool Education

Preschool education or Infant education is the provision of education for children before the commencement of statutory and obligatory education, usually between the ages of zero or three and five, depending on the jurisdiction.

In British English, nursery school or simply "nursery" or playgroup is the usual term for preschool education. In the United States preschool and Pre-K are used, while "nursery school" is an older term.

Preschool work is organized within a framework that professional educators create. The framework includes structural (administration, class size, teacher-child ratio, services, etc.), process (quality of classroom environments, teacher-child interactions, etc), and alignment (standards, curriculum, assessments) components that are associated with each individual unique child that has both social and academic outcomes. Arguably the first pre-school institution was opened in 1816 by Robert Owen in New Lanark, Scotland. The Hungarian countess Theresa Brunszvik followed in 1828. In 1837, Friedrich Fröbel opened one in Germany, coining the term "kindergarten".

Developmental Areas

The areas of development which preschool education covers varies from country to country. However, the following main themes are represented in the majority of systems.

- Personal, social, economical, and emotional development
- Communication, including sign language, talking and listening
- Knowledge and understanding of the world
- Creative and aesthetic development
- Educational software

- Mathematical awareness and development
- Physical development
- Playing
- Self-help skills
- Social skills.

Allowing preschool aged children to discover and explore freely within each of these areas of development is the foundation for developmental learning. While the National Association for the Education of Young Children (NAEYC) and the National Association of Child Care Professionals (NACCP) have made tremendous strides in publicizing and promoting the idea of developmentally appropriate practice, there is still much work to be done. It is widely recognized that although many preschool educators are aware of the guidelines for developmentally appropriate practice, putting this practice to work effectively in the classroom is more challenging. The NAEYC published that although 80% of Kindergarten classrooms claim to be developmentally appropriate, only 20% actually are.

Age and Importance

Preschool is generally considered appropriate for children between zero or three and five years of age, between the baby or toddler and school stages. During this stage of development, children learn and assimilate information rapidly, and express interest and fascination in each new discovery.

It is well established that the most important years of learning are begun at birth. A child's brain at this age is making connections that will last the rest of their life. During these early years, a human being is capable of absorbing more information at a time than they will ever be able to again. The environment of the young child influences the development of cognitive skills and emotional skills due to the rapid brain growth that occurs in the early years. Studies have shown that high quality preschools have a short and long term effect in improving the outcomes of a child, especially a disadvantaged child. However, some more recent studies dispute the accuracy of the earlier results which cited benefits to preschool education, and actually point at preschool being detrimental to a child's cognitive and social development. A study by UC Berkeley and Stanford University on 14,000 Kindergarteners revealed that while there is a temporary cognitive boost in pre-reading and math, preschool holds detrimental effects on social development and cooperation.

The Universal Preschool movement is an international effort to make access to preschool available to families in a similar way to compulsory primary education. Various jurisdictions and advocates have differing priorities for access, availability and funding sources. There has been a shift from preschools that operated primarily as controlled play groups to educational settings in which children learn specific, if basic, skills. It examines several different perspectives on teaching in kindergarten, including those of the developmentally appropriate practice, the academic approach, the child-centered approach, and the Montessori approach to the curriculum.

Gratuity

The gratuity of infant education has been established in some countries, as Spain, beginning in the second cycle (from three to six years), but extending to the first cycle (from birth to three years).

History of Preschool in the United States

Head Start, the first publicly funded preschool program, was created in 1965 by President Johnson. The federal government helped create this half-day program for preschool children from low-income families. Head Start began as a summer pilot program that included an education component, nutrition and health screenings for children, and support services for families (CPE, 2007). In the 1960s only ten percent of the nations three and four year olds were enrolled in a classroom setting. Due to a large amount of people interested, and a lack of funding for Head Start, during the 1980s a handful of states started their own version of a program for students from low-income families. The positive success and effects of preschool meant many state leaders were showing interest in educational reform of these young students (CPE, 2007). By 2005 sixty-nine percent, or over 800,000, four year-old children nationwide participated in some type of state preschool program (CPE, 2007). The yearly increase in enrollment of preschool programs throughout the years is due to an increase of higher maternal employment rates, national anti-poverty initiatives, and research showing the link between early childhood experiences and the brain development of young children. These factors have caused the rate of attendance in preschool programs to grow each year (CPE, 2007).

In most states, there are multiple preschool or Pre-K options for young children. Parents have the choice of sending their child to a federally funded Head Start program, if their income is at the poverty level, state-funded preschool, government-funded special education programs, and for-profit and not-for-profit providers (Levin & Schartz, 2007), including those that accept government subsidies that help low income parents pay. Currently, in the United States, Georgia, Illinois, Florida, Oklahoma, West Virginia, and New York are the only states with legislation underway or which already have universal preschool for all four year olds in the state, and Preschool For All in Illinois is the only universal preschool program that serves three year olds as well.

Methods of Preschool Education

Some preschools have adopted specialized methods of teaching, such as Montessori, Waldorf, Head Start, HighReach Learning, High Scope, *The Creative Curriculum*, Reggio Emilia approach, Bank Street, Forest kindergartens, and various other pedagogies which contribute to the foundation of education.

Creative Curriculum has an interactive website where parents and teachers can work together in evaluating preschool age children. The website is very user friendly and prints off many reports that are helpful in evaluating children and the classroom itself. The web site has a variety of activities that are targeted to each of the fifty goals on the continuum.

The International Preschool Curriculum adopted a bilingual approach to teaching and offers a curriculum that embraces international standards and recognizes national requirements for preschool education. In the United States most preschool advocates support the National Association for the Education of Young Children's Developmentally Appropriate Practices. Family childcare can also be nationally accredited by the National Association of Family Childcare if the provider chooses to go through the process. National accreditation is only awarded to those programs who demonstrate the quality standards set forth by the NAFCC.

Funding for Preschool Programs

While a majority of American preschool programs remain tuition-based, support for some public funding of early childhood education has grown over the years. As of 2008, 38 states and the District of Columbia invested in at least some pre-kindergarten programs, and many school districts were providing preschool services on their own, using local and federal funds.

The benefits and challenges of a public preschool are closely tied to the amount of funding provided. Funding for a public preschool can come in a variety of sources. According to Levin and Schwartz (2007) funding can range from federal, state, local public allocations, private sources, and parental fees. The problem of funding a public preschool occurs not only from limited sources but from the cost per child. The average cost across the 48 states is $6,582 (Levin and Schwartz, 2007). There are four categories that determine the costs of public preschools: personnel ratios, personnel qualifications, facilities and transportation, and health and nutrition services. According to Levin and Schwartz (2007) these structural elements depend heavily on the cost and quality of services provided. The main personnel factor related to cost is the qualifications each preschool require for a teacher. Another determinate of cost is the length of a preschool day. The longer the session, the more increase in cost. Therefore, the quality of program accounts presumably for a major component of cost.

Collaboration has been a solution for funding issues in several districts. Wilma Kaplan, principal, turned to collaborating with the area Head Start and other private preschool to fund a public preschool in her district. "We're very pleased with the interaction. It's really added a dimension to our program that's been very positive" (Reeves, 2000). The National Head Start Bureau has been looking for more opportunities to partner with public schools. Torn Schultz of the National Head Start Bureau states, "We're turning to partnership as much as possible, either in funds or facilities to make sure children get everything necessary to be ready for school". The goal for funding is to develop a variety of sources that provide for all children to benefit from early learning within a public preschool.

Primary Education

Primary (or elementary) education consists of the first 5–7 years of formal, structured education. In general, main education consists of six or eight years of schooling starting at the age of five or six, although this varies between, and sometimes within, countries. Globally, around 70% of primary-age children are enrolled in primary education, and this proportion is rising. Under the Education for All programs driven by UNESCO, most countries have committed to achieving universal enrollment in primary education by 2015, and in many countries, it is compulsory for children to receive primary education. The division between primary and secondary education is somewhat arbitrary, but it generally occurs at about eleven or twelve years of age. Some education systems have separate middle schools, with the transition to the final stage of secondary education taking place at around the age of fourteen. Schools that provide primary education, are mostly referred to as *primary schools*. Primary schools in these countries are often subdivided into infant schools and junior school.

Secondary Education

In most contemporary educational systems of the world, secondary education comprises the formal education that occurs during adolescence. It is characterized by transition from the typically compulsory, comprehensive primary education for minors, to the optional, selective tertiary, "post-secondary", or "higher" education (e.g., university, vocational school for adults. Depending on the system, schools for this period, or a part of it, may be called secondary or high schools, gymnasiums, lyceums, middle schools, colleges, or vocational schools. The exact meaning of any of these terms varies from one system to another. The exact boundary between primary and secondary education also varies from country to country and even within them, but is generally around the seventh to the tenth year of schooling. Secondary education occurs mainly during the teenage years. In the United States, Canada and Australia primary and secondary education together are sometimes referred to as K-12 education, and in New Zealand Year 1-13 is used. The purpose of secondary education can be to give common knowledge, to prepare for higher education or to train directly in a profession.

The emergence of secondary education in the United States did not happen until 1910, caused by the rise in big businesses and technological advances in factories (for instance, the emergence of electrification), that required skilled workers. In order to meet this new job demand, high schools were created and the curriculum focused on practical job skills that would better prepare students for white collar or skilled blue collar work. This proved to be beneficial for both the employer and the employee, because this improvement in human capital caused employees to become more efficient, which lowered costs for the employer, and skilled employees received a higher wage than employees with just primary educational attainment.

In Europe, the grammar school or academy existed from as early as the 16th century; public schools or fee paying schools, or charitable educational foundations have an even longer history.

Higher Education

Higher education, also called tertiary, third stage, or post secondary education, is the non-compulsory educational level that follows the completion of a school providing a secondary education, such as a high school, secondary school. Tertiary education is normally taken to include undergraduate and postgraduate education, as well as vocational education and training. Colleges and universities are the main institutions that provide tertiary education. Collectively, these are sometimes known as tertiary institutions. Tertiary education generally results in the receipt of certificates, diplomas, or academic degrees. Higher education includes teaching, research and social services activities of universities, and within the realm of teaching, it includes both the *undergraduate* level (sometimes referred to as tertiary education) and the *graduate* (or *postgraduate*) level (sometimes referred to as graduate school). Higher education generally involves work towards a degree-level or foundation degree qualification. In most developed countries a high proportion of the population (up to 50%) now enter higher education at some time in their lives. Higher education is therefore very important to national economies, both as a significant industry in its own right, and as a source of trained and educated personnel for the rest of the economy.

Adult Education

Adult education has become common in many countries. It takes on many forms, ranging from formal class-based learning to self-directed learning and e-learning. A number of career specific courses such as veterinary assisting, medical billing and coding, real estate license, bookkeeping and many more are now available to students through the Internet.

Alternative Education

Alternative education, also known as *non-traditional education* or *educational alternative*, is a broad term that may be used to refer to all forms of education outside of traditional education (for all age groups and levels of education). This may include not only forms of education designed for students with special needs (ranging from teenage pregnancy to intellectual disability), but also forms of education designed for a general audience and employing alternative educational philosophies and methods.

Alternatives of the latter type are often the result of education reform and are rooted in various philosophies that are commonly fundamentally different from those of traditional compulsory education. While some have strong political, scholarly, or philosophical orientations, others are more informal associations of teachers and students dissatisfied with certain aspects of traditional education. These alternatives, which include charter schools, alternative schools, independent schools, and home-based learning vary widely, but often emphasize the value of small class size, close relationships between students and teachers, and a sense of community.

Indigenous Education

Increasingly, the inclusion of indigenous models of education (methods and content) as an alternative within the scope of formal and non-formal education systems, has come to represent a significant factor contributing to the success of those members of indigenous communities who choose to access these systems, both as students/learners and as teachers/instructors.

As an educational method, the inclusion of indigenous ways of knowing, learning, instructing, teaching and training, has been viewed by many critical and postmodern scholars as important for ensuring that students/learners and teachers/ instructors (whether indigenous or non-indigenous) are able to benefit from education in a culturally sensitive manner that draws upon, utilizes, promotes and enhances awareness of indigenous traditions.

For indigenous students or learners, and teachers or instructors, the inclusion of these methods often enhances educational effectiveness, success and learning outcomes by providing education that adheres to their own inherent perspectives, experiences and worldview. For non-indigenous students and teachers, education using such methods often has the effect of raising awareness of the individual traditions and collective experience of surrounding indigenous communities and peoples, thereby promoting greater respect for and appreciation of the cultural realities of these communities and peoples.

In terms of educational content, the inclusion of indigenous knowledge, traditions, perspectives, worldviews and conceptions within curricula, instructional materials, textbooks and coursebooks have largely the same effects as the inclusion of indigenous methods in education. Indigenous students and teachers benefit from enhanced academic effectiveness, success and learning outcomes, while non-indigenous students/learners and teachers often have greater awareness, respect, and appreciation for indigenous communities and peoples in consequence of the content that is shared during the course of educational pursuits.

The subjects of indigenous cultures, outdoor education and environmental awareness are exceptionally pertinent now that we are in this sixth global species extinction (the Holocene extinction). The term indigenous refers to those cultures who exist and grow naturally in a particular region or country; often called natives. Indigenous cultures usually live in a particular bioregion for many generations and have learned how to live there sustainably. This quality often puts truly indigenous cultures in a unique position in modern times to be aware of and knowledgeable about the interrelationships, needs, benefits and dangers of their bioregion. This is not true of natives whose cultures have been eroded or whom have been displaced.

A prime example of how indigenous methods and content can be used to promote the above outcomes is demonstrated within higher education in Canada. Due to certain jurisdictions' focus on enhancing academic success for Aboriginal learners and promoting the values of multiculturalism in society, the inclusion of indigenous methods and content in education is often seen as an important obligation and duty of both governmental and educational authorities.

Process

Curriculum

An academic discipline is a branch of knowledge which is formally taught, either at the university, or via some other such method. Each discipline usually has several sub-disciplines or branches, and distinguishing lines are often both arbitrary and ambiguous. Examples of broad areas of academic disciplines include the natural sciences, mathematics, computer science, social sciences, humanities and applied sciences.

Learning Modalities

There has been work on learning styles over the last two decades. Dunn and Dunn focused on identifying relevant stimuli that may influence learning and manipulating the school environment, at about the same time as Joseph Renzulli recommended varying teaching strategies. Howard Gardner identified individual talents or aptitudes in his Multiple Intelligences theories. Based on the works of Jung, the Myers-Briggs Type Indicator and Keirsey Temperament Sorter focused on understanding how people's personality affects the way they interact personally, and how this affects the way individuals respond to each other within the learning environment. The work of David Kolb and Anthony Gregorc's Type Delineator follows a similar but more simplified approach. It is currently fashionable to divide education into different learning "modes". The learning modalities are probably the most common:

- Visual: learning based on observation and seeing what is being learned.
- Auditory: learning based on listening to instructions/ information.
- Kinesthetic: learning based on hands-on work and engaging in activities.

Although it is claimed that, depending on their preferred learning modality, different teaching techniques have different levels of effectiveness, recent research has argued "there is no adequate evidence base to justify incorporating learning styles assessments into general educational practice."

A consequence of this theory is that effective teaching should present a variety of teaching methods which cover all three learning modalities so that different students have equal opportunities to learn in a way that is effective for them. Guy Claxton has questioned the extent that learning styles such as VAK are helpful, particularly as they can have a tendency to label children and therefore restrict learning.

A student might find a particular question threatening and intimidating in one context yet stimulating and challenging in a different context. What makes one learning context unpleasant and another pleasant?

Many Factors Influence Learning

Learning depends on several factors, but a crucial step is the engagement of the learner. This is affected by their motivation and perception of relevance. These, in turn, can be affected by learners' previous experiences and preferred learning styles and by the context and environment in which the learning is taking place. In adult learning theories, teaching is as much about setting the context or climate for learning as it is about imparting knowledge or sharing expertise.

Motivation

Motivation can be intrinsic (from the student) and extrinsic (from external factors). Assessments are usually a strong extrinsic motivator for learners. Individual learners' intrinsic motivation can be affected by previous experiences, by their desire to achieve, and the relevance of the learning to their future.

A teacher's role in motivation should not be underestimated. Enthusiasm for the subject, interest in the students' experiences, and clear direction (among other things) all help to keep students' attention and improve assimilation of information and understanding.

Maslow's hierarchy of needs for motivating learning. Adapted from Maslow A H. *Motivation and Personality*, New York: Harper and Row, 1954.

Even with good intrinsic motivation, however, external factors can demotivate and disillusion. Distractions, unhelpful attitudes of teachers, and physical discomfort will prompt learners to disengage. Maslow described a model to illustrate the building blocks of motivation. Each layer needs to be in place before the pinnacle of "self actualisation" is reached.

Physiological Needs

Although the need to be fed, watered, and comfortable seems trite, many teachers will have experienced, for example, the difficulties of running sessions in cold or overheated rooms, in long sessions without refreshments.

10

Personality Development and Measurement

Personality can be defined as a dynamic and organized set of characteristics possessed by a person that uniquely influences his or her cognitions, motivations, and behaviours in various situations.

The word "personality" originates from the Latin *persona*, which means mask. Significantly, in the theatre of the ancient Latin-speaking world, the mask was not used as a plot device to *disguise* the identity of a character, but rather was a convention employed to represent or *typify* that character.

The pioneering American psychologist, Gordon Allport (1937) described two major ways to study personality, the nomothetic and the idiographic. *Nomothetic psychology* seeks general laws that can be applied to many different people, such as the principle of self-actualization, or the trait of extraversion. *Idiographic psychology* is an attempt to understand the unique aspects of a particular individual.

The study of personality has a broad and varied history in psychology, with an abundance of theoretical traditions. The major theories include dispositional (trait) perspective, psychodynamic, humanistic, biological, behaviorist and social learning perspective. There is no consensus on the definition of "personality" in psychology. Most researchers and psychologists do not explicitly identify themselves with a certain perspective and often take an eclectic approach. Some research is empirically driven such as the "Big 5" personality model whereas other research emphasizes theory development such as psychodynamics. There is also a substantial emphasis on the applied field of personality testing. In psychological education and training, the study of the nature of personality and its psychological development is usually reviewed as a prerequisite to courses in abnormal or clinical psychology.

Philosophical Assumptions

Many of the ideas developed by historical and modern personality theorists stem from the basic philosophical assumptions they hold. The study of personality is not a purely empirical discipline, as it brings in elements of art, science, and philosophy to draw general conclusions. The following five categories are some of the most fundamental philosophical assumptions on which theorists disagree:

Freedom Versus Determinism

This is the debate over whether we have control over our own behaviour and understand the motives behind it (Freedom), or if our behaviour is causally determined by forces beyond our control (Determinism). Determinism has been considered unconscious, environmental, or biological by various theories.

Heredity Versus Environment

Personality is thought to be determined largely by genetics and biology, by environment and experiences, or by some combination resulting thereof. There is evidence for all possibilities. Contemporary research suggests that most personality traits are based on the joint influence of genetics and environment. One of the forerunners in this arena is C. Robert Cloninger with the Temperament and Character model.

Uniqueness Versus Universality

The argument over whether we are all unique individuals (Uniqueness) or if humans are basically similar in their nature (Universality). Gordon Allport, Abraham Maslow, and Carl Rogers were all advocates of the uniqueness of individuals. Behaviorists and cognitive theorists, in contrast, emphasized the importance of universal principles such as reinforcement and self-efficacy.

Active Versus Reactive

Do we primarily act through our own initiative (Active), or react to outside stimuli (Reactive)? Behavioral theorists typically believe that humans are passively shaped by their environments, whereas humanistic and cognitive theorists believe that humans are more active.

Optimistic Versus Pessimistic

Personality theories differ on whether people can change their personalities (Optimism), or if they are doomed to remain the same throughout their lives (Pessimism). Theories that place a great deal of emphasis on learning are often, but not always, more optimistic than theories that do not emphasize learning.

Personality Theories

Critics of personality theory claim personality is "plastic" across time, places, moods, and situations. Changes in personality may indeed result from diet (or lack thereof), medical effects, significant events, or learning. However, most personality theories emphasize stability over fluctuation. The definition of personality that is most widely supported to date is attributed to the neurologist Paul Roe. He stated personality to be "an individual's predisposition to think certain patterns of thought, and therefore engage in certain patterns of behaviour".

Trait Theories

According to the *Diagnostic and Statistical Manual* of the American Psychiatric Association, personality traits are "enduring patterns of perceiving, relating to, and thinking about the environment and oneself that are exhibited in a wide range of social and personal contexts." Theorists generally assume a) traits are relatively stable over time, b) traits differ among individuals (e.g. some people are outgoing while others are reserved), and c) traits influence behaviour.

The most common models of traits incorporate three to five broad dimensions or factors. The least controversial dimension, observed as far back as the ancient Greeks. is simply extraversion and introversion (outgoing and physical-stimulation-oriented vs. quiet and physical-stimulation-averse).

- Gordon Allport delineated different kinds of traits, which he also called dispositions. *Central traits* are basic to an individual's personality, while *secondary traits* are more peripheral. *Common traits* are those recognized within a culture and thus may vary from culture to culture. *Cardinal traits* are those by which an individual may be strongly recognized.
- Raymond Cattell's research propagated a two-tiered personality structure with sixteen "primary factors" (16 Personality Factors) and five "secondary factors."
- Hans Eysenck believed just three traits—extraversion, neuroticism and psychoticism—were sufficient to describe human personality. Differences between Cattell and Eysenck emerged due to preferences for different forms of factor analysis, with Cattell using oblique, Eysenck orthogonal, rotation to analyse the factors that emerged when personality questionnaires were subjected to statistical analysis. Today, the Big Five factors have the weight of a considerable amount of empirical research behind them, building on the work of Cattell and others.
- Lewis Goldberg proposed a five-dimension personality model, nicknamed the "Big Five":
  1. Openness to Experience: the tendency to be imaginative, independent, and interested in variety vs. practical, conforming, and interested in routine.
  2. Conscientiousness: the tendency to be organized, careful, and disciplined vs. disorganized, careless, and impulsive.
  3. Extraversion: the tendency to be sociable, fun-loving, and affectionate vs. retiring, somber, and reserved.
  4. Agreeableness: the tendency to be softhearted, trusting, and helpful vs. ruthless, suspicious, and uncooperative.
  5. Neuroticism: the tendency to be calm, secure, and self-satisfied vs. anxious, insecure, and self-pitying.

The Big Five contain important dimensions of personality. However, some personality researchers argue that this list of major traits is not exhaustive. Some support has been found for two additional factors: excellent/ordinary and evil/decent. However, no definitive conclusions have been established.

- John L. Holland's *RIASEC* vocational model, commonly referred to as the Holland Codes, stipulates that six personality traits lead people to choose their career paths. In this circumplex model, the six types are represented as a hexagon, with adjacent types more closely related than those more distant. The model is widely used in vocational counseling.

Trait models have been criticized as being purely descriptive and offering little explanation of the underlying causes of personality. Eysenck's theory, however, does propose biological mechanisms as driving traits, and modern behaviour genetics researchers have shown a clear genetic substrate to them. Another potential weakness of trait theories is that they lead people to accept oversimplified classifications, or worse offer advice, based on a superficial analysis of their personality. Finally, trait models often underestimate the effect of specific situations on people's behaviour. It is important to remember that traits are statistical generalizations that do not always correspond to an individual's behaviour.

Type Theories

Personality type refers to the psychological classification of different types of people. Personality types are distinguished from personality traits, which come in different levels or degrees. For example, according to type theories, there are two types of people, introverts and extraverts. According to trait theories, introversion and extraversion are part of a continuous dimension, with many people in the middle. The idea of psychological types originated in the theoretical work of Carl Jung and William Marston, whose work is reviewed in Dr. Travis Bradberry's *Self-Awareness*. Jung's seminal 1921 book on the subject is available in English as *Psychological Types*.

Building on the writings and observations of Jung, during World War II, Isabel Briggs Myers and her mother, Katharine

C. Briggs, delineated personality types by constructing the Myers-Briggs Type Indicator. This model was later used by David Keirsey with a different understanding from Jung, Briggs and Myers. In the former Soviet Union, Lithuanian Auðra Augustinavièiûtë independently derived a model of personality type from Jung's called Socionics.

The model is an older and more theoretical approach to personality, accepting extraversion and introversion as basic psychological orientations in connection with two pairs of psychological functions:

- Perceiving functions: sensing and intuition (trust in concrete, sensory-oriented facts vs. trust in abstract concepts and imagined possibilities)
- Judging functions: thinking and feeling (basing decisions primarily on logic vs. considering the effect on people).

Briggs and Myers also added another personality dimension to their type indicator to measure whether a person prefers to use a judging or perceiving function when interacting with the external world. Therefore they included questions designed to indicate whether someone wishes to come to conclusions (judgment) or to keep options open (perception).

This personality typology has some aspects of a trait theory: it explains people's behaviour in terms of opposite fixed characteristics. In these more traditional models, the sensing/intuition preference is considered the most basic, dividing people into "N" (intuitive) or "S" (sensing) personality types. An "N" is further assumed to be guided either by thinking or feeling, and divided into the "NT" (scientist, engineer) or "NF" (author, humanitarian) temperament. An "S", by contrast, is assumed to be guided more by the judgment/perception axis, and thus divided into the "SJ" (guardian, traditionalist) or "SP" (performer, artisan) temperament. These four are considered basic, with the other two factors in each case (including always extraversion/introversion) less important. Critics of this traditional view have observed that the types can be quite strongly stereotyped by professions (although neither Myers nor Keirsey engaged in such stereotyping in their type descriptions), and thus may arise more from the need to categorize people for purposes of guiding their career choice.

This amorg other objections led to the emergence of the five-factor view, which is less concerned with behaviour under work conditions and more concerned with behaviour in personal and emotional circumstances. (It should be noted, however, that the MBTI is not designed to measure the "work self," but rather what Myers and McCaulley called the "shoes-off self.") Some critics have argued for more or fewer dimensions while others have proposed entirely different theories (often assuming different definitions of "personality").

Type A and Type B personality theory: During the 1950s, Meyer Friedman and his co-workers defined what they called Type A and Type B behaviour patterns. They theorized that intense, hard-driving Type A personalities had a higher risk of coronary disease because they are "stress junkies." Type B people, on the other hand, tended to be relaxed, less competitive, and lower in risk. There was also a Type AB mixed profile. Dr. Redford Williams, cardiologist at Duke University, refuted Friedman's theory that Type A personalities have a higher risk of coronary heart disease; however, current research indicates that only the hostility component of Type A may have health implications. Type A/B theory has been extensively criticized by psychologists because it tends to oversimplify the many dimensions of an individual's personality.

Psychoanalytic Theories

Psychoanalytic theories explain human behaviour in terms of the interaction of various components of personality. Sigmund Freud was the founder of this school. Freud drew on the physics of his day (thermodynamics) to coin the term psychodynamics. Based on the idea of converting heat into mechanical energy, he proposed psychic energy could be converted into behaviour. Freud's theory places central importance on dynamic, unconscious psychological conflicts.

Freud divides human personality into three significant components: the id, ego, and super-ego. The id acts according to the *pleasure principle*, demanding immediate gratification of its needs regardless of external environment; the ego then must emerge in order to realistically meet the wishes and demands of the id in accordance with the outside world, adhering to the *reality principle*. Finally, the superego (conscience) inculcates moral judgment and societal rules upon the ego, thus forcing the demands of the id to be met not only realistically but morally. The superego is the last function of the personality to develop, and is the embodiment of parental/social ideals established during childhood. According to Freud, personality is based on the dynamic interactions of these three components.

The channeling and release of sexual (libidal) and aggressive energies, which ensues from the "Eros" (sex; instinctual self-preservation) and "Thanatos" (death; instinctual self-annihilation) drives respectively, are major components of his theory. It is important to note that Freud's broad understanding of sexuality included all kinds of pleasurable feelings experienced by the human body.

Freud proposed five psychosexual stages of personality development. He believed adult personality is dependent upon early childhood experiences and largely determined by age five. Fixations that develop during the Infantile stage contribute to adult personality and behaviour.

One of Sigmund Freud's earlier associates, Alfred Adler, did agree with Freud early childhood experiences are important to development, and believed birth order may influence personality development. Adler believed the oldest was the one that set high goals to achieve to get the attention they lost back when the younger siblings were born. He believed the middle children were competitive and ambitious possibly so they are able to surpass the first-born's achievements, but were not as much concerned about the glory. Also he believed the last born would be more dependent and sociable but be the baby. He also believed that the only child loves being the center of attention and matures quickly, but in the end fails to become independent.

Heinz Kohut thought similarly to Freud's idea of transference. He used narcissism as a model of how we develop our sense of self. Narcissism is the exaggerated sense of one self in which is believed to exist in order to protect one's low self esteem and sense of worthlessness. Kohut had a significant impact on the field by extending Freud's theory of narcissism and introducing what he called the 'self-object transferences' of mirroring and idealization. In other words, children need to idealize and emotionally "sink into" and identify with the idealized competence of admired figures such as parents or older siblings. They also need to have their self-worth mirrored by these people. These experiences allow them to thereby learn the self-soothing and other skills that are necessary for the development of a healthy sense of self.

Another important figure in the world of personality theory was Karen Horney. She is credited with the development of the "real self" and the "ideal self". She believes all people have these two views of their own self. The "real self" is how you really are with regards to personality, values, and morals; but the "ideal self" is a construct you apply to yourself to conform to social and personal norms and goals. Ideal self would be "I can be successful, I am CEO material"; and real self would be "I just work in the mail room, with not much chance of high promotion".

Behaviorist Theories

Behaviorists explain personality in terms of the effects external stimuli have on behaviour. It was a radical shift away from Freudian philosophy. This school of thought was developed by B. F. Skinner who put forth a model which emphasized the mutual interaction of the person or "the organism" with its environment. Skinner believed children do bad things because the behaviour obtains attention that serves as a reinforcer. For example: a child cries because the child's crying in the past has led to attention. These are the *response*, and *consequences*. The response is the child crying, and the attention that child gets is the reinforcing consequence. According to this theory, people's behaviour is formed by processes such as operant conditioning. Skinner put forward a "three term contingency model" which helped promote analysis of behaviour based on the "Stimulus-Response-Consequence Model" in which the critical question is: "Under which circumstances or antecedent 'stimuli' does the organism engage in a particular behaviour or 'response', which in turn produces a particular 'consequence'?"

Richard Herrnstein extended this theory by accounting for attitudes and traits. An attitude develops as the response strength (the tendency to respond) in the presences of a group of stimuli become stable. Rather than describing conditionable traits in non-behavioral language, response strength in a given situation accounts for the environmental portion. Herrstein also saw traits as having a large genetic or biological component as do most modern behaviorists.

Ivan Pavlov is another notable influence. He is well known for his classical conditioning experiments involving dogs. These physiological studies led him to discover the foundation of behaviourism as well as classical conditioning.

Social Cognitive Theories

In cognitivism, behaviour is explained as guided by cognitions (e.g. expectations) about the world, especially those about other people. Cognitive theories are theories of personality that emphasize cognitive processes such as thinking and judging.

Albert Bandura, a social learning theorist suggested the forces of memory and emotions worked in conjunction with environmental influences. Bandura was known mostly for his "Bobo Doll experiment". During these experiments, Bandura video taped a college student kicking and verbally abusing a bobo doll. He then showed this video to a class of kindergarten children who were getting ready to go out to play. When they entered the play room, they saw bobo dolls, and some hammers. The people observing these children at play saw a group of children beating the doll. He called this study and his findings observational learning, or modeling.

Early examples of approaches to cognitive style are listed by Baron (1982). These include Witkin's (1965) work on field dependency, Gardner's (1953) discovering people had consistent preference for the number of categories they used to categorise heterogeneous objects, and Block and Petersen's (1955) work on confidence in line discrimination judgments. Baron relates early development of cognitive approaches of personality to ego psychology. More central to this field have been:

- Self-efficacy work, dealing with confidence people have in abilities to do tasks;
- Locus of control theory dealing with different beliefs people have about whether their worlds are controlled by themselves or external factors;
- Attributional style theory dealing with different ways in which people explain events in their lives. This

approach builds upon locus of control, but extends it by stating we also need to consider whether people attribute to stable causes or variable causes, and to global causes or specific causes.

Various scales have been developed to assess both attributional style and locus of control. Locus of control scales include those used by Rotter and later by Duttweiler, the Nowicki and Strickland (1973) Locus of Control Scale for Children and various locus of control scales specifically in the health domain, most famously that of Kenneth Wallston and his colleagues, The Multidimensional Health Locus of Control Scale. Attributional style has been assessed by the Attributional Style Questionnaire, the Expanded Attributional Style Questionnaire, the Attributions Questionnaire, the Real Events Attributional Style Questionnaire and the Attributional Style Assessment Test.

Walter Mischel (1999) has also defended a cognitive approach to personality. His work refers to "Cognitive Affective Units", and considers factors such as encoding of stimuli, affect, goal-setting, and self-regulatory beliefs. The term "Cognitive Affective Units" shows how his approach considers affect as well as cognition.

Personal Construct Psychology (PCP) is a theory of personality developed by the American psychologist George Kelly in the 1950s. From the theory, Kelly derived a psychotherapy approach and also a technique called *The Repertory Grid Interview* that helped his patients to uncover their own "constructs" (defined later) with minimal intervention or interpretation by the therapist. The Repertory Grid was later adapted for various uses within organizations, including decision-making and interpretation of other people's world-views. From his 1963 book, *A Theory of Personality*:

- Fundamental Postulate: A person's processes are psychologically channelized by the ways in which the person anticipates events.
- Construction Corollary: A person anticipates events by construing their replications.
- Individuality Corollary: People differ from one another in their construction of events.

- Organization Corollary: Each person characteristically evolves, for convenience in anticipating events, a construction system embracing ordinal relationships between constructs.
- Dichotomy Corollary: A person's construction system is composed of a finite number of dichotomous constructs.
- Choice Corollary: People choose for themselves the particular alternative in a dichotomized construct through which they anticipate the greater possibility for extension and definition of their system.
- Range Corollary: A construct is convenient for the anticipation of a finite range of events only.
- Experience Corollary: A person's construction system varies as the person successively construes the replication of events.
- Modulation Corollary: The variation in a person's construction system is limited by the permeability of the constructs within whose ranges of conveniences the variants lie.
- Fragmentation Corollary: A person may successively employ a variety of construction subsystems which are inferentially incompatible with each other.
- Commonality Corollary: To the extent that one person employs a construction of experience which is similar to that employed by another, the psychological processes of the two individuals are similar to each other.
- Sociality Corollary: To the extent that one person construes another's construction processes, that person may play a role in a social process involving the other person.

Humanistic Theories

In humanistic psychology it is emphasized people have free will and they play an active role in determining how they behave. Accordingly, humanistic psychology focuses on subjective experiences of persons as opposed to forced, definitive factors that determine behaviour. Abraham Maslow and Carl Rogers were proponents of this view, which is based on the "phenomenal field" theory of Combs and Snygg (1949). Maslow spent much of his time studying what he called "self-actualizing persons", those who are "fulfilling themselves and doing the best they are capable of doing". Maslow believes all who are interested in growth move towards self-actualizing (growth, happiness, satisfaction) views. Many of these people demonstrate a trend in dimensions of their personalities. Characteristics of self-actualizers according to Maslow include the four key dimensions:

1. Awareness-maintaining constant enjoyment and awe of life. These individuals often experienced a "peak experience". He defined a peak experience as an "intensification of any experience to the degree there is a loss or transcendence of self". A peak experience is one in which an individual perceives an expansion of his or herself, and detects a unity and meaningfulness in life. Intense concentration on an activity one is involved in, such as running a marathon, may invoke a peak experience.
2. Reality and problem centered-they have tendency to be concerned with "problems" in their surroundings.
3. Acceptance/Spontaneity-they accept their surroundings and what cannot be changed.
4. Unhostile sense of humour/democratic-they do not like joking about others, which can be viewed as offensive. They have friends of all backgrounds and religions and hold very close friendships.

Maslow and Rogers emphasized a view of the person as an active, creative, experiencing human being who lives in the present and subjectively responds to current perceptions, relationships, and encounters. They disagree with the dark, pessimistic outlook of those in the Freudian psychoanalysis ranks, but rather view humanistic theories as positive and optimistic proposals which stress the tendency of the human personality toward growth and self-actualization. This progressing self will remain the center of its constantly changing world; a world that will help mold the self but not necessarily confine it. Rather, the self has opportunity for maturation based on its encounters with this world. This understanding attempts to reduce the acceptance of hopeless redundancy. Humanistic therapy typically relies on the client for information of the past and its effect on the present, therefore the client dictates the type of guidance the therapist may initiate. This allows for an individualized approach to therapy. Rogers found patients differ in how they respond to other people. Rogers tried to model a particular approach to therapy-he stressed the reflective or empathetic response. This response type takes the client's viewpoint and reflects back his or her feeling and the context for it. An example of a reflective response would be, "It seems you are feeling anxious about your upcoming marriage". This response type seeks to clarify the therapist's understanding while also encouraging the client to think more deeply and seek to fully understand the feelings they have expressed.

Biopsychological Theories

Some of the earliest thinking about possible biological bases of personality grew out of the case of Phineas Gage. In an 1848 accident, a large iron rod was driven through Gage's head, and his personality apparently changed as a result (although descriptions of these psychological changes are usually exaggerated).

In general, patients with brain damage have been difficult to find and study. In the 1990s, researchers began to use Electroencephalography (EEG), Positron Emission Tomography (PET) and more recently functional Magnetic Resonance Imaging (fMRI), which is now the most widely used imaging technique to help localize personality traits in the brain. One of the founders of this area of brain research is Richard Davidson of the University of Wisconsin–Madison. Davidson's research lab has focused on the role of the prefrontal cortex (PFC) and amygdala in manifesting human personality. In particular, this research has looked at hemispheric asymmetry of activity in these regions. Neuropsychological experiments have suggested that hemispheric asymmetry can affect an individual's personality (particularly in social settings) for individuals with NLD (non-verbal learning disorder), which is marked by the impairment of nonverbal information controlled by the right hemisphere of the brain. Progress will arise in the areas of gross motor skills, inability to organize visual-spatial relations, or adapt to novel social situations. Frequently, a person with NLD is unable to interpret non-verbal cues, and therefore experiences difficulty interacting with peers in socially normative ways.

One integrative, biopsychosocial approach to personality and psychopathology, linking brain and environmental factors to specific types of activity, is the hypostatic model of personality, created by Codrin Stefan Tapu.

Personality Tests

There are two major types of personality tests. Projective tests assume personality is primarily unconscious and assess an individual by how he or she responds to an ambiguous stimulus, like an ink blot. The idea is unconscious needs will come out in the person's response, e.g. an aggressive person may see images of destruction. Objective tests assume personality is consciously accessible and measure it by self-report questionnaires. Research on psychological assessment has generally found objective tests are more valid and reliable than projective tests.

Examples of personality tests include:

- Holland Codes
- Personality Assessment Inventory
- Keirsey Temperament Sorter
- Kelly's Repertory Grid
- Minnesota Multiphasic Personality Inventory
- Morrisby Profile
- Myers-Briggs Type Indicator
- NEO PI-R
- ProScan Survey by PDP
- Rorschach test
- Thematic Apperception Test.

Critics have pointed to the Forer effect to suggest some of these appear to be more accurate and discriminating than they really are.

An individual's personality is an aggregate conglomeration of decisions we've made throughout our lives (Bradshaw). There are inherent natural, genetic, and environmental factors that contribute to the development of our personality. According to process of socialization, "personality also colors our values, beliefs, and expectations... Hereditary factors that contribute to personality development do so as a result of interactions with the particular social environment in which people live." There are several personality types as Katharine Cook Briggs and Isabel Briggs Myers illustrated in several personalities typology tests. These tests only provide enlightenment based on the preliminary insight scored according to the answers judged by the parameters of the test. Other theories on personality development are Jean Piaget stages of development, and personality development in Sigmund Freud's theory being formed through the interaction of id, ego, and super-ego. Personality is defined as the enduring personal characteristics of individuals. Although some psychologists frown on the premise, a commonly used explanation for personality development is the psychodynamic approach. The term psychodynamic describes any theory that emphasizes the constant change and development of the individual. Perhaps the best known of the psychodynamic theories is Freudian psychoanalysis.

Freud's Psychoanalytic Theory

Drives

Freud believed that two basic drives—sex and aggression—motivate all our thoughts and behaviours. He referred to these as Eros (love) and Thanatos. Eros represents the life instinct, sex being the major driving force. Thanatos represents the death instinct (characterised by aggression), which, according to Freud, allowed the human race to both procreate and eliminate its enemies.

Structure of Personality

Freud conceived the mind as only having a fixed amount of psychic energy (libido). The outcome of the interaction between the id, ego and the superego, (each contending for as much libidinal energy as possible) determines our adult personality.

Tripartite Personality

Freud believed that personality had three parts—the id, ego, and super-ego—referring to this as the tripartite personality. The id allows us to get our basic needs met. Freud believed that the id is based on the pleasure principle, i.e. it wants immediate satisfaction, with no consideration for the reality of the situation.

As a child interacts more with the world, the ego begins to develop. The ego's job is to meet the needs of the id, whilst taking into account the constraints of reality. The ego acknowledges that being impulsive or selfish can sometimes hurt us, so the id must be constrained. The superego develops during the phallic stage, as a result of the moral constraints placed on us by our parents. It is generally believed that a strong superego serves to inhibits the biological instincts of the id (resulting in a high level of guilt), whereas a weak superego allows the id more expression (resulting in a low level of guilt).

Defence Mechanisms

The ego, having a difficult time trying to satisfy both the needs of the id and the superego, employs defence mechanisms. Repression is perhaps the most powerful of these. Repression is the act by which unacceptable id impulses (most of which are sexually related) are "pushed" out of awareness and into the unconscious mind. Another example of a defence mechanism is projection. This is the mechanism that Freud used to explain Little Hans' complex. Little Hans is said to have projected his fear for his father onto horses, which is why he was afraid of horses.

Psychosexual Stages

Freud believed that at particular points in the child's development, a single part of the body is particularly sensitive to sexual stimulation. These erogenous zones are the mouth, anus and the genital region. At any given time, the child's libido is focused on the primary eurogenous zone for that age. As a result, the child has certain needs and demands that are related to the eurogenous zones for that stage. Frustration occurs if these needs are not met, but, a child may also become overindulged, and so may be reluctant to progress beyond the stage. Both frustration and overindulgence may lead to fixation—some of the child's libido remains locked into that stage. If a child is fixated at a particular stage, the method of obtaining satisfaction that characterised that stage will dominate their adult personality.

Although many people view Freud's descriptions of personality development as pure fantasy, his ideas have endured and have had far reaching influences both in and outside psychology. Freud has changed the way we think about the importance of childhood, and also made us aware of the unconscious elements of our psyche that are essential for development.

Personality Assessment

Personality assessment, the measurement of personal characteristics. Assessment is an end result of gathering information intended to advance psychological theory and research and to increase the probability that wise decisions will be made in applied settings (*e.g.*, in selecting the most promising people from a group of job applicants). The approach taken by the specialist in personality assessment is based on the assumption that much of the observable variability in behaviour from one person to another results from differences in the extent to which individuals possess particular underlying personal characteristics (traits). The assessment specialist seeks to define these traits, to measure them objectively, and to relate them to socially significant aspects of behaviour.

A distinctive feature of the scientific approach to personality measurement is the effort, wherever possible, to describe human characteristics in quantitative terms. How much of a trait manifests itself in an individual? How many traits are present? Quantitative personality measurement is especially useful in comparing groups of people as well as individuals. Do groups of people from different cultural and economic backgrounds differ when considered in the light of their particular personality attributes or traits? How large are the group differences?

Overt behaviour is a reflection of interactions among a wide range of underlying factors, including the bodily state of the individual and the effects of that person's past personal experiences. Hence, a narrowly focused approach is inadequate to do justice to the complex human behaviour that occurs under the constantly changing set of challenges, pleasures, demands, and stresses of everyday life. The sophisticated measurement of human personality inescapably depends on the use of a variety of concepts to provide trait definitions and entails the application of various methods of observation and evaluation. Personality theorists and researchers seek to define and to understand the diversity of human traits, the many ways people have of thinking and perceiving and learning and emoting. Such nonmaterial human dimensions, types, and attributes are constructs—in this case, inferences drawn from observed behaviour. Widely studied personality constructs include anxiety, hostility, emotionality, motivation, and introversion-extroversion. Anxiety, for example, is a concept, or construct, inferred in people from what they say, their facial expressions, and their body movements.

Personality is interactional in two senses. As indicated above, personal characteristics can be thought of as products of interactions among underlying psychological factors; for example, an individual may experience tension because he or she is both shy and desirous of social success. These products, in turn, interact with the types of situations people confront in their daily lives. A person who is anxious about being evaluated might show debilitated performance in evaluative situations (for example, taking tests), but function well in other situations in which an evaluative emphasis is not present. Personality makeup can be either an asset or a liability depending on the situation. For example, some people approach evaluative situations with fear and foreboding, while others seem to be motivated in a desirable direction by competitive pressures associated with performance.

Measuring Constructs

Efforts to measure personality constructs stem from a variety of sources. Frequently they grow out of theories of personality; anxiety and repression (the forgetting of unpleasant experiences), for example, are among the central concepts of the theory of psychoanalysis. It is understandable that efforts would be made to quantify one's degree of anxiety, for example, and to use the score thus obtained in the assessment of and in the prediction of future behaviour. Among the major issues in the study of personality measurement is the question of which of the many personality constructs that have been quantified are basic or fundamental and which can be expected to involve wasted effort in their measurement because they represent poorly defined combinations of more elemental constructs; which measurement techniques are most effective and convenient for the purpose of assessment; and whether it is better to interview people in measuring personality, or to ask them to say, for example, what an inkblot or a cloud in the sky reminds them of.

Efforts to measure any given personality construct can fail as a result of inadequacies in formulating or defining the trait to be measured and weaknesses in the assessment methods employed. An investigator might desire to specify quantitatively the degree to which individuals are submissive in social and competitive situations. His effectiveness will depend on the particular theory of submissiveness he brings to bear on the problem; on the actual procedures he selects or devises to measure submissiveness; and on the adequacy of the research he performs to demonstrate the usefulness of the measure. Each of these tasks must be considered carefully in evaluating efforts to measure personality attributes.

The methods used in personality description and measurement fall into several categories that differ with regard to the type of information gathered and the methods by which it is obtained. While all should rely on data that come from direct observations of human behaviour if they are to have at least the semblance of scientific value, all may vary with regard to underlying assumptions, validity, and reliability (consistency, in this case).

Assessment Methods

Personality tests provide measures of such characteristics as feelings and emotional states, preoccupations, motivations, attitudes, and approaches to interpersonal relations. There is a diversity of approaches to personality assessment, and controversy surrounds many aspects of the widely used methods and techniques. These include such assessments as the interview, rating scales, self-reports, personality inventories, projective techniques, and behavioral observation.

The Interview

In an interview the individual under assessment must be given considerable latitude in "telling his story." Interviews have both verbal and nonverbal (*e.g.*, gestural) components. The aim of the interview is to gather information, and the adequacy of the data gathered depends in large part on the questions asked by the interviewer. In an employment interview the focus of the interviewer is generally on the job candidate's work experiences, general and specific attitudes, and occupational goals. In a diagnostic medical or psychiatric interview considerable attention would be paid to the patient's physical health and to any symptoms of behavioral disorder that may have occurred over the years.

Two broad types of interview may be delineated. In the interview designed for use in research, face-to-face contact between an interviewer and interviewee is directed toward eliciting information that may be relevant to particular practical applications under general study or to those personality theories (or hypotheses) being investigated. Another type, the clinical interview, is focused on assessing the status of a particular individual (*e.g.*, a psychiatric patient); such an interview is action-oriented (*i.e.*, it may indicate appropriate treatment). Both research and clinical interviews frequently may be conducted to obtain an individual's life history and biographical information (*e.g.*, identifying facts, family relationships), but they differ in the uses to which the information is put.

Although it is not feasible to quantify all of the events occurring in an interview, personality researchers have devised ways of categorizing many aspects of the content of what a person has said. In this approach, called content analysis, the particular categories used depend upon the researchers' interests and ingenuity, but the method of content analysis is quite general and involves the construction of a system of categories that, it is hoped, can be used reliably by an analyst or scorer. The categories may be straightforward (*e.g.*, the number of words uttered by the interviewee during designated time periods), or they may rest on inferences (*e.g.*, the degree of personal unhappiness the interviewee appears to express). The value of content analysis is that it provides the possibility of using frequencies of uttered response to describe verbal behaviour and defines behavioral variables for more-or-less precise study in experimental research. Content analysis has been used, for example, to gauge changes in attitude as they occur within a person with the passage of time. Changes in the frequency of hostile reference a neurotic makes toward his parents during a sequence of psychotherapeutic interviews, for example, may be detected and assessed, as may the changing self-evaluations of psychiatric hospital inmates in relation to the length of their hospitalization.

Sources of erroneous conclusions that may be drawn from face-to-face encounters stem from the complexity of the interview situation, the attitudes, fears, and expectations of the interviewee, and the interviewer's manner and training. Research has been conducted to identify, control, and, if possible, eliminate these sources of interview invalidity and unreliability. By conducting more than one interview with the same interviewee and by using more than one interviewer to evaluate the subject's behaviour, light can be shed on the reliability of the information derived and may reveal differences in influence among individual interviewers. Standardization of interview format tends to increase the reliability of the information gathered; for example, all interviewers may use the same set of questions. Such standardization, however, may restrict the scope of information elicited, and even a perfectly reliable (consistent) interview technique can lead to incorrect inferences.

Rating Scales

The rating scale is one of the oldest and most versatile of assessment techniques. Rating scales present users with an item and ask them to select from a number of choices. The rating scale is similar in some respects to a multiple choice test, but its options represent degrees of a particular characteristic.

Rating scales are used by observers and also by individuals for self-reporting. They permit convenient characterization of other people and their behaviour. Some observations do not lend themselves to quantification as readily as do simple counts of motor behaviour (such as the number of times a worker leaves his lathe to go to the restroom). It is difficult, for example, to quantify how charming an office receptionist is. In such cases, one may fall back on relatively subjective judgments, inferences, and relatively imprecise estimates, as in deciding how disrespectful a child is. The rating scale is one approach to securing such judgments. Rating scales present an observer with scalar dimensions along which those who are observed are to be placed. A teacher, for example, might be asked to rate students on the degree to which the behaviour of each reflects leadership capacity, shyness, or creativity. Peers might rate each other along dimensions such as friendliness, trustworthiness, and social skills. Several standardized, printed rating scales are available for describing the behaviour of psychiatric hospital patients. Relatively objective rating scales have also been devised for use with other groups.

A number of requirements should be met to maximize the usefulness of rating scales. One is that they be reliable: the ratings of the same person by different observers should be consistent. Other requirements are reduction of sources of inaccuracy in personality measurement; the so-called halo effect results in an observer's rating someone favourably on a specific characteristic because the observer has a generally favourable reaction to the person being rated. One's tendency to say only nice things about others or one's proneness to think of all people as average (to use the midrange of scales) represents other methodological problems that arise when rating scales are used.

Self-report Tests

The success that attended the use of convenient intelligence tests in providing reliable, quantitative (numerical) indexes of individual ability has stimulated interest in the possibility of devising similar tests for measuring personality. Procedures now available vary in the degree to which they achieve score reliability and convenience. These desirable attributes can be partly achieved by restricting in designated ways the kinds of responses a subject is free to make. Self-report instruments follow this strategy. For example, a test that restricts the subject to true-false answers is likely to be convenient to give and easy to score. So-called personality inventories tend to have these characteristics, in that they are relatively restrictive, can be scored objectively, and are convenient to administer. Other techniques (such as inkblot tests) for evaluating personality possess these characteristics to a lesser degree.

Self-report personality tests are used in clinical settings in making diagnoses, in deciding whether treatment is required, and in planning the treatment to be used. A second major use is as an aid in selecting employees, and a third is in psychological research. An example of the latter case would be where scores on a measure of test anxiety—that is, the feeling of tenseness and worry that people experience before an exam—might be used to divide people into groups according to how upset they get while taking exams. Researchers have investigated whether the more test-anxious students behave differently than the less anxious ones in an experimental situation.

Personality Inventories

Among the most common of self-report tests are personality inventories. Their origins lie in the early history of personality measurement, when most tests were constructed on the basis of so-called face validity; that is, they simply appeared to be valid. Items were included simply because, in the fallible judgment of the person who constructed or devised the test, they were indicative of certain personality attributes. In other words, face validity need not be defined by careful, quantitative study; rather, it typically reflects one's more-or-less imprecise, possibly erroneous, impressions. Personal judgment, even that of an expert, is no guarantee that a particular collection of test items will prove to be reliable and meaningful in actual practice.

A widely used early self-report inventory, the so-called Woodworth Personal Data Sheet, was developed during World War I to detect soldiers who were emotionally unfit for combat. Among its ostensibly face-valid items were these: Does the sight of blood make you sick or dizzy? Are you happy most of the time? Do you sometimes wish you had never been born? Recruits who answered these kinds of questions in a way that could be taken to mean that they suffered psychiatric disturbance were detained for further questioning and evaluation. Clearly, however, symptoms revealed by such answers are exhibited by many people who are relatively free of emotional disorder.

Rather than testing general knowledge or specific skills, personality inventories ask people questions about themselves. These questions may take a variety of forms. When taking such a test, the subject might have to decide whether each of a series of statements is accurate as a self-description or respond to a series of true-false questions about personal beliefs.

Several inventories require that each of a series of statements be placed on a rating scale in terms of the frequency or adequacy with which the statements are judged by the individual to reflect his tendencies and attitudes. Regardless of the way in which the subject responds, most inventories yield several scores, each intended to identify a distinctive aspect of personality.

One of these, the Minnesota Multiphasic Personality Inventory (MMPI), is probably the personality inventory in widest use in the English-speaking world. Also available in other languages, it consists in one version of 550 items (*e.g.*, "I like tall women") to which subjects are to respond "true," "false," or "cannot say." Work on this inventory began in the 1930s, when its construction was motivated by the need for a practical, economical means of describing and predicting the behaviour of psychiatric patients. In its development efforts were made to achieve convenience in administration and scoring and to overcome many of the known defects of earlier personality inventories. Varied types of items were included and emphasis was placed on making these printed statements (presented either on small cards or in a booklet) intelligible even to persons with limited reading ability.

Most earlier inventories lacked subtlety; many people were able to fake or bias their answers since the items presented were easily seen to reflect gross disturbances; indeed, in many of these inventories maladaptive tendencies would be reflected in either all true or all false answers. Perhaps the most significant methodological advance to be found in the MMPI was the attempt on the part of its developers to measure tendencies to respond, rather than actual behaviour, and to rely but little on assumptions of face validity. The true-false item "I hear strange voices all the time" has face validity for most people in that to answer "true" to it seems to provide a strong indication of abnormal hallucinatory experiences. But some psychiatric patients who "hear strange voices" can still appreciate the socially undesirable implications of a "true" answer and may therefore try to conceal their abnormality by answering "false." A major difficulty in placing great reliance on face validity in test construction is that the subject may be as aware of the significance of certain responses as is the test constructor and thus may be able to mislead the tester. Nevertheless, the person who hears strange voices and yet answers the item "false" clearly is responding to something—the answer still is a reflection of personality, even though it may not be the aspect of personality to which the item seems to refer; thus, careful study of responses beyond their mere face validity often proves to be profitable.

Much study has been given to the ways in which response sets and test-taking attitudes influence behaviour on the MMPI and other personality measures. The response set called acquiescence, for example, refers to one's tendency to respond with "true" or "yes" answers to questionnaire items regardless of what the item content is. It is conceivable that two people might be quite similar in all respects except for their tendency toward acquiescence. This difference in response set can lead to misleadingly different scores on personality tests. One person might be a "yea-sayer" (someone who tends to answer true to test items); another might be a "nay-sayer"; a third individual might not have a pronounced acquiescence tendency in either direction.

Acquiescence is not the only response set; there are other test-taking attitudes that are capable of influencing personality profiles. One of these, already suggested by the example of the person who hears strange voices, is social desirability. A person who has convulsions might say "false" to the item "I have convulsions" because he believes that others will think less of him if they know he has convulsions. The intrusive potentially deceiving effects of the subjects' response sets and test-taking attitudes on scores derived from personality measures can sometimes be circumvented by varying the content and wording of test items. Nevertheless, users of questionnaires have not yet completely solved problems of bias such as those arising from response sets. Indeed, many of these problems first received widespread attention in research on the MMPI, and research on this and similar inventories has significantly advanced understanding of the whole discipline of personality testing.

Attributes of the MMPI

The MMPI as originally published consists of nine clinical scales (or sets of items), each scale having been found in practice to discriminate a particular clinical group, such as people suffering from schizophrenia, depression, or paranoia. Each of these scales (or others produced later) was developed by determining patterns of response to the inventory that were observed to be distinctive of groups of individuals who had been psychiatrically classified by other means (*e.g.*, by long-term observation). The responses of apparently normal subjects were compared with those of hospital patients with a particular psychiatric diagnosis—for example, with symptoms of schizophrenia. Items to which the greatest percentage of "normals" gave answers that differed from those more typically given by patients came to constitute each clinical scale.

In addition to the nine clinical scales and many specially developed scales, there are four so-called control scales on the inventory. One of these is simply the number of items placed by the subject in the "cannot say" category. The L (or lie) scale was devised to measure the tendency of the test taker to attribute socially desirable attributes to himself. In response to "I get angry sometimes" he should tend to mark false; extreme L scorers in the other direction appear to be too good, too virtuous. Another so-called F scale was included to provide a reflection of the subjects' carelessness and confusion in taking the inventory (*e.g.*, "Everything tastes the same" tends to be answered true by careless or confused people). More subtle than either the L or F scales is what is called the K scale. Its construction was based on the observation that some persons tend to exaggerate their symptoms because of excessive openness and frankness and may obtain high scores on the clinical scales; others may exhibit unusually low scores because of defensiveness. On the K-scale item "I think nearly anyone would tell a lie to keep out of trouble," the defensive person is apt to answer false, giving the same response to "I certainly feel useless at times." The K scale was designed to reduce these biasing factors; by weighting clinical-scale scores with K scores, the distorting effect of test-taking defensiveness may be reduced.

In general, it has been found that the greater the number and magnitude of one's unusually high scores on the MMPI, the more likely it is that one is in need of psychiatric attention. Most professionals who use the device refuse to make assumptions about the factualness of the subject's answers and about his personal interpretations of the meanings of the items. Their approach does not depend heavily on theoretical predilections and hypotheses. For this reason the inventory has proved particularly popular with those who have strong doubts about the eventual validity that many theoretical formulations will show in connection with personality measurement after they have been tested through painstaking research. The MMPI also appeals to those who demand firm experimental evidence that any personality assessment method can make valid discriminations among individuals.

In recent years there has been growing interest in actuarial personality description—that is, in personality description based on traits shared in common by groups of people. Actuarial description studies yield rules by which persons may be classified according to their personal attributes as revealed by their behaviour (on tests, for example). Computer programs are now available for diagnosing such disorders as hysteria, schizophrenia, and paranoia on the basis of typical group profiles of MMPI responses. Computerized methods for integrating large amounts of personal data are not limited to this inventory and are applicable to other inventories, personality tests (*e.g.*, inkblots), and life-history information. Computerized classification of MMPI profiles, however, has been explored most intensively.

Comparison of the MMPI and CPI

The MMPI has been considered in some detail here because of its wide usage and because it illustrates a number of important problems confronting those who attempt to assess personality characteristics. Many other omnibus personality inventories are also used in applied settings and in research. The California Psychological Inventory (CPI), for example, is keyed for several personality variables that include sociability, self-control, flexibility, and tolerance. Unlike the MMPI, it was developed specifically for use with "normal" groups of people. Whereas the judgments of experts (usually psychiatric workers) were used in categorizing subjects given the MMPI during the early item-writing phase of its development, nominations by peers (such as respondents or friends) of the subjects were relied upon in work with the CPI. Its technical development has been evaluated by test authorities to be of high order, in part because its developers profited from lessons learned in the construction and use of the MMPI. It also provides measures of response sets and has been subjected to considerable research study.

From time to time, most personality inventories are revised for a variety of reasons, including the need to take account of cultural and social changes and to improve them. For example, a revision of the CPI was published in 1987. In the revision, the inventory itself was modified to improve clarity, update content, and delete items that might be objectionable to some respondents. Because the item pool remained largely unchanged, data from the original samples were used in computing norms and in evaluating reliability and validity for new scales and new composite scores. The descriptions of high and low scorers on each scale have been refined and sharpened, and correlations of scale scores with other personality tests have been reported.

Other Self-report Techniques

Beyond personality inventories, there are other self-report approaches to personality measurement available for research and applied purposes. Mention was made earlier of the use of rating scales. The rating-scale technique permits quantification of an individual's reactions to himself, to others, and, in fact, to any object or concept in terms of a standard set of semantic (word) polarities such as "hot-cold" or "good-bad." It is a general method for assessing the meanings of these semantic concepts to individuals.

Another method of self-report called the Q-sort is devised for problems similar to those for which rating scales are used. In a Q-sort a person is given a set of sentences, phrases, or words (usually presented individually on cards) and is asked to use them to describe himself (as he thinks he is or as he would like to be) or someone else. This description is carried out by having the subject sort the items on the cards in terms of their degree of relevance so that they can be distributed along what amounts to a rating scale. Examples of descriptive items that might be included in a Q-sort are "worries a lot," "works hard," and "is cheerful."

Typical paper-and-pencil instruments such as personality inventories involve verbal stimuli (words) intended to call forth designated types of responses from the individual. There are clearly stated ground rules under which he makes his responses. Paper-and-pencil devices are relatively easy and economical to administer and can be scored accurately and reliably by relatively inexperienced clerical workers. They are generally regarded by professional personality evaluators as especially valuable assessment tools in screening large numbers of people, as in military or industrial personnel selection. Assessment specialists do not assume that self-reports are accurate indicators of personality traits. They are accepted, rather, as samples of behaviour for which validity in predicting one's everyday activities or traits must be established empirically (*i.e.*, by direct observation or experiment). Paper-and-pencil techniques have moved from their early stage of assumed (face) validity to more advanced notions in which improvements in conceptualization and methodology are clearly recognized as basic to the determination of empirical validity.

Projective Techniques

One group of assessment specialists believes that the more freedom people have in picking their responses, the more meaningful the description and classification that can be obtained. Because personality inventories do not permit much freedom of choice, some researchers and clinicians prefer to use projective techniques, in which a person is shown ambiguous stimuli (such as shapes or pictures) and asked to interpret them in some way. (Such stimuli allow relative freedom in projecting one's own interests and feelings into them, reacting in any way that seems appropriate.) Projective techniques are believed to be sensitive to unconscious dimensions of personality.

Defence mechanisms, latent impulses, and anxieties have all been inferred from data gathered in projective situations. Personality inventories and projective techniques do have some elements in common; inkblots, for example, are ambiguous, but so also are many of the statements on inventories such as the MMPI. These techniques differ in that the subject is given substantially free rein in responding to projective stimuli rather than merely answering true or false, for example. Another similarity between projective and questionnaire or inventory approaches is that all involve the use of relatively standardized testing situations.

While projective techniques are often lumped together as one general methodology, in actual practice there are several approaches to assessment from a projective point of view. Although projective techniques share the common characteristic that they permit the subject wide latitude in responding, they still may be distinguished broadly as follows: (1) associative techniques, in which the subject is asked to react to words, to inkblots, or to other stimuli with the first associated thoughts that come to mind; (2) construction techniques, in which the subject is asked to create something—for example, make up a story or draw a self-portrait; (3) completion techniques, in which the subject is asked to finish a partially developed stimulus, such as adding the last words to an incomplete sentence; (4) choice or ordering techniques, in which the subject is asked to choose from among or to give some orderly sequence to stimuli—for example, to choose from or arrange a set of pictures or inkblots; (5) expressive techniques, in which the subject is asked to use free expression in some manner, such as in finger painting.

Hidden personality defence mechanisms, latent emotional impulses, and inner anxieties all have been attributed to test takers by making theoretical inferences from data gathered as they responded in projective situations. While projective stimuli are ambiguous, they are usually administered under fairly standardized conditions. Quantitative (numerical) measures can be derived from subjects' responses to them. These include the number of responses one makes to a series of inkblots and the number of responses to the blots in which the subject perceives what seem to him to be moving animals.

11

Age: Differences and Changes

What is the nature of age-related changes in intelligence? Most of the literature has focused on changes in mean levels of different types of ability across the adult life span. A broad inference, supported by both cross-sectional and longitudinal evidence, is that abilities differ in patterns of mean change during adulthood. Reasoning, spatial ability, perceptual speed, verbal fluency, and episodic memory decline during adulthood, whereas word knowledge, verbal comprehension, and other aspects of specific knowledge show relative maintenance or improvement until after age 60. This generalization is widely accepted, although scientists still differ on issues such as the magnitude and age of onset of intellectual decline or the importance of cohort effects in biasing estimates of age changes in cross-sectional data. In terms of current hierarchical theories of the structure of intelligence, the available data suggest that there are age changes in multiple second-order abilities, including especially fluid intelligence, spatial visualization, and general information processing speed.

One of the earliest arguments concerning age changes in psychometric intelligence was that age changes in the speed of behaviour limited intelligence test performance of older adults. According to this perspective, speed of processing acts as a confounded methodological factor that inflates estimated age differences in test performance. Essentially, this hypothesis states that speed relations to intellectual abilities are performance-specific rather than construct-relevant (Hertzog, 1989). That is, the relationship of processing speed to test performance produces systematic measurement errors that inflate age differences and reduce the construct validity of the test, perhaps differentially so for older adults. Hertzog (1989) found that the Primary Mental Abilities (PMA) Verbal Meaning test yielded larger age differences than other vocabulary tests and that these differences between tests were eliminated when partialling for processing speed. This pattern was interpreted as a performance-specific speed effect on the test that was independent of age differences in verbal ability, conceptualized as the amount of accessible knowledge about word meanings in the lexicon.

Alternatively, age-related changes in the speed of information processing may affect ability constructs because of the importance of speed of execution of cognitive mechanisms for successful higher-level cognitive functioning. Birren (1965) and Birren, Woods, and Williams (1980) originally argued that age-related changes in information processing speed were ubiquitous in the central nervous system and potentially affected all aspects of cognition, including intelligence. More recently, Salthouse (1991, 1996) advanced the theory that age changes in information processing speed, as reflected by psychometric tests of the Perceptual Speed factor, mediates much of the age-related decline in working memory, fluid intelligence, spatial visualization, and episodic memory. A large number of cross-sectional studies provide evidence that has been taken as support of this argument. Certainly, much of the age-related variance in various types of psychometric intelligence is shared with perceptual speed, although the theoretical interpretation of this empirical phenomenon is actually somewhat controversial. Verhaeghen and Salthouse (1997) suggested that age-related slowing in processing rate may be, at minimum, an excellent index of a common factor of rates of cognitive aging that applies to many aspects of cognition.

On the other hand, some studies do not suggest a strong shared relationship between processing speed and the observed age differences in cognitive performance. Such findings increase the likelihood that virtual elimination of age differences in cognition by statistical control of processing speed, when observed, is influenced by the nature of the measures, sampling design, and measurement conditions. Such findings may favor the performance-specific view of speed/cognition relations.

Moreover, the limited longitudinal evidence now available does not demonstrate that individual differences in age-related changes in processing speed strongly relate to changes in memory and other intellectual abilities.

Age-related changes in speed of information processing may also affect the factor structure of intelligence for older adults. The question is: are there age changes in the structure of intelligence, and if so, are these changes due to influences of age-related slowing in information processing? There has been scattered evidence for age changes in the structure of intelligence, although much of the early research is equivocal given the use of exploratory factor analysis and problematic criteria for age comparisons of factor solutions. Adult age changes in factor structure are predicted by the dedifferentiation hypothesis, which states that aging will increase the correlations of ability factors and increase the communalities of primary ability factors on a higher-order intelligence factor. A strong form of the dedifferentiation hypothesis states that aging will tend to collapse the dimensionality of the factor space, reducing the number of distinct primary ability factors. Such effects would have profound theoretical and methodological significance. The developmental interpretation of well-established findings of age changes in level of intelligence test performance would be complicated if there were qualitative changes in the structure of intelligence factors in late life.

Optimal assessment of cross-sectional age differences in intellectual factor structure requires use of confirmatory factor analysis, in which a hypothesized factor structure is simultaneously fit to data from multiple age groups. Confirmatory factor analysis can identify multiple kinds of age differences in factor structure. Possible types include (a) age changes in number and/or definition of ability factors; (b) age differences in the metric factor loadings regressing individual tests on ability factors; (c) age differences in the magnitude of factor correlations; and (d) age differences in communalities (variance in tests determined by common factors).

Over the last two decades, a number of confirmatory factor analytic studies of cross-sectional ability data has been conducted. The evidence is mixed, but virtually all studies indicate configural invariance of intellectual factor structure. That is, the same primary and secondary ability factors can be found in different age groups. Moreover, the magnitude of the metric factor loadings (unstandardized regressions of variables on factors) have been found in some cases to be invariant across adult age groups. Such findings are consistent with Meredith's (1964, 1991) argument that selection into groups differing in mean levels of ability factors and tests, by itself, will not change the factors or their metric factors loadings, although group mean differences can affect factor variances, error variances, and factor covariances. A weak form of the dedifferentiation hypothesis — higher factor correlations in older groups — has been supported in multiple studies. However, some studies have even suggested age-related invariance in the covariance structure of ability factors.

The distinction between configural and metric invariance is to a degree arbitrary unless variables being factored are developed with the a priori goal of conforming to factorial simple structure, i.e., when variables are congeneric and measure one and only one latent variable. It may be unreasonable to expect age-related metric invariance for Verbal and Performance factors for the WAIS-R, for example, because the WAIS subtests were not designed with factorial purity or homogeneity in mind.

Under such conditions, age differences in the covariances of underlying abilities might be absorbed into covariances of factorially complex subtests, leading to age differences in factor loadings when tests are factored. Thus, tests of age-related factorial invariance are probably best conducted with test batteries designed a priori to conform to simple structure at the first-order or primary ability level. However, configural but not metric invariance across age groups has been found even when variables were selected in advance to conform to a simple structure configuration (e.g., Schaie et al., 1998).

The possible role of age changes in speed of information processing in any observed age differences in ability factor structure is supported by outcomes from multiple studies. First, there appear to be at least some age differences in the correlations of speeded ability factors themselves. Babcock,

Laguna, and Roesch (1997) found that three narrowly defined speed factors (which they labeled Motor Speed, Alphanumeric Speed, and Geometric Speed) were more highly intercorrelated in an older adult sample than in a young adult sample. Two studies have found age differences in second-order factor loadings of Perceptual Speed (measured by tests such as WAIS-R Digit Symbol Substitution), Semantic Information Processing Speed (measured by RT tasks such as Category Verification), and Choice RT on a second-order general speed factor. Older adults showed higher correlations of between speeded tasks involving cognitive evaluation of stimulus attributes than did younger adults. However, this pattern has not been universally found (Tomer & Cunningham, 1993).

Second, dedifferentiation of factor correlations in older adults often is manifested most prominently in correlations involving information processing speed factors. Schaie et al. (1998) found that multiple age/cohort groups from a sequential sample had significant differences in factor correlations and showed significant changes in factor correlations over a 7-year period. Several of the prominent developmental changes involved speeded ability tests or factors.

For example, the factor correlation of Spatial Orientation with Perceptual Speed was.36 in the youngest age group but increased to.69 in the oldest age group. Over the 7-year interval, the oldest age group showed further longitudinal dedifferentiation; the two factors correlated.78 at the second occasion of measurement. To be sure, not all speeded ability factor correlations in the Seattle Longitudinal Study battery showed major increases with age. For example, the correlations of Induction with Perceptual Speed were high throughout the life span.

Hultsch et al. (1998) produced similar results. They divided their sample into young-old and old-old groups. The groups differed in factor correlations, with higher factor correlations in the older group. Two speeded latent factors, Semantic Speed and Comprehension Speed, showed a significant longitudinal increase in correlation with each other over the 6-year interval, and both speeded factors increased in correlation with latent variables of working memory and episodic memory. These latter longitudinal increases were also reflected in the cross-sectional age group correlations. Comprehension Speed correlated about-.5 with the memory-related latent variables in the young-old group but about-.7 with the same variables in the old-old group.

Third, the performance-specific speed effects on PMA Verbal Meaning observed by Hertzog (1989) are consistent with other factor analytic evidence from the Seattle Longitudinal Study that this test loads on both a Verbal Ability factor and a Perceptual Speed factor.

Thus, in at least some cases, a lack of simple structure for speeded tests, when factored in the presence of relevant measures of information processing speed, may indicate performance-specific speed contamination.

Early Adulthood

— ages 20-40y

— peak of physical health & fitness (occurs on average at approximately age 30)

— height of cognitive abilities

— healthy, vigorous, energetic.

Physical Development

— in 20's

— may still gain height

— gain in muscle, fat

— brain still increasing in size & weight (although no new neurons are being formed)

— senses optimal.

Cognitive Development

— Piagetan view: adult thinking quantitatively different

— incr. knowledge, skills

— no qualitative change after adolescence

— new view: adult think qualitatively different

— post-formal stage i/subjective, ii/pragmatic, iii/ relativistic.

Subjectivity (Giesela Labouvie-Vief)

— thinking is based on personal experience and perceptions

— adults learn to confront society's paradoxes

— objectivity can limit understanding (need to know what others think and feel and respond to that)

— subjective thinking may be especially adaptive for this purpose (allows one to make decisions that others will accept

— various possibilities in real life situation (more than one "right" solution)

— the solution does not always require logic (formal operations)

— adult predicaments must sometimes be solved by recognizing subjective world

— (pragmatism, relativity).

Pragmatism (K. Warner Shaie)

— Shaie's theory of adult cognition is a stage theory

— adults maintain style of formal-operational stage (logic)

— according to him, Piaget's stages described a period of acquisition

— acquire basic skills/abilities required for adulthood

— adults, on the other hand, must move beyond acquisition

— enter the achieving stage

— make use of skills previously obtained to *achieve* goals (career goals, domestic goals)

— to do so, they must consider contexts, consequences before decisions

— (therefore similar to concept of relativity)

— based upon personal needs/desires (therefore associated with concept of subjectivity).

Relativity (Perry)

— adolescent cognition is noted for its basic dualism

— something is either true or false, right or wrong

— adult experience, on the other hand, leads to reflection which, in turn, leads to contextual relativism
— "truth" often depends on context
— not absolute
— why is adult thinking like this?
— must respond to real world demands?
— but: research is based on university students (comprise most research subjects)
— recent research suggests that these findings may be an artifact of university demands
— thus, this type of thinking would be less common in "real world".

Psychosocial Development

Continuity From Childhood;

— adult personality has fewer extremes and a narrower range of expression
— longitudinal studies, i/if child has easy temperament from 3-5 yrs
— become well-adjusted adults
— if child has difficult temperament, more likely to lead to adjustment problems in adulthood
— ii/boys with difficult temperament
— less likely to continue education
— if girls, increased marital conflict in adulthood
— iii/for inhibited children
— in adulthood, likely to be less assertive, have less social support, longer delay in career development
— iv/poor emotional self control as child
— problem with self control as adults.

Summary:

— some continuity, but variable
— many exceptions
— due to intervening variables?.

Relationships

a) Introduction;

— Erikson: stage of intimacy vs. isolation

— after identity resolved

— crisis if no intimacy

— but intimacy could mean loss of identity

— recent view is that identity and intimacy both sought

— often inseperable

— i/identity seen in terms of intimacy

— ii/identity adjusted for new relationship.

b) Attachment;

— for non-clinical populations,

— 50-60% securely attached

— likely to have successful relationships

— self-aware, realistic

— likely to have had secure attachment as children

— 25-30% insecure-dismissing

— unsuccessful relationships

— focus on negative experiences

— unwilling to discuss relationships

— likely to be insecure as children

— 15% insecure preoccupied

— unsuccessful

— focus on relationships, willing to discuss

— disorganized, inconsistent

— likely insecure childhood

— note: 1994 study — 30% change attachment styles during young adulthood.

c) Friendships;

— gender differences:

— in *general*

— females: emotional sharing of confidences
— males: shared activities, interests
— if discuss same topics
— females in greater depth
— more self-revealing
— confide less about strengths, victories, achievements
— why?
— control theory
— females:
— less desire for control, more willing to show dependency, vulnerability
— males:
— must protect against loss of control
— implications for health behaviour/care
— cross-gender friendships
— females: little difference
— males: more self-disclosure, dependency, emotional involvement
— females: consider interactions with friends as less than relationship with partner
— males: difference not as great
— more likely to see female friends potential partners.

d) Close Relationships;

1. changes over time;

i/delay before marriage;

— 1950's, average age of marrying 20/23 y for females/ males
— (lowest since recorded)
— 1995: 24/26 y.

ii/increased number of relationships;

— but still monogamous during each one
— 90% still marry.

2. relationship maturity (Kathleen White);

i/self-focused level;

— earliest level (adolescence)

— perspective of other concerned with effect on self

— little intimate communication

— little awareness of needs of other.

ii/role-focused level;

— more perception of others as individual

— aware of expected behaviour (but often stereotyped)

iii/individuated-connected level;

— adult level

— deeper understanding of other's needs, motivations

— able to anticipate

— able to provide emotional support.

Health in Early Adulthood

— generally, good health

— but: problem behaviours

— often, same as adolescence

— cumulative: after many years, problems develop

— 3 areas:

1/sexual activity;

— almost 90% of STD occur before age of 30 yrs

— up to 50% of pregnancies unintended

— half due to contraceptive failure.

2/eating & nutrition;

— basal metabolism declines from puberty

— adolescence: still very active

— young adults, less so

— increased weight gain

— from ages 20-50 y.: body fat doubles for males

— 50% increase for females

— often end up in diet-binging cycles.

3/substance abuse;

— more than 40% college students report bouts of heavy drinking
— by mid 20's, usually reduce
— if not, can lead to health problems, addiction
— addiction
— pattern of behaviour: overwhelming involvement with using a drug and securing its supply
— disease model of addiction
— addiction of drug due to inherent reinforcing properties of particular drugs
— quickly lead to withdrawal upon abstinance
— some people more susceptible due to biology, genetics, etc.
— life-process model of addiction
— addiction *not* a disease
— habitual response
— source of gratification or security understood only in the context of personal and social experience.

In early adulthood, an individual is concerned with developing the ability to share intimacy, seeking to form relationships and find intimate love. Long-term relationships are formed, and often marriage and children result. The young adult is also faced with career decisions.

- Choices concerning marriage and family are often made during this period. Research shows that divorce is more likely among people who marry during adolescence, those whose parents were divorced, and those who are dissimilar in age, intelligence, personality, or attractiveness. Separation is also more frequent among those who do not have children. Most people who have divorced remarry; consequently, children may experience more than one set of parents.
- Such alternatives to marriage as "living together" (cohabitation) have become more common. In 1997, the Census Bureau estimated that 4.13 million unwed couples lived in the United States.

- Work/career choice affects not only socioeconomic status but also friends, political values, residence location, child care, job stress, and many other aspects of life. And while income is important in both career selection and career longevity, so are achievement, recognition, satisfaction, security, and challenge. In the modern cultures of many nations, the careers of both spouses or partners frequently must be considered in making job choices.

Middle adulthood. In middle adulthood, an important challenge is to develop a genuine concern for the welfare of future generations and to contribute to the world through family and work. Erik Erikson refers to the problem posed at this stage as generativity vs. self-absorption.

Robert Havighurst lists seven major tasks in the middle years.

- accepting and adjusting to physiological changes, such as menopause
- reaching and maintaining satisfaction in one's occupation
- adjusting to and possibly caring for aging parents
- helping teenage children to become responsible adults
- achieving adult social and civic responsibility
- relating to one's spouse as a person
- developing leisure-time activities.

While a midlife crisis is not regarded as a universal phenomenon, during one's 40s and 50s comes the recognition that more than half of one's life is gone. That recognition may prompt some to feel that the clock is ticking and that they must make sudden, drastic changes in order to achieve their goals, while others focus on finding satisfaction with the present course of their lives.

Health

Young adults are generally in good health, subject neither to disease nor the problems of senescence. Biological function and physical performance reach their peak from 20–35 years of age, waning after 35. Strength peaks around 25 years of age, plateaus through 35 or 40 years of age, and then declines. Flexibility also decreases with age throughout adulthood. However, there are large individual differences and a fit 40-year-old may outcompete a sedentary 20-year-old.

Women reach their peak fertility in their early 20s. Assuming unprotected intercourse with a man of the same age, women aged 19–26 have about a 50% chance of becoming pregnant during a given menstrual cycle, compared with 40% in the 27-34 age group and below 30% for women 35-39.

In developed countries, mortality rates for the 18-40 age group are typically very low. Men are more likely to die at this age than women, particularly in the 18-25 group: reasons include car accidents and suicide. Mortality statistics among men and women level off during the late twenties and thirties, due in part to good health and less risk-taking behaviour.

Regarding disease, cancer is much less common in young than in older adults. Exceptions are testicular cancer, cervical cancer, and Hodgkin's lymphoma. In sub-Saharan Africa, HIV/AIDS has hit the early adult population particularly hard. According to a United Nations report, AIDS has significantly increased mortality of between ages 20 to 55 for African males and 20 to 45 for African females, reducing the life expectancy in South Africa by 18 years and in Botswana by 34 years.

Early Adulthood

According to Erikson, the young adult stage involves the personal need for intimacy and sex. Failure to achieve this need results in isolation, which is avoided, and as a result the young adult strives for love and compassion. The young adult learns that love and compassion may get him what he wants.

In modern societies, young adults in their late teens and early 20s encounter a number of issues as they finish school and begin to hold full-time jobs and take on other responsibilities of adulthood.

Settling Down

After the upheaval of the early 30s, the middle to late 30s (roughly ages 34–39) are often characterized by settling down.

People in their 30s may increase the financial and emotional investments they make in their lives. Many have been employed long enough to gain promotions and raises. They often become more focused on advancing their careers and gaining stability in their personal lives. They may have started a family.

Middle Age

Middle age is the period of age beyond young adulthood but before the onset of old age. Various attempts have been made to define this age, which is around the third quarter of the average life span of human beings.

According to Collins Dictionary, this is "... *usually considered to occur approximately between the ages of 40 and 60*".

The Oxford English Dictionary gives a similar definition but with a later start point "... *the period between youth and old age, about 45 to 60*".

The US Census lists middle age as including both the age categories 35 to 44 and 45 to 54, while prominent social scientist, Erik Erikson, sees it ending a little later and defines middle adulthood as between 40 and 65.

Health

Middle-aged adults often show visible signs of aging such as loss of skin elasticity and graying of the hair. Physical fitness usually wanes, with a 5–10 kg (10-20 lb) accumulation of body fat, reduction in aerobic performance and a decrease in maximal heart rate. Strength and flexibility also decrease throughout middle age. However, people age at different rates and there can be significant differences between individuals of the same age.

Both male and female fertility declines with advancing age. Advanced maternal age increases the risk of a child being born with some disorders such as Down syndrome. Advanced paternal age sharply increases the risk of miscarriage and many birth defects, including Down syndrome, schizophrenia, autism, decreased intellectual capacity, and bipolar disorder. Most women go through menopause, which ends natural fertility, in their late 40s or 50s. Cannon, Mary (2003-06-26). "Male Biological Clock is Ticking, Too". *WebMD Health News*.

In developed countries, yearly mortality begins to increase more noticeably from age 40 onwards, mainly due to age-related health problems such as heart disease and cancer. However, the majority of middle-age people in industrialized nations can expect to live into old age. Life expectancy in developing countries is much lower and the risk of death at all ages is higher.

Midlife Crisis

Midlife crisis is a term coined in 1965 by Elliott Jaques and used in Western societies to describe a period of dramatic self-doubt that is felt by some individuals in the "middle years" or middle age of life, as a result of sensing the passing of their own youth and the imminence of their old age. Sometimes, a crisis can be triggered by transitions experienced in these years, such as extramarital affairs, andropause or menopause, the death of parents or other causes of grief, unemployment or underemployment, realizing that a job or career is hated but not knowing how else to earn an equivalent living, or children leaving home. The result may be a desire to make significant changes in core aspects of day-to-day life or situation, such as in career, work-life balance, marriage, romantic relationships, big-ticket expenditures, or physical appearance.

Academic research since the 1980s rejects the notion of midlife crisis as a phase that most adults go through. In one study, fewer than 10% of people in the United States had psychological crises due to their age or aging. Personality type and a history of psychological crisis are believed to predispose some people to this "traditional" midlife crisis. People going through this suffer a variety of symptoms and exhibit a disparate range of behaviours.

Many middle aged adults experience major life events that can cause a period of psychological stress or depression, such as the death of a loved one, or a career setback. However, those events could have happened earlier or later in life, making them a "crisis," but not necessarily a midlife one. In the same study, 15% of middle-aged adults experienced this type of midlife turmoil. Some studies indicate that some cultures may be more sensitive to this phenomenon than others, one study found that there is little evidence that people undergo midlife crises in

Japanese and Indian cultures, raising the question of whether a midlife crises is mainly a cultural construct. The authors hypothesized that the "culture of youth" in Western societies accounts for the popularity of the midlife crisis concept there.

Occurrence

For the approximately 10% of middle aged adults who go through an age-related midlife crisis, the condition is most common ranging from the ages of 40-60 (a large study in the 1990s found that the average age at onset of a self-described midlife crisis was 46). Midlife crises last about 3–10 years in men and 2–5 years in women.

A midlife crisis could be caused by aging itself, or aging in combination with changes, problems, or regrets over:

- work or career
- spousal relationships
- maturation of children
- aging or death of parents
- physical changes associated with aging.

Midlife crises seem to affect men and women differently. Researchers have proposed that the triggers for midlife crisis differ between men and women, with male midlife crisis more likely to be caused by work issues.

Some have hypothesized that another cause of the male midlife crisis is the imminent menopause of the female partner and end of her reproductive career.

Characteristics

Individuals experiencing a midlife crisis have some of these feelings:

- search of an undefined dream or goal
- a deep sense of remorse for goals not accomplished
- desire to achieve a feeling of youthfulness
- need to spend more time alone or with certain peers.

They exhibit some of these behaviours:

- abuse of alcohol

- acquisition of unusual or expensive items such as motorbikes, boats, clothing, sports cars, jewelry, gadgets, tattoos, piercings, etc.
- depression
- blaming themselves for their failures
- paying special attention to physical appearance such as covering baldness, wearing "younger" designer clothes etc.
- entering relationships with younger people (either/or sexual, professional, parental, etc.)
- placing overimportance (and possibly a psychologically damaging amount) on their children to excel in areas such as sports, arts or academics.

Theoretical Basis

"The notion of the midlife crisis began with followers of Sigmund Freud, who thought that during middle age everyone's thoughts were driven by the fear of impending death". Although midlife crisis has lately received more attention in popular culture than serious research, there are some theoretical constructs supporting the notion. Jungian theory holds that midlife is key to individuation, a process of self-actualization and self-awareness that contains many potential paradoxes. Although Carl Jung did not describe midlife crisis per se, the midlife integration of thinking, sensation, feeling, and intuition that he describes could, it seems, lead to confusion about one's life to date and one's goals. Erik Erikson held that in life's seventh stage, middle adulthood, people struggle to find new meaning and purpose to their lives; their questioning, he believed, could lead to what we now call a midlife crisis.

Some psychologists believe men's midlife crisis is a psychological reaction to the imminent menopause and end of reproductive career of their spouses. Their genes may be influencing men to be more attracted to reproductive women, and less attached to their non-reproductive spouses.

Criticism

Some people have challenged the existence of midlife crises altogether. One study found that 23% of participants had what they called a "midlife crisis," but in digging deeper, only one-third of those—8% of the total—said the crisis was associated with realizations about aging.

The balance (15% of those surveyed) had experienced major life experiences or transitions such as divorce or loss of a job in middle age and described them as "midlife crisis." While there is no doubt these events can be traumatic—the associated grief reactions can be indistinguishable from depression — these upheavals aren't unique to middle age and aren't an age-related midlife crisis. University of California-Davis researchers Carolyn Alwin and Michael Levenson presented the current view of midlife crisis in a 2001 article:

Costa and McCrae (1980) found little evidence for an increase in neuroticism in midlife... While they did find that some people were likely to experience such crises,... these individuals were likely to experience crises in their 20s and 30s, and these experiences were not unique to midlife....Robinson, Rosenberg, and Farrell (1999) reinterviewed (500) men. Looking back over their midlife period, it became evident that while not necessarily entailing crisis, it was a time for re-evaluation."

Wrapping up their review of men's midlife crisis, Alwin and Levenson wrote that "... Given the bulk of the data, it is likely that, for most men, midlife is a time of achievement and satisfaction. For a certain proportion of men, however, the passage is not at all smooth." They found a similar pattern when they reviewed research on what are commonly thought to be triggers for women's midlife crisis: menopause, children leaving home, the "sandwich" of caring for both parents and children. Most women navigated those periods without a traumatic psychological "crisis."

The enduring popularity of the midlife crisis concept may be explained by another finding by Robinson et al. As Alwin and Levenson summarize: "... younger men, now middle-aged Baby Boomers, used the term "midlife crisis" to describe nearly any setback, either in their career or family life."

Levinson's findings were research about the possible existence of a midlife crisis and its implications. Whereas Levinson (1978) found that 80% of middle-aged participants had a crisis, and Ciernia (1985) reported that 70% of men in midlife said they had a crisis (Shek, 1996) others could not replicate those findings including Shek (1996), Kruger (1994), McCrae and Costa (1990), and Whitbourne (2010). The debate of whether or not there is a midlife crisis is being answered through recent research that attempts to balance such factors as response bias and experimenter effects in order to establish internal validity. The above mentioned research does not support Levinson's model of a single age in the middle years that is a designated time of transition and potential "crisis." Instead, changes in personality can occur throughout the adult years with no peak in general distress or psychosocial crisis.

For the most part, at all ages researchers in Positive Adult Development have found improvement or at worst, stasis for most of the population.

In Popular Culture

The midlife crisis has been the subject of many television series and films, often the source of amusement in sitcoms, soaps and other television productions. The 1970s Polish television series, *Czterdziestolatek* meaning "The 40-Year-Old" was entirely geared towards covering midlife crisis issues in a comedy series. In the Australian television series, *Neighbours*, Karl Kennedy went though a midlife crisis dating young women and changing his appearance.

While the classic 1955 movie The Seven Year Itch deals with the supposed decline of marital quality after seven years of marriage, the protagonist Richard Sherman (played by Tom Ewell) is obviously going through a midlife crisis.

In fact, the book that proposes the seven-year-itch hypothesis, entitled "Of Man and the Unconscious", even has a chapter on "The Repressed Urge in the Middle-Aged Male: Its Roots and Its Consequences" connecting it to the midlife crisis in men. As an editor for a publishing house, Sherman reads – and reads into – this psychological study which he believes directly corresponds to increasingly erotic, frenetic, and ultimately frantic daydreams stemming from his flirtation with the new nubile neighbor upstairs (Marilyn Monroe in one of her most memorable roles).

Decidedly more serious takes on the subject include John Cheever's short stories, "The Country Husband" and "The Swimmer", shedding light on modern '60s era suburbia, as well as more bittersweet and timely turns at the turn of the millennium in the films *American Beauty* (2000 Academy Awards Best Picture winner) and *Lost in Translation*.

English progressive rocker, Roger Waters, formerly of Pink Floyd, also released a solo album, *The Pros and Cons of Hitch-Hiking*, which explores a man and his midlife crisis as he dreams of having an affair and tries desperately to find solutions to his problems.

Old Age

Old age (also referred to as one's eld) consists of ages nearing or surpassing the average life span of human beings, and thus the end of the human life cycle. Euphemisms and terms for old people include seniors (American usage), senior citizens (British and American usage) and the elderly. As occurs with almost any definable group of humanity, some people will hold a prejudice against others — in this case, against old people. This is one form of ageism.

Old people have limited regenerative abilities and are more prone to disease, syndromes, and sickness than other adults. For the biology of ageing. The medical study of the aging process is gerontology, and the study of diseases that afflict the elderly is geriatrics.

Definition

The boundary between middle age and old age cannot be defined exactly because it does not have the same meaning in all societies. People can be considered old because of certain changes in their activities or social roles. Examples: people may be considered old when they become grandparents, or when they begin to do less or different work — retirement.

In the United States of America, and the United Kingdom, the age of 65 was traditionally considered the beginning of the senior years because, until recently, United States and British people became eligible to retire at this age with full Social Security benefits. In 2003, the age at which a US citizen became eligible for full Social Security benefits began to increase gradually, and will continue to do so until it reaches 67 in 2027. Currently, it is 66.

Physical Changes

There is often a general physical decline, and people become less active. Old age can cause, amongst other things:

- Wrinkles and liver spots on the skin
- Change of hair color to gray or white
- Hair loss
- Lessened hearing
- Diminished eyesight
- Slower reaction times and agility
- Reduced ability to think clearly
- Difficulty recalling memories
- Lessening or cessation of sex, sometimes because of physical symptoms such as erectile dysfunction in men, but often simply a decline in libido
- Greater susceptibility to bone diseases such as osteoarthritis.

Demographic Changes

In the industrialized countries, life expectancy has increased consistently over the last decades. In the United States the proportion of people aged 65 or older increased from 4% in 1900 to about 12% in 2000. In 1900, only about 3 million of the nation's citizens had reached 65. By 2000, the number of senior citizens had increased to about 35 million. Population experts estimate that more than 50 million Americans — about 17 percent of the population — will be 65 or older in 2020. The number of old people is growing around the world chiefly because of the post-war 'baby boom', and increases in the provision and standards of health care.

Life Expectancy

In most parts of the world, women live, on average, longer than men; even so, the disparities vary between 9 years or more in countries such as Sweden and the United States to no difference or higher life expectancy for men in countries such as Zimbabwe and Uganda.

Psychosocial Aspects

According to Erik Erikson's "Eight Stages of Life" theory, the human personality is developed in a series of eight stages that take place from the time of birth and continue on throughout an individual's complete life. He characterises old age as a period of "Integrity vs. Despair", during which a person focuses on reflecting back on their life. Those who are unsuccessful during this phase will feel that their life has been wasted and will experience many regrets. The individual will be left with feelings of bitterness and despair. Those who feel proud of their accomplishments will feel a sense of integrity. Successfully completing this phase means looking back with few regrets and a general feeling of satisfaction. These individuals will attain wisdom, even when confronting death. Health and physical in old age

We will all be geriatric individuals one day. As we age, we face many physical and emotional changes that can affect our level of function and well-being. Our baby-boomer population is aging, and people are living longer. We must maintain our functional independence in the elderly and address the needs of our older generation. Rehabilitation of geriatric patients is imperative for the patients' well-being and for society, so that we can thrive socially and economically.

Classification of old age:

Young old — 65-74 yrs

Old-75-84

Very old –more than 85 years

What are the major problems in elderly?

1. Visual impairment
2. Hearing loss
3. Cognitive impairment (dementia)
4. Malnutrition
5. Psycological problems (depression/poor confidence levels)

6. Bone loosening (osteoporosis)
7. Imbalance (multifactorial)
8. Falls/mobility issues
9. Infections
10. Elderly abuse.

Organ Changes with Ageing

Brain: Nerve: Cell Loss/degeneration—memory impairment

Lungs: Rreduced elasticity, reduced immune function-susceptible for infection, and causes shortness of breath

Heart and blood vessels: reduced elasticity of aorta-increase in blood pressure (one of the factor).

Decreased Heart Muscle Function

Endocrine function: reduced sensitivity to insulin

Stomach and intestine: slowing of motility leading to-constipation

Bones: reduced mineral density –prone for fractures

Auditory impairment/Visual impairment.

Hearing loss has a major contribution to communication and quality-of-life issues. People who use hearing aids are more likely than others to report improvements in their physical, emotional, and social comfort.With aging, the gradual deterioration of sensory modalities, including vision, can interfere with one's daily activities. Nearly 7% of patients admitted to inpatient rehabilitation units have a severe visual impairment. A visual impairment is defined as visual acuity of 20/40 or worse and legal blindness is defined as visual acuity of 20/200 or worse. Consequences of visual impairment Vision impairment exerts a more wide-ranging impact on functional status than does hearing impairment. Visual impairment is associated with increased physical disability, increased social isolation, low employment rates, reduced self-image, and depression.

Falls

Falls and near-falls occur in more than 30% of people aged

65 years or older. Every year, 50% of people in the community older than 80 years have a fall, and approximately 60% of nursing home residents fall each year. Those most susceptible to falling are older women with a low body mass index (BMI), greater height, lower bone mineral density (BMD), and history of a cerebrovascular accident (STROKE). Alcohol-related falls are more common in men than in women.

Age-related physiologic factors that can lead to falls include the following: decreased muscle mass (which decreases overall strength), postural changes of the hips with increasing valgus deformity, change in the center of gravity to behind the hips, increased postural sway, decreased righting reflexes, increased reaction time, visuoperceptual decline, decreased vibratory sensation and altered proprioception (poor lower-extremity sensory input), impaired mobility, orthostatic hypotension (systolic blood pressure [SBP] <20 mm Hg), balance disorders, and vasovagal syncope. Depression, confusion, dementia, and other cognitive deficits also contribute to falls. Cognitive impairment, depressive symptoms, and orthostatic hypotension most contribute to gait dysfunction.

Dementia

Dementia is a problem with decline in memory and at least 1 other cognitive function. The World Health Organization defines dementia as memory decline, especially in the learning of new information, lasting longer than 6 months. Dementia is not a normal part of aging. Dementia disrupts one's daily activities and leads to a decline in memory and previous functioning, and it can also lead to social impairment.

Malnutrition

In geriatric rehabilitation, malnutrition affects a patient's functional status and global medical condition. Malnutrition occurs when a deficiency of caloric, vitamin, mineral, protein, water, and/or nutrient uptake is present. However, no exact definition of malnutrition has been established in the elderly.

Risk Factors for Malnutrition

Physiologic factors of aging may lead to malnutrition. These factors are reduced metabolic requirements, decreased total body protein level, decreased total body water, decreased BMD, decreased taste and smell sensation, diminished levels of neurotransmitters that increase appetite, and early satiety. Physical conditions include reduced physical activity; poor dentition; digestive disorders etc.

Depression

Depression is the most common mood disorder in the geriatric population. Some symptoms of depression, such as weight loss, sleep disturbance, and fatigue, may be associated with other concurrent medical conditions. These medical issues must be ruled out prior to establishing a diagnosis of depression. Cognitive disorders may also interfere with the diagnosis of geriatric depression.

What can we do to Take Care of Elderly People?

Essential to geriatric rehabilitation is communication, specifically improving any sensory impairment, including those related to vision and hearing.

The prevention of falls and osteoporosis can improve the Patient's health and longevity. Addressing malnutrition can promote healing and vitalize the patient to participate in a formal rehabilitation program. Depression is common in the older population if a functional loss of mobility and an inability to perform activities of daily living (ADLs) predominates.

Personality Problems in Old Age

Personality in later life does not differ much from younger years. Happy young people grow into happy older people, but life's heaviest punches seem to be reserved for later life.

Diseases and deaths of friends and life mates are extremely unhappy moments, and they force great changes in our ways of life. In spite of these sobering events, the mature personality still reflects a fairly steady manner of living, almost the same at all ages.

It is a source of wonderment that the brandishments of life do not effect more mental problems but generally, the human mind stands up remarkably well under the beating of life.

The Self-displeased Personality

Some people are actually displeased with themselves and must continuously try to prove to themselves that they are as good or better than others. If they cannot prove this to their satisfaction, extreme displeasure overtakes them. This group of people has several distinct characteristics. They are very self-conscious and keenly aware of their own shortcomings; they can never admit that they are wrong; they fear and avoid all honest competition; they must have more money, more power, and more fame than anyone else; they avoid all situations which may detract from them; they must always have the last word; they are difficult to satisfy, and are apt to be very selfish; and they are very difficult persons to live with.

Personality problems involving displeasure with self, are likely to be found in the little Napoleon, the severe inferiority complex with the exaggerated way of compensating. These unfortunate persons need the uplifting influence of charity and love in their lives. It is difficult for the extremely selfish or self-centered person to love himself or anyone else, until he learns concern and charity for others. Then he may forget himself and begin to love life itself.

Displeasure with others, Causing Personality Difficulties

Some people seem anti-social. They do not enjoy the company of others, and actually seem hostile in their attitudes to other people. They are obviously anything but joiners and have several identifying characteristics: they feel continuously alone, and display little concern for anyone else; they have very few friends and they are possessed with the idea that others are against them; they trust very few people whom they can love or enjoy; they are inclined to impose upon others and show little respect, if any, for their fellowman. The personality problem displeased with others around him, is likely to be found in thieves, racketeers and other enemies of society. These people need to experience a strong feeling of trust in others, and to be trusted in turn, as well. Their lot is indeed a hard one, for without sharing the problems of life with loved and trusted friends, it is indeed a lonely and bitter road.

Displeasure with the World as a Cause of Personality Troubles

Some people are always down on their luck or are always getting the bad breaks. The world of reality is too cold and hard for them to endure, and they dream of an unreal future through their rose-colored glasses. Some characteristics of this group are: They deftly avoid and shirk any real responsibility; they shun hard work in favor of an angle; they waste any real talents that they may have in their search for the proverbial rainbow; they shun making decisions, and new ideas or change of any kind are avoided at all costs.

Personality problems involving the world at large are likely to be found in the ne'er-do-wells, the alcoholics, and people with very shallow personalities. The great need of these people is the satisfaction enjoyed from hard work well done. Without this, they can experience very little real satisfaction or enjoyment in life, and their readjustment is very difficult. Their need to excel in something is very great indeed.

Death

Life Meaning and Death

Human beings think about the impact and inevitability of death throughout much of their lives. Most children understand by the ages of 5 to 7 that death is the irreversible ending of all life functions, and that it happens to all living beings. Adolescents fully comprehend the meaning of death, but they often believe that they are somehow immortal. As a result, they may engage in risky behaviour, such as driving recklessly or smoking, with little thought of dangerous consequences.

Although most young and middle adults have gained a more realistic view of death through the death of some family members or friends, anxiety about death may be more likely to peak in middle adulthood. As people continue aging, they gradually learn to accept the eventual deaths of loved ones, as well as their own deaths. By later adulthood, most people come to accept—perhaps with some tranquility if they feel they have lived meaningfully—the inevitability of their own demise, which prompts them to live day by day and make the most of whatever time remains. If they do not feel they have lived meaningfully, older adults may react to impending death with feelings of bitterness or even passivity.

Old age is advanced years the latter period of life. Changes in any particular order for example, experience vision problems with no noticeable loss of hearing. Fatigue; appetite loss; insomnia; difficulty concentrating; loss of interest in life or the ability to enjoy it; feelings of emptiness, guilt, sadness, and hopelessness; wishing for death; and thinking of suicide.

The people who live past sixty years of age or so are commonly known as aged or elderly. Old age is still an inevitable physiological process, which cannot be postponed indefinitely. One has to perceive both physical and socio-psychological aspects of life of the aged to understand life conditions of elderly. Parents abusing children, husbands abusing wives, and older persons being abused and neglected by spouses, daughters-in-law, sons, brothers and other members of the family and relatives. The youngsters do not wish to accept them as part of their social setup, their life-style at all. Changing priorities of younger generation, and replacement of "We" concept by "I" concept. Very few research studies emphasize on the needs and problems of the elderly.

Being 'old' is a psychic perception while being labeled 'old' is a social ascription according to Ghosh maulik. Older are dependent on those who abuse them for their physical and financial need and support. During 1980s elder abuse gained rapid recognition in USA. It is estimated that in USA alone, around 500,000 cases to 2.5 million cases of elderly are subjected to physical violence annually. "late time of life; "old age is not for sissies," "he's, showing his years"; "age hasn't slowed him down at all"; "a beard white with eld"; "on the brink of geezerhood"

Some cases exemplify the nature of abuse in our society: There was 70 years old widower living with his son. A few years back, his son started demanding transfer of father's property to his name. When the father refused to comply, he started abusing him physical and verbally.

While in other case one poor widow woman of about 60 years of age lived with he young unemployed son. Due to economic hardship she had to sell her small room and after some time she lost her legs in a road accident. Her son one day discarded her who had become a liability for him.

The definition given by Council of Europe includes all the aspects, "the physical and psychological integrity of an older person or harms the development of his/her personality and undermines or damages his/her financial security."

Elders are talkative, but nobody listens to them, nobody to share their grievances. Older persons are least or not wanted in the social setup of a family or the society at large resulting in loneliness and the death anxiety according to Mullins. While Kogan & Wallach found that everyone evaluated death negatively, the elderly rated it more positive than others.

Children do not care, they neglect, and they don't look after their elder. The problem for older persons did not seem to be lake of money but lack of time by the 'others'. The other thing is lack of emotional support from family members. Sense of insecurity and feeling of burden and old age itself was a disease.

Old people are sent away to old age homes even when families can taken care of them. If ole person is sick children stay away. The other problem is older couple being asked to live separately when they had more than one child.

Such as the older woman to stay with one child and than man to stay with another according to the convenience of their support in whatever housework they could contribute to. While in the case or rotation, the parents stayed with one child for a particular period of time and then moved over to the other child to stay with him for the same period of time.

Death of spouses in old age caused greatest mental anguish. Aged widows could manage to spend time with grand children but the old widowers of their wife as their link with the family was snapped. Women perceived financial dependency and no access to money whenever required especially for health problems and buying of medicines as a form of maltreatment. The cause of abuse is because there is no communication between old and young. Person was abused when he/she got pension and children wanted to take away the money.

Bibliography

Ahlawat, Neetu : *Developmental Psychology*, RBSA, Delhi, 2010.

Allport, G. W. : *Becoming: Basic Considerations for a Psychology of Personality,* Yale Univ. Press, New Haven, CT. 1955.

Allport, Gordon : *Pattern and Growth in Personality*, Holt, Rinehart and Winston, New York, 1961.

Angell, J. R.: *The evolution of intelligence*. New Haven, CT: Yale University Press, 1922.

Arndt, William B. Jr. : *Theories of Personality*, Macmillan, New York, 1974.

Asch, M. : *Abnormal and Developmental Psychology*, Ivy Pub, Delhi, 2003.

Baldwin, B., Fillmore, E., & Hadley, L : *Farm Children: An investigation of rural child life in selected areas of Iowa*. New York: Appleton, 1930.

Baldwin, J.M.: *Social and Ethical Interpretations of Mental Development*. New York: Macmillan, 1897.

Benjamin, L.: *Harry Kirke Wolfe: Pioneer in psychology*. Lincoln: University of Nebraska Press, 1991.

Blumenthal, A.: *Language and Psychology: Historical aspects of psycholinguistics*. New York: John Wiley, 1970.

Boring, E.G.: *A History of Experimental Psychology*. New York: The Century Company, 1929.

Bottery, M. : *The Ethics of Educational Management: Personal, Social and Political Perspectives on School Organization*, London, Cassell, 1992.

Burgess, R. L. & MacDonald: *Evolutionary Perspectives on Human Development,* Thousand Oaks, CA: Sage Publications, 2004.

Damon, William : *Social and Personality Development, Infancy through Adolescence,* New York: Norton, 1983.

Dubey, K.C. : *Experimental and Developmental Psychology*, Omega Pub, Delhi, 2009.

Ellis, A. :*Humanistic Psychology, The Rational-emotive Approach,* Julian Press, New York, 1973.

Eysenck, Hans : *Psychoticism as a Dimension of Personality*, Pergamon, Elsevier Science Inc, Amsterdam, 1997.

Georgi, A. : *Psychology as a Human Science*, Harper & Row, New York, 1970.

Grace, G. : *School Leadership: Beyond Educational Development*, London, Falmer, 1995.

Hurt, K. F. : *The Quest of the Psychological Jesus*, Unitarian Universalist Christian, 1982.

Kaur, Rajpal : *Developmental Psychology : New Trends and Innovations*, Deep and Deep, Delhi, 2006.

Keen, E. A. : *Primer in Phenomenological Psychology*, Holt, Rinehart, & Winston, New York, 1975.

Kluger, R. S. : *Psyche and Bible, Three Old Testament Themes,* Zurich, New York, Spring Publications, 1974.

Laub, D. : *Testimony, Crises of Witnessing in Literature, Psychoanalysis and History*, Routledge, New York, 1992.

Lifton, R. : *The Nazi Doctors, Medical Killing and the Psychology of Genocide*, Basic Books, New York, 1986.

MacDonald, K. : *Evolutionary Perspectives on Human Development*, Thousand Oaks, CA: Sage, 2004.

Maslow, A. H. : *Motivation and Personality,* Harper & Bros, New York, 1954.

Moustakas, S.: *Existential Psychotherapy and the Interpretation of Dreams,* J. Aronson, C., Northvale, NJ, 1994.

Sen, Anuradha : *An Introduction to Developmental Psychology*, Indian Pub, Delhi, 2010.

Sharma, K.K. : *Principles of Developmental Psychology*, Sublime, Delhi, 2003.

Strasser, S.: *Phenomenology and the Human Science,* Duquesne University Press, Pittsburgh, PA, 1963.

Verma, R.B. : *Developmental Psychology and Human Development*, Alfa, Delhi, 2006.

Index